NORTH WESTERN
ROAD CAR COMPANY LIMITED

A nearside view of No. 507 (FDB 507), an Atkinson Alpha with Weymann bodywork, clearly showing the rear entrance detail. It is working a Bramhall service and is pictured in Stockport in August 1965, en route to Cheadle to take up service.

A 1949 Leyland Titan PD2/1, with a Leyland body, No. 241 (CDB 241) works service 55, Stockport to Brinnington, and is pictured at Stockport on 20th August 1965.

NORTH WESTERN
ROAD CAR COMPANY LIMITED

A Driver's Reminiscences

PETER CAUNT

Oxford Publishing Company

Typesetting by:
Aquarius Typesetting Services, New Milton, Hants.

Printed in Great Britain by:
Netherwood Dalton & Co. Ltd., Huddersfield, Yorks.

Published by:
Oxford Publishing Co.
Link House
West Street
POOLE, Dorset

My thanks go to Mr G. R. Mills of Colchester, who has kindly provided additional photographic material for use in this book. These photographs can be found on pages 2, 5, 9, 25, 26, 27, 36, 38, 39, 42, 51, 52, 53, 54, 58, 66, 69, 76, 83 and 94.

No. 933 (VDB 933), an AEC Reliance with a Willowbrook body, poses in Charles Street yard, when new in 1963, showing off the 'Banana Split' livery.

Contents

Differing designs of the North Western fleet are shown in this view, at Stockport, in August 1965. Preparing to take out service 77 to Wilmslow is No. 168 (DDB 168C), a Daimler Fleetline with Alexander bodywork, whilst alongside is a Weymann-bodied Leyland PD2/21, No. 661 (KDB 661). The Fleetline has a seating capacity of 75 whilst the PD2/21 has only 58 seats.

DEDICATION

To my mother and father; for their patience and encouragement whilst I pursued an unusual hobby.

For assistance in several ways, I should like to thank: my wife, for her support and for typing the final manuscript; Mrs Susan Gaskell, for so ably translating my hand-written notes into a readable draft; Chris Bowles, for his valued service information to supplement my memory, and for attending to proof reading; and to my colleagues and friends who have been aware of this task, and for their good wishes.

Peter E. Caunt
Umina
Australia
January 1983

A design for a New Image Company symbol drawn up on 9th August 1959. A much simplified design, using the compass rose, was used on AEC Reliance coach No. 845 which was used for a Directors' Tour.

Chapter One ~ Introduction

The following account of the workings of the North Western Road Car Co. Ltd., particularly reference to my personal experiences at the Manchester Depot of the Company, are based on the period from May 1963 to February 1967.

Certain abbreviations used will be familiar to readers, but others, may not. The abbreviation 'N—N' relates to North Western Road Car Company Limited and was the style of abbreviation used by employees in the Company's head office, in Charles Street, Stockport, when writing memos, duty boards or allied paperwork that would then be typed. In order to ease the boredom of the proof checking tasks, it was often that the phrase 'North Western Jam Jar Company' would be read out as a friendly dig at the Company's title. This latter title is not used in the text!

In order to avoid confusion, the twenty four hour clock is used throughout although North Western used a.m. and p.m. during my time at Manchester Garage until early 1965.

Working from the Manchester Depot of the North Western Road Car Company provided me with a wide experience in both routes and vehicle types. After a couple of years, I reached the dizzy heights of a roster which included, almost daily, express and 'limited stop' workings. With, for example, the jointly-operated Leeds to Liverpool service, the additional experience of other operators' vehicles was opened to me, sometimes with amusing results.

During five years of work in the head office at Charles Street, Stockport, I was able to obtain my PSV badge. This had been a dream of mine, as a bus enthusiast, since the buses and their technical intrigues had alway been the predominant aspect of my enthusings. My visits to scrapyards had provided me with a drive in a pre-war Crosville Regent when the man in the yard was unable to find reverse and asked me to 'have a go'. What dizzy heights of success! Between one or two other odd 'goes' in scrapyards and depots, a Ford Koln coach, owned by the Royal Air Force during my two year stay with the forces at RAF Geilenkirchen, was my sole experience until my training started for the PSV test.

Of all the N—N depots, Manchester had the most varied list of services, or perhaps in the largest quantity. Several local services were jointly operated with Manchester Corporation, and other locals were 'by arrangement' with Manchester Corporation and these tended to be the longer distance local services to Alderley, Hayfield, Buxton or Macclesfield. The regular express services generally started from Manchester, although seasonal express services departed from most of the Company's centres in the summer with a fair variety of destinations available. This aspect of N—N operation was to provide a splendid opportunity for me to gain experience on a variety of vehicles, including types not to be found in the Company's remarkably varied fleet. Even where

types such as the Leyland Leopard and AEC Reliance were concerned, the other operators' vehicles helped one to maintain a sense of balance, since it was possible to compare the performance of the vehicles from the different fleets. On the whole, I think North Western did rather well.

Within the Company, of course, similar comparisons were possible and Buxton, Matlock and Glossop garages, with forty three, twenty six and twenty respectively, would have a reputation for looking after their buses and for taking an interest in their condition. This was doubtless a product of the small depot, but Northwich also had a remarkably good name despite Imperial Chemical Industries Limited's works' requirement, giving Northwich a reason for its sixty six vehicle fleet. Stockport had one hundred and fifty vehicles which tended to reflect its 'float' for engineering purposes, whilst Manchester's allocation came out at sixty six, of which a healthy thirty were coaches. This, however, did not exclude the use of those thirty coaches from stage carriage work. Several of the Manchester duties worked a two and a half to three hours early peak hour portion of service duplication using a coach, prior to going on to express work. The peak hour work, in this case would often be to Bramhall, Cheadle Hulme or Wilmslow, although single deck vehicles would sometimes be allocated to Flixton or Urmston duplication, an area normally served on the Manchester routes by double deck vehicles. North Western made remarkably economic use of their coaches throughout their empire.

It was this use of coaches which helped to brighten life for the crews at Manchester and, no doubt, other North Western depots, although if the work was purely a job that provided a wage every Thursday, then the buses and coaches were immaterial. My own attitude was that of an enthusiast. After almost four years as a full time road staff driver, I was loath to leave the job. In fact, a decision to move on to a 'better' job, a year earlier, had been abandoned simply because I felt that I really must try those newly-delivered pneumocyclic Leopards! These were times when a two week holiday period felt more like a penance than a vacation.

My very early enthusiasm, stemming from holidays on the Lancashire Coast, where we were well-served by Ribble buses, continued at home by 'spotting' the buses of Manchester Corporation and emptying used ticket boxes, not always with the conductors' approval, at the Ben Brierley terminus in Moston. This was where the trolley bus services 33 and 37 turned, as short workings on services 32 and 36 which went on to Moston, Gardeners Arms, having come from Manchester via Rochdale and Oldham Road respectively. Later, these services were renumbered, 37 to 31X, 36 to 31 and later, they went into the trolley bus service number series, 211 and 212 (ex-31 and 32).

The tickets which I obtained in this semi-official manner fed my interest in buses, and filled my home-made ticket racks with most of the range of Manchester Corporation issues, although higher values came from friends and relatives who travelled afar on the system. The 2½d ticket (yellow), being the fare to Ben Brierley from town, meant that I became heartily sick of these tickets and at one time I possessed hundreds of them.

Occasional visits to relatives in other towns enabled me to obtain some long 'Willibrew' tickets from North Western buses, whilst the holidays in Ribble territory brought their 'Willibrew' tickets into my possession as well. The initial Ribble interest showed itself in my having painted their fleet name on all my 'Dinky' buses. Later I became more discerning and replaced the standard 'Dinky Toy' livery of cream and red with a Ribble cherry red, with three cream bands of course! Needless to say 'Dinky' buses received as gifts rarely came into my fleet with green as their lower colour, most of my uncles and aunts being well trained.

In the days before I was able to obtain copies of the Ribble fleet allocation lists, in fact, I probably hadn't heard of them at the time, I was fortunate enough to have an elderly friend of the family who was a farmer. He visited relatives in Lea, near Preston, changing buses at that shrine of Ribble Motor Services Limited. He used to note the fleet numbers of Ribble buses for me so that I could make inspired guesses as to where I might find a particular type of Ribble bus. People must have stared at this elderly gentleman 'bus spotter' but I shall be eternally grateful to him for his kindness.

When mother's outing with the local Mothers' Union went into Ribble territory, I received the fruits of a coachload of 'spotters'; a good supply of Ribble bus numbers! I often wonder what their coach driver thought, although he would, at that time, be confined to his half cab in the Burlingham-bodied Albion Valkyrie of Makinsons of Moston Lane, Harpurhey, whose fleet was in purple livery with cream flash.

A new Bedford VAL, No. 130 (AJA 130B), with specially-built low-roofed bodywork by Strachans, to enable it to pass beneath Dunham Bridge, near Altrincham, is seen in Charles Street Works, in May 1964, on its delivery check.

No. 780 (LDB 780), an AEC Reliance with Harrington Contender coachwork, photographed, when new, in April 1959, at Stockport Garage, and decorated for a 'Courtesy Campaign'.

Alas, the Mothers' Union degenerated to Bedford Duples whilst Makinson was taken over and eventually ended up in the arms of Yelloway of Rochdale.

My bus interest remained a hobby when I left school and went to work in an insurance office. The 'natural break' of National Service provided the impetus I needed and I never returned to the insurance profession. I joined North Western at their Charles Street, Stockport offices. By this time I was well aware of North Western's interesting fleet and operations, although Ribble took up a good part of my interest. I joined North Western just as Melba Motors Limited of Reddish had been taken over and their operation came under head office's control.

My period in the Traffic and Private Hire offices taught me many basic aspects of the industry as well as helping me to become reasonably competent in Welsh pronunciation! This, I should explain, came about when I was working alongside a fellow traffic office clerk who was Welsh. During our conversation on one occasion, I commented on the Menai Bridge between the Welsh mainland and Anglesey. My pronunciation of the name left much to be desired, judging from my friend's reaction. There and then, I was given a thorough grounding in the pronunciation of Welsh which has since been of considerable assistance when reading Crosville timetables. Despite my ignorance, my Welsh teacher and I have remained good friends since then, and we have experienced the joint ownership and preservation of a North Western Bristol K5G vehicle.

Towards the end of my head office career, I bought my first car and soon became embroiled in its maintenance and became particularly interested in driving buses, although I had, by then, acquired my PSV driver's licence. I left my office job with North Western for a short period and returned to get the bus driving 'bug' out of my system by enrolling on the driving staff of Manchester Depot. The move was not successful. I enjoyed my driving life so much that I had to make a conscious effort to leave after four years.

I remember, before I had a PSV badge, taking a coach holiday for a seven day trip round Devon and Cornwall with Kingfisher Holidays, the Auty's Tour section of Ribble Motor Services Limited. A Ribble Burlingham Seagull-bodied Tiger Cub was used. We were a small party of twelve, compact and friendly, yet I spent much of the time wishing the driver would be taken ill and give me an opportunity to drive the coach! He was a splendid chap and, happily, my desire to drive had no effect on his health whatsoever. My driving interest has declined very little, despite the passing of time.

Eventually, I went to work in the offices of Salford City Transport, where I met an ex-North Western employee, much to my surprise and, when SELNEC came into being on 1st November 1969, it set the scene for a change in North Western so that the dear old firm fell apart at the seams, which was very sad.

Meanwhile, in June 1970, Lancashire United Transport Limited had started a five day week for road staff, so that weekend work required part-time staff. I enrolled, and drove until 1978, their Guy Arabs, Fleetlines, old and new, Bristol LHs, Tiger Cubs and Leopards, in a sort of semblance of the old North Western.

The observations, reminiscences and comments that follow stem from my interest in buses that has evolved over a period of about thirty five years, not being too specific, and my practical work with North Western in both clerical and driving capacities which, in turn, have been added to by experiences with the undertakings both in full and part-time positions. It is interesting to note that of the fleet of approximately six hundred buses and coaches, my records show that I actually drove two hundred and ninety one of these vehicles at least once! Needless to say, some I drove so often that I became heartily sick and tired of them!

It is not the intention that the information, relative to technical details, be of 'workshop manual' quality. The experiences of the writer are practical everyday occurrences and whatever a mechanical unit is supposed to do, it does not always do it as the manufacturer intended after several hundred drivers have tried out their own personal brand of driving on it! An example of this is the pneumocyclic gearbox. I have stated elsewhere that the earlier electric changes were more positive than the later air changes. The makers may well consider this not to be so, but from my point of view as a driver, it certainly appears to be.

A Guy Arab of the Lancashire United fleet, No. 108 (572 TD), similar to the type driven by the author in the early 1970s. This vehicle is fitted with Northern Counties bodywork and is pictured at Atherton Garage on 19th August 1965.

Chapter Two ~ Manchester Garage and Lower Mosley Street Omnibus Station

I started work at Manchester Garage in May 1963, just in time for the Whitsun weekend rush. Although I lived in Manchester, I saw very few North Western buses since I lived in Moston, to the north of the city, and the nearest of the Company's routes was service 2, Manchester, Stevenson Square to New Hey, which travelled along Broadway, New Moston. Other than this, the 'limited stop' services used Oldham Road together with services 10, 13 and 14 from Stevenson Square to Greenfield and Uppermill; all these stage carriage services being jointly operated by the Company together with Manchester and Oldham Corporations.

A similar distance from home was Middleton Junction where the 159 service passed on its ramblings between Middleton and Woodhouses, which further on used Broadway, as far as Moston Lane East, making this route an outpost on the boundary of the Manchester and Oldham Corporation territories. This route, which was operated by Oldham Depot, originally had Bristol L5Gs working on it until these were withdrawn and Tiger Cubs took over. The low bridge at Middleton Junction restricted this service to a single deck operation, although the bridge at Failsworth Station would certainly have required the use of lowbridge double deckers if that had been the only restriction. Since Manchester Garage worked to the south of the city, a number of routes were unknown to me in their finer detail. I certainly knew where Stretford, Urmston and Flixton were, but the ramifications of where services 11 and 23 went in relation to services 3 and 5, and later service 12, needed some clarification for me. As for Partington, that, indeed, was only a name on a bus indicator. Buxton, Hayfield, Higher Poynton and the Bramhall area were reasonably clear, although I found that some things had changed, as will be seen.

The normal arrangement was for a driver to be passed by the training school at Stockport and report to his parent depot to go through the local procedures, and travel as a passenger on a list of routes which then provided the appropriate familiarization. Armed with his route list, the driver would board each bus in turn, travel along the route, and the conductor would sign his list to show that the trainee had actually been on the bus and theoretically, at least, knew the route. Fortunately, I was lucky since I have a good sense of direction and can learn new routes quickly but, nevertheless, I agreed with the garage foreman at Manchester that since I would prefer to look at Flixton, Urmston and Partington in detail, then I could ignore Higher Poynton and Middlewood, Woodford and Lostock Road, Hayfield and Buxton; an arrangement which worked out well in the end.

My downfall very nearly took place on service 51, a route I had driven over on my very first driving duty from Stockport. On that occasion, I had worked from Stockport to Torkington as service 165, then as service 51 from Torkington to Manchester, Chorlton

Street Bus Station. The 51 route went via Cheadle. Because of having worked the service, I nearly left this one out of my list but did, in fact, train on it. It was just as well. Particularly when a bus was a single deck underfloor type, where a driver could be given directions easily, the general practice was for the trainee driver to do the driving and the official driver to put his feet up and fling occasional instructions and directions to his trainee. This was an arrangement to which I was delighted to agree, although I had the feeling that it would have happened without my agreement. On this run, the official driver almost had kittens as I headed towards Cheadle at the Parrs Wood stop. Fortunately, he could anticipate my intentions since I stayed in the nearside lane, and I was able to correct my error and head along the Kingsway Extension to The Griffin Hotel, Heald Green, where the route then headed towards Cheadle Hulme. The remainder of the route went off without upset.

Partington was a service which took a good share of the Manchester Garage workings. Its ramifications in later years became quite complicated but, in May 1963, the terminal was either The Greyhound or Wood Lane, the latter in the main housing estate at Partington, three minutes further than The Greyhound. There were two service numbers, 222 and 223, of which 223 operated through the works of Shell Chemicals Limited. This was the vast petrochemicals complex close to Carrington, Moss Lane, where one of the 11 and 12A variant services terminated. Once I had these areas sorted, I was happy to get down to the brass tacks of driving the buses, my route training having done nothing to curb my enthusiasm.

One of the minor problems that I had encountered during my part-time driving, whilst based at Charles Street office, was the difficulty in knowing where the bus stops were situated. This became even more important in my full-time driving career, particularly in view of the stopping restrictions resulting from the agreements between the Company and Manchester Corporation Transport Department. The rural areas could be even more confusing.

When travelling over main bus routes, stop signs are usually clear and noticeable but on roads, even within relatively short distances from a town centre, trees tend to obscure the bus stop signs and this becomes even more prevalent as more rural sections prevail. A further complication is that the rural areas often have only one footpath so that a bus stop on one side of the road will suffice for both directions, although it is unlikely that this will be stated on the stop itself. As yet, further complication for the unwary, the assumption that the stop on the other side of the road is the one for your direction also will, inevitably, be wrong and apart from odd looks from the passengers who have been decanted at the wrong spot, one feels a fool, when leaving the assumed stop, to find the

No. 731 (LDB 731), an AEC Reliance with a Weymann dual-purpose body, is seen on the wash at Manchester Garage in May 1958.

No. 102 (AJA 102B), a Daimler Fleetline with Alexander bodywork, stands at the rear entrance of the Greyhound Hotel, Partington in June 1965. Buses terminating here would park at The Green until ready to draw on to the inward stop.

correct alighting stop twenty yards further down the road, obscured by the inevitable tree! The excellent efficient system of undertakings who take the trouble to show all service numbers on the appropriate stop plates is not the Utopia that it may at first seem. On 'limited stop' services, the unwary or novice will find himself responding to a bell signal to stop at the next stop, only to find, when almost stationary, that the stop is not in use for the service which he is operating. The problem is whether to show one's ignorance to all and sundry by carrying on to the next, official, stop for the service, or stop, let the passengers off and continue, on the basis that most passengers do not know which stops are which anyway. These situations illustrate that the 'limited stop' system tends to lead to a battle of wits between road staff and passenger, and intending passengers at bus stops are never averse to putting out their hands on the off chance that the approaching bus will stop, even though the service number shows that it should not officially stop! Mind you, that is always assuming that the service number is correct. It has been known for 'cowboy' crews to try to reduce their workload by displaying the wrong number or destination on the principle of reducing the stopping opportunities and, therefore, the opportunities for passengers to board.

The industry has long laughed at the established joke of their staff that the job would be a good one if it were not for the passengers! Fortunately, the majority of staff accept it as a joke but, alas, some do not, and make every effort not to pick up passengers.

Despite North Western's method of allocating different duties each day, the weeks alternating as early or late weeks, it was often found that one's least-liked route would feature prominently every so often. Take my heartily disliked services 11X and 23. Those were Manchester (Piccadilly) to Davyhulme (Nags Head), service 11X and to Flixton (Red Lion), service 23. The Nags Head service was 29 minutes running time from Piccadilly, whilst The Red Lion was along the same route and a further 10 minutes run.

By the time half a duty of 'Nags and Lions' had passed, I was inevitably driving on 'automatic pilot'. This was achieved by driving along thinking of how to sort out my current problem on my Crossley Regis car! Unfortunately, this neutral state of driving led to a few problems.

One would be given two bells to start from a stop, and one to stop at the next stop. I often found that a bell to stop would intrude into my thoughts, so that I would be jerked to reality only to find that I had no idea what the bell was for! Not being able to decide whether the previous signal to start was still ringing in my ears or not, I would have to twist round, to squint through the bulkhead window behind me, to see whether passengers were on the platform ready to alight. If so, I knew I had to stop at the next alighting point. This was not an infallible check, however, since the absence of passengers on the platform could mean

that those intending to alight were still coming down the stairs and had not arrived on the platform. Assuming that the bell did not indicate that the next stop was required, one would keep going, only to be jerked into realization of the position as half a dozen irritated rings of the bell told their own story. The passengers were not happy to be deposited yards past their stop!

My main aim was now achieved. I was driving buses all day and every day, within the limits of duties and the Road Traffic Act, of course. The more I worked, the more conversant I became with the routes and the stops and generally, any doubts about routes could be dispelled by the conductor. This was often a fallacy, however, since Murphy's Law is such that on the occasions when the driver does not know a route, or part of it, then the chances are that his conductor is new to the job and doesn't know either!

Although I was by now well-versed in the service 32 route to Higher Poynton and Middlewood, the first time I had encountered this service was in my part-time days from head office. I often helped out by delivering buses to Manchester from Stockport Works or Garage. Sometimes I would receive a telephone call at the office asking if I was available for work during the evening. Usually, I leapt at the chance and I would then be asked to convey myself to Lower Mosley Street Bus Station by delivering a bus from the Works. On this occasion, I pulled into Lower Mosley Street and parked my bus, to be quickly ushered to a waiting Tiger Cub, No. 651 (KDB 651) on the service 32 stand. I asked the conductor leaning on the front of the bus if he was working that duty and he replied that he was when he got a driver! As I was not in uniform, he was surprised to find that he had a driver, so off we went. It turned out that he was not sure of the route. However, I was able to successfully reach Cheadle via the correct route but from there, matters became rather hazy. The conductor, who was a sociable chap, both to his ignorant driver and the passengers, managed to chat up a young lady on the front nearside seat who, no doubt, did not believe a word of the conductor's story about being lost. She laughingly called out directions of left, right and so on, until she got up to alight at Church Inn, Cheadle Hulme. Service 32 bears left here to Bramhall, but service 31, also to Bramhall, turns right. Faced with this choice, we again sought this last snippet of information from our alighting young lady. Luckily she was able to direct us but the look of horror on her face confirmed our suspicions that she had not believed we were lost at Cheadle. From Bramhall, I was able to find the route without difficulty although, in retrospect, I find it odd that I did not know the Cheadle to Bramhall section. Drivers at Manchester Garage came under the control of the garage foreman, at this time Mr W. Broadbent, and were, of course, based at the garage at Hulme Hall Road, which was surrounded by the River Irwell and tributaries of the Bridgewater Canal. The road was also an access to part of Pomona Dock and was

A Daimler Fleetline waits at the terminus of service 11X, Nags Head, Davyhulme, in August 1965.

One of two Leyland Olympics with integral Weymann body, No. 396 (EDB 323), on service 32, in February 1960, at Lower Mosley Street, Manchester.

No. 670 (KDB 670) was originally a Northwich car and the smartness of that depot's vehicles is reflected in the fact that this is the sole example of the class to retain its front wheel nut guard. A Leyland PD2/21 with Weymann lowbridge body, it is seen at Manchester Garage in May 1964.

In May 1958, an AEC Reliance with a Weymann body, No. 735 (LDB 735), stands outside Manchester Garage. When demoted to buses, these vehicles were not very popular with Manchester drivers.

used by lorries delivering to the docks. Otherwise, there was little cause for traffic to use the road further than the premises of firms on the Chester Road side of the canal bridge. After the bridge, the road widened on the right and continued to the garage entrance and to another firm's entrance next door. The road itself, curved to the left and entered the docks under one of the railway arches.

The road surface gave more than a hint of its origins since the side road, used by docks' transport leaving the docks and having to climb the slight slope fully-

laden, had two lines of smooth paving stones laid from the dock entrance arch to the canal bridge on Hulme Hall Road, the remainder being a cobbled surface. This was the old method of assisting horse-drawn lurries to climb gradients, by making the way smooth for the wheels but by leaving cobblestones between for the horses' hooves for a better grip. The pavement edges, near the garage entrance, were fitted with angle iron inserts which prevented the steel-tyred horse-drawn lurry wheels from crumbling the kerb edges away.

The arches of the railway viaduct, crossed the end of the road, like the bar of a letter 'T', and formed one wall of the North Western Garage so that buses inside the garage would be parked inside some of these arches. Two arches, which were situated near to the garage entrance, were equipped with service pits, tyre store and associated benches. Immediately inside the gate, another arch was built up and provided a crew room and toilet facilities. On the right of the entrance was the garage foreman's office and accommodation for garage staff and stores, and signing-on window for drivers. Lower Mosley Street Bus Station had a wonderful appeal for bus enthusiasts, but Manchester Garage had an equally devastating appeal, at least to me! In its jumbled layout, the garage was probably no different to the jumbled garages owned by BET companies throughout England and Wales, where premises have been secured in the only available space and the best use made of that space. A similar example was the Ribble garage at Trafalgar Street, Burnley, which was converted from the shell of a mill. It was a sort of split level arrangement which, as a modern house, would have won architectural awards hands down. As a bus garage it was a dump, but was one of the most interesting and appealing dumps I have known.

The area outside Manchester Garage and down to the dock entrance provided several arches in the viaducts for parking single deck vehicles and, when these had gone out into service, for cars belonging to the drivers. Opposite the arches was a timber fence between roadway and canal where the overflow of double deck buses could be parked. Other buses of all types, could be parked between the canal bridge and the garage entrance where the road widened. Just before I left Manchester Garage in 1967, the premises were extended on to the site of St. George's Finishing Works. Its impressive array of sliding doors and the North Western nameboard looked very professional. It was, but it had lost a lot of its old appeal.

No. 227 (FJA 227D), a Duple-bodied Leyland Leopard, is pictured in Manchester Garage in June 1966.

Lower Mosley Street, Manchester, in February 1961, seen from Lower Mosley Street inward bus stop where crew changeovers took place. The enquiry office is on the ground floor with Ribble and N—N offices above. Through Calder Street can be seen part of the Blackpool stand, complete with clock.

All drivers signed-on at the garage when a bus had to be taken out. Since conductors signed-on at Lower Mosley Street Station where there was an inspector in charge, it was necessary for a bus from garage to go to Lower Mosley Street to pick up the conductor. Twenty minutes signing-on time was given to a driver to collect his bus, get to Lower Mosley Street for his conductor and then depart in service. Most drivers arrived early enough to get to Lower Mosely Street and call in at the Golden Horse for a tea or coffee. Very often, that was the first port of call with conductors, making their way to the cafe after signing-on and collecting their ticket machine and duty board at the office.

Early duties usually signed-off at Lower Mosley Street so that drivers could make their way home, unless they had a car parked at the garage. Split duties often took the bus back to garage or, at least, put the morning bus on the parking ground at Lower Mosley Street and took another bus to garage. A brisk trade was done between drivers wanting to go straight home from Lower Mosley Street and those with cars at the garage, without a bus to take to garage. Usually all worked out well, with an empty bus station, when the arguing was over. The station inspector saw to that.

At night, when all duties had to return buses to garage and sign-off there, the Corporation's all-night services provided a useful means of reaching home if other transport was not available. The all-night departures started at 23.15, then 23.45 and 00.15. A staff bus left Manchester Garage at 23.35 and 00.05 to connect with the appropriate departure of buses from Piccadilly and went via Lower Mosley Street for the benefit of conductors. As in all bus undertakings, there was considerable effort put into the last journey to garage to ensure that the staff bus could be caught.

The feeling of working for N–N was that the Company worked well within the B E T Company Limited and loyalty to the Company was apparent, together with a fair amount of inter-depot rivalry. It must be admitted that where buses from different depots ran on the same routes, there was a certain amount of bad feeling when one bus 'pushed' the other along the road. This aspect of the industry, as a whole, of letting another bus do all the work, tends to even itself out as drivers and conductors progress through the rosters, the 'pushers' finding themselves on the duty where it is their turn to be 'pushed', although some crews are particularly expert or knowledgeable on timetables to prevent themselves being 'pushed'.

On the Manchester Depot routes to Flixton and Urmston, Manchester and Urmston Depots operated jointly, together with Manchester Corporation Transport Department. No doubt, due to the lack of express work to break the monotony of stage carriage work, the Corporation crews were, by far, the most expert at 'pushing' the bus in front, be it N–N or Corporation! The Corporation crews were rostered to a duty for a full week and this helped them to weigh

up the possibilities for 'pushing' on the first day and take advantage for the remainder of the week.

I was never too sure of the passenger loyalty to N–N since I was never convinced that they could tell a red Corporation bus from a red N–N vehicle. A passenger once told my conductor that she would report him to 'No. 55 Piccadilly' for some small offence, which suited my conductor beautifully since 'No. 55 Piccadilly' was the Corporation office!

North Western was a well-known Company due to its far-flung express service network. It also had a major attraction, certainly to the enthusiast, that it shared with Ribble Motor Services Limited and, to a much lesser degree, with other operators. This was Lower Mosley Street Bus Station, Manchester, which was run by Omnibus Stations Limited, a company jointly-owned by N–N and Ribble. With several jointly-operated services using the bus station, many operators' vehicles could be seen there.

Ribble operated its Manchester-based express and 'limited stop' network from here and had road staff signing-on facilities in the office block. The major operation was N–N's, since all conductors signed-on here and collected ticket machines and boxes and, of course, returned them here after duty. N–N drivers, signing-on at Lower Mosley Street when not taking a bus from garage would report to the inspector at the bus station.

The bus station was under the general supervision of a manager, Mr Williamson, who had the unenviable task of sorting out everyone's problems, whilst for operational purposes, both North Western and Ribble employed a senior inspector and superintendent, respectively, to look after their interests. Possibly, because the Ribble interests seemed to be less than that of North Western on the main part of the bus station, Mr Clitheroe, the superintendent, made up for it in personality. During peak operations, he could often be seen assisting his Inspectorate staff with much arm-waving, as he directed his drivers to the correct service stands, to ensure that the station was kept as free as possible of congestion. Despite these pressing problems, he was always ready to answer passengers' enquiries, as he rushed about the bus station, and I must record my own indebtedness to him for his help in furthering my bus enthusiasm for some years prior to my joining North Western at Stockport, and later whilst I was a driver for 'the other lot'.

It should not be supposed that North Western had a less efficient supervisor. The inspector in charge is still employed by the Company's successors elsewhere, so must remain nameless. In North Western's case, however, the steady puff of the incumbent's pipe indicated that all was well!

The atmosphere of this small bus station must have affected more people than its size would have one believe. Bus enthusiasts and passengers alike have made their way to this Manchester 'Mecca'. The famous X60 service to Blackpool has catered for vast queues of people, particularly at weekends in the

North Western vehicle No. 893 (RDB 893) stands parked on the Ribble side of Lower Mosley Street Bus Station in April 1965. It has arrived from Blackpool with an X60 service.

A quiet period at Lower Mosley Street in June 1966, showing a Ribble Leopard coach on service X9, Oldham to Blackpool. A N—N AEC Renown is also seen working service 28 for Little Hayfield.

Ribble Leyland Leopard, with a Marshall bus body, No. 548 (ARN 548B) is seen, in April 1965, on service X43, Manchester to Skipton, at Lower Mosley Street. This type of vehicle was used on joint services and was driven by N—N staff.

summer and on Bank Holidays. Buses on service X60 have been culled from all corners of the operators' garages, and local municipalities have hired buses, at the height of the season, to Ribble or North Western for use as duplicates on X60 services. Lancashire United Transport Limited also operated on the X60 service from Lower Mosely Street, usually with a varied selection of their Guy Arab fleet. Bolton and Leigh Corporations tended to operate 'on hire' to Ribble, with Manchester Corporation operating for N–N. Manchester's route number system with 'X'

suffixes gave rise to the latter's buses invariably displaying 60X on X60 journeys. Most of the duplicates operated fully-loaded to Blackpool, leaving the main operators to leave Lower Mosley Street with seats available for intermediate passengers. N–N or Ribble conductors in peak times would either collect fares on a hired bus, prior to its departure, from Lower Mosley Street, or travel to Bolton collecting fares before transferring to another bus. This latter method enabled several buses to be serviced by one conductor and was also applied to duplicates hired

No. 958 (GCK 293), of the Ribble fleet, a Leyland Tiger Cub with Burlingham Seagull coachwork, waits to take out the X14 service to Burnley in April 1965. These coaches were often used on the joint services between Blackpool and Nottingham.

Ribble's allocation for the X60, Manchester to Blackpool, service often turned out to be an Atlantean with an MCW body in semi-coach guise, not normally driven by N–N drivers. No. 1273 (RRN 422) is seen on this service at Lower Mosley Street in April 1965.

for other services, such as Scarborough and North Wales. My own initial contact with Lower Mosley Street came when I bought my first Ribble fleet list, one of the well known 'ABC' editions. This was July 1952 and I began to 'spot' Ribble buses. I think that Ribble was my predominant interest, at that time, due to several wartime holidays at Knott End, over the River Wyre from Fleetwood, where Ribble operated services to Blackpool, Lancaster and Garstang, amongst other local destinations. In retrospect, I realized that the buses that had fired my interest had been Leyland Cheetahs of LZ2A or LZ5 types. However, living in North Manchester meant that I saw little of the Ribble fleet other than those on X4 or X14 services, the nearest routes, which operated along Rochdale Road. This led me to visit their Manchester bus station, Lower Mosley Street.

My 'spotting' days were brief and I quickly became a photographer of buses and in view of the gaps in the Ribble fleet list, I started to take an interest in the vehicle history. Sadly, I had a one-track mind at this stage and took far less interest in other operators, than in Ribble, for the first couple of years.

This is worthy of a slight digression. At the time, one of the main recipients of ex-BET buses was the dealer, Frank Cowley Limited, Salford. This firm had office premises in Blackfriars Road, Salford, with space for one bus, which would be serviced, or generally tidied up, ready for sale. Depending, presumably, on how sales were progressing, several other vehicles would be parked, nearby, on Blackfriars Road or in adjoining back streets. Cowley had a larger bus park at Fallowfield, at the corner of Moseley Road and Wilmslow Road, where, on my first visit in 1952, it was possible to see, through gaps in the fence, 1936 ex-Ribble Cheetah coaches and a varied assortment of ex-BET vehicles. Further afield, was the yard at Pennington, near Leigh (Lancashire) where an even larger and varied collection was housed.

I remember one visit to this location when I saw a Leyland TD1 with a Hall Lewis body, (later, this company became Park Royal Limited) which was of the lowbridge variety, but with seats centrally-placed in the upper saloon with a gangway along both sides of the saloon. The mid-1950s was a time when many time-expired vehicles were sold to dealers after their lives had been extended by the shortages of the war years, 1939–45.

My visits to Cowley's sites and other yards confirmed fleet details of many examples of the Ribble fleet, usually culled by squinting through gaps in fences, so that registration and fleet numbers could be checked. Visits to Lower Mosley Street invariably included a trip to Cowley's yard at Blackfriars Road or Fallowfield to see his latest acquisitions!.

For the first two years, or so, of my enthusings, I probably visited Lower Mosley Street virtually every Saturday, early summer Saturdays being particularly interesting, in view of the necessity for the operators to dredge vehicles from all the extremities of their empires. Enthusiasts from all parts of the north-west, and sometimes from further afield, would meet at Lower Mosley Street at the height of the season and I feel that no other bus station, in this corner of the country, could have given so much pleasure and provided such a varied diet of vehicles and services as did Lower Mosley Street Bus Station. Having known Chorlton Street Bus Station, albeit, closer to the city centre than Lower Mosley Street, since it was first built, and later roofed with a multi-storey car-park, I find that it does not have any attraction, to me at least, as a centre for Ribble or N–N, and yet the routes and fluctuations of service brought about by N–N's demise and reorganization, in NBC and National Travel, must have equal interest, to some enthusiasts, as Lower Mosley Street had for me in the 1950s and 1960s. The operations to and from Lower Mosley Street, in the 1950s, required buses from many far-flung depots and these were parked overnight, on Saturdays, under the railway on Great Bridgewater Street, in the case of Ribble, with the Scottish companies using Whitworth Street West. North Western, too, used Whitworth Street West as a

Having just been repainted, No. 666 (KDB 666), one of the PD2/21 vehicles with Weymann bodywork, stands in Whitworth Street West, in July 1965, ready to go on to the Liverpool stand at Lower Mosley Street, as a 'duplicate', on service X97. Behind, stands a Leyland Leopard, of the Sheffield Joint Omnibus Committee's fleet, probably on the X48, the Woodhead service to Sheffield.

parking spot, prior to bringing a coach or bus on to a crowded stand in the bus station. Drivers used to park there en route from the Manchester Depot, report to the stand inspector, and then join their colleagues in the Golden Horse for a tea or coffee. Inspectors found this a useful rallying point. The buses, so parked, would enter the bus station via Trumpet Street past the Ribble Depot (it held six Royal Tigers, with careful manoeuvring), and so on to the more open part of Lower Mosley Street, opposite the well-known and well-photographed site, where offices and bus stands were provided. This section, divided from the rest of the bus station by Great Bridgewater Street, was a coach parking area which was used, District services, together with N–N's London and North Wales services. PMT's Stoke-on-Trent and Hanley service also terminated on this side. In the season when the morning departures were loading, the area was a turmoil of buses and people. It was to this side of the bus station that N–N buses, coming from garage in the early morning or mid afternoon to collect conductors ready for peak hour work, parked. The times of buses from garage for such work did not normally clash with the express loadings.

Behind the petrol station, next to Lower Mosley Street, was a coaching parking area which was used, at busy times, for loading services to points such as Great Yarmouth, Scarborough, Skegness and the like. It teemed with vehicles and people, as did the bus station proper. On a special parking lot in this area was parked an ex-Rochdale Corporation TD5 (DDK 117). In a very smart green livery with neat lining, this was the Manchester Depot canteen and had been fitted out by the Works at Charles Street, Stockport. This was another rallying point for crews. Snacks and cups of tea, coffee, Bovril and the like were dispensed efficiently by the lady behind the counter, which was situated in the lower saloon. Tables were arranged between seats upstairs and I think the arrangement worked well. The adverse comments one might hear were no different from those made about the most modern canteens and restaurants that I have heard during my years in the industry. The usual rule applies, I think, that the grass on the other side of the street is always greener, until you get there! This was to be the case in many other ways.

A number of staff joined the Company from Manchester, or one of the surrounding Corporation Transport departments. They looked forward to some long distance work including the famous X60 service to Blackpool. Inevitably, their desire would be fulfilled during the summer months, when additional buses were required, or because a more senior man wanted his rest day 'off'. Purely coincidentally, this was a time of heavy traffic, and after the first Blackpool journey, most newcomers realized that the two hour, eleven minutes trip to Blackpool became vastly longer, after the traffic jam through Preston had been negotiated, and also due to the jams when entering Blackpool. The result was a late arrival in Blackpool with time for a quick 'cuppa' whilst the inspector directed the queue to your bus, if you were lucky, and then a traffic-packed journey home. After this, express work was not sought after to quite the same degree. I can speak with authority on this subject as this is how I found the work!

In some cases, drivers joining the Company from local municipalities had already experienced the 'limited stop' routes of the Company since both N–N and Ribble hired buses, usually double deckers, from local Corporation Transport Departments, in the summer peak periods. N–N tended to recruit Manchester Corporation for Blackpool duplicates. What enthusiast had not seen the inevitable indicator display, on Manchester Corporation vehicles on X60 services showing 60X, the nearest that their blinds could get to the official number?

Leigh Corporation's AEC Regents were often used by Ribble to cover their service X50 to Morecambe, whilst they supplemented service X60 with hirings from Bolton Corporation, usually starting at Bolton. In more recent years, changed circumstances have brought Fylde Borough buses on to the X60 scene, although the present NBC service is 952, part of the Nottingham to Blackpool service, X60 having gone the way of many rural local services, something that seemed impossible not too many years ago.

Mention of the use of duplicates brings to mind the fact that N–N has always been famous for its use of the destination display 'Duplicate'. It seemed that on any occasion when an extra bus was needed on a service, 'Duplicate' was the display, even if the name of the destination was actually on the blind. No doubt, this could be compared to the use of the display, 'Relief' by so many of the Eastern Coachworks-bodied Bristols of the BTC companies.

When one thinks about duplication on long distance services, it will be realized that the traffic jam situation is natural, since it is on Bank Holidays or peak summer 'Wakes' weekends when the passengers wish to travel. Equally so, these are days when one stays away from popular busy roads when having a run out in the car, the same busy roads from which, as driver of the Nottingham service, you cannot deviate on a Bank Holiday. It may, of course, be possible to un-officially leave the licensed route to miss a 'pinch' point for traffic in a town, but the deviation will be small in comparison to, for example, the eighty miles between Manchester and Nottingham.

Returning to the bus stations stands, if the London side of the bus station and the Isherwood's Garage extension sound chaotic, what of the main section? This section had offices, public toilet, waiting-rooms and passenger queueing facilities on the side adjoining Lower Mosley Street, none of which catered for the numbers of passengers using them at busy periods. Buses entered from this street via Calder Street, alongside the College of Further Education, leaving the bus station via Great Bridgewater Street. A three lane width adjoined the offices, etc., followed by a passenger shelter and refuge, and another three lane section with another shelter (for X60 and X70 Blackpool departures), as the far boundary of the bus station. All dimensions catered for 1930s sizes of buses but, by now, were accepting the new maximum 36 ft. x 8 ft. 2½ in. types. The lanes nearest the offices catered for Buxton, Macclesfield, Bradford, Leeds and beyond. Against the centre shelter were stands for services 32, X19/X20 and Hayfield, service 32 being at the Great Bridgewater Street end. On the other side of this shelter started the Ribble territory,

The Ribble side of the bus station at Lower Mosley Street, where departures for the Lake District and Scotland waited. The Plaxton-bodied Leyland Leopard has arrived on service X30 from Glasgow, in April 1965, whilst the Burlingham-bodied Tiger Cub waits to depart for Ambleside on service X40.

No. 432 arouses interest on the 'spare' stand at Lower Mosley Street, in December 1965, when flanked by a Ribble 'White Lady' and No. 148 of the N–N Leopard Y type fleet.

covering services X3, X13, X4, X14, X23, X43 and X53. Although a long list, these services dovetailed to a 30 minute Burnley service and beyond, and a similar frequency operated to Great Harwood and beyond. On the far side of these three lanes were services X60/X70, as already mentioned. At the rear of the X3 service, etc., were services X1 and 6. Service 6 was operated by Manchester and Ashton Corporations, and the SHMD Board (Stalybridge, Hyde, Mossley and Dukinfield), who operated to Glossop on this service. Both service 6 and service 28 were, possibly, the least fortunate of all those using the bus station. Being at the rear of their respective stands, they could depart by using the middle of the three lanes in their section of the bus station. With Hayfield services leaving at 20 and 50 minutes past each hour, there would often be a Buxton bus on its stand with a service 32 from Middlewood or Higher Poynton against the opposite stand, having arrived slightly earlier than the official 22 or 52 minutes past the hour. If a Leeds or Liverpool duplicate had arrived, the centre lane would be blocked and reversing would be the only answer. Service 6 had a similar problem, again departing at 20 and 50 minutes past the hour. Here, however, service X43 left at 52 minutes past, and services X4, X14 or X53 at 22 past the hour. If blocked in, it was a question

of wait or reverse. Needless to say, it was rare for the Blackpool stand to be empty. Service 6 was, incidentally, the only regular operation of any of its municipal operators into Lower Mosley Street.

The services of the bus station were reasonably comprehensive, although the 'overflow' necessities of Isherwood's Garage car-park, or the London side of the bus station, lacked ample waiting facilities, either seats or shelters, except for one central shelter and refuge in the centre of the London side. This was later demolished and replaced by a large waiting-room and staff canteen fashioned from the old Ribble garage premises. This was possible after North Western's depot had been rebuilt and extended, around 1968, and Ribble took a share of the maintenance facilities.

The enquiry office was comprehensively equipped and almost always busy, so that telephones rang incessantly as enquirers tried to obtain information. A popular departure point in the summer, Lower Mosley Street positively 'bent' under the weight of travellers in the rail strikes of the early 1960s.

The transfer of bus station facilities, in 1973, to Chorlton Street Bus Station ended an era in the histories of the companies running into Manchester. By then, of course, the BET had given way to the National Bus Company.

Chorlton Street Bus Station facilities in Corporation ownership were varied. The Leyland Royal Tiger with Northern Counties 'Crush Loader' (standee type) body, No. 25 (NNB 25), was a waiting-room for passengers. The Leyland TS1, No. A87 (VR 5742) with Manchester Corporation 'Car Works' body, was a crew room for road staff! The scene was photographed in March 1964.

Some spare duties that used Lower Mosley Street, as the signing-on point for both drivers and conductors, also covered Chorlton Street Bus Station in the days when services to Torkington (51), Woodford (20), Wilmslow (52) and Macclesfield (30) used these facilities. These covered late duties or the second parts of split duties which were signing-on at Lower Mosley Street and then, after walking to Chorlton Street, would take over on one of these services. Any crew failure here could be quickly covered with the spare crew 'on the spot'. Wilmslow and Torkington, not being the most popular of services, meant that spare duty 166 at Chorlton Street would rarely reach the end of the afternoon without taking over some

work, often having to complete the full duty. I always felt out of the way at Chorlton Street with its mainly Corporation operation, although the inspector on duty was a friendly sort.

This was a feeling that also applied at Piccadilly or Parker Street Bus Station, the stronghold of Manchester Corporation. Whilst there were no crew reliefs at Piccadilly itself, other than service 64, North Western crews were very much in the minority in the canteen but, at least, there were enough North Western operations to provide another North Western crew to talk to. Despite these comments, the MCTD crews were, generally, friendly enough, most of their rivalry being saved for their 'oppos' from other

Corporation garages. A service which was separate from other North Western routes, was service 64, Piccadilly to Moss Nook, Styal or Ringway Airport. This service was operated mainly by MCTD, with one bus being provided by North Western. Since the operation along the Wilmslow Road corridor, Palatine Road, through Northenden and Gatley was all Corporation territory, there was no friendly face to wave to, except for the occasional view of a Stockport or Altrincham car on service 80 in the Northenden area, and again on service 71 in the Gatley area. The Airport terminus at Outwood Road, to which the service operated in my part-time days, was replaced by a more elaborate bus lay-by in the new airport development, and even this has now been improved.

Service 64 was alone in having St. Peter's Square as its unofficial relieving point, since crews were normally scheduled to travel up to Piccadilly. However, most crews walked the short distance to St. Peter's Square and relieved the off-going crew in the square, then continuing to Piccadilly terminus.

The summer months at Lower Mosley Street Bus Station provided a spectacle worth seeing, particularly on Saturday mornings. Head office published a weekly list of bus requirements which covered, in the main, the Saturday operation but also those of

Sunday and any other day, when one or other part of the North Western empire had a 'Wakes' or special operation, for which duplicate vehicles were required. This list of serial spares would identify all the duplicates in numerical order, and the buses, operating these journeys, would have a paper number stuck in the windscreen for identification purposes. A passing inspector could tell, at a glance, what the vehicle was doing by referring to his spares sheet. In this way, ten buses allocated to service X60 duplicates could be identified, although it was by no means unknown for one of these spares to be found elsewhere on the Company's routes, especially if the vehicle was a single decker.

This was often apparent from the roster sheets showing a driver's, or conductor's, work for the week. I remember being listed for '1020 Hayfield Duplicate' on one Bank Holiday when it was usual for the bus station to disappear amongst the throngs of hikers searching for buses to Hayfield, Buxton, Higher Poynton and the more exotic destinations of Barnsley or Leeds, when they could alight at various points in the Pennine Hills. When the Sheffield routes via Snake Pass (X39), Woodhead (X48) and Castleton (X72) arrived, they also did a good trade in hikers. My bus, on this occasion, was a faithful K5G, No. 406 (JA 7722), a normal Hayfield service type of

No. 219 (CDB 219), a Leyland PD1 with ECW bodywork, on service 5 for Flixton, stands at Piccadilly Bus Station, Manchester, in April 1960.

In May 1964, No. 406 (JA 7722) a 1938 Bristol K5G with a 1951 Willowbrook body, is seen at Canning Place, Liverpool on an X97 'duplicate'. A West Yorkshire service car is behind. No. 406 was withdrawn in 1965 and the lack of brightwork tends to reflect this as the radiator is no longer kept polished but is painted, as are the headlight bezels.

vehicle. Arriving at Lower Mosley Street, however, I was instructed to park on the spare stand and eventually became the '1040 Liverpool Duplicate'. This was the last season of K5G operation, 1965, and whilst it made a change to take No. 406 to Liverpool instead of on an ordinary stage carriage route, I feel sure that the passengers were not impressed. So much for serial spares!

The duty rosters at North Western worked on the basis of drivers having different conductors each day and, to this end, the drivers proceeded down the roster lists each week whilst conductors' names moved up their lists. This did mean, unfortunately, that conductors with a reasonable 'bus enthusiast' interest worked with me infrequently, which was probably just as well since I have occasionally talked of buses and forgotten to leave the terminus on time.

It is difficult to include comments about the characters of the industry who helped to make up the atmosphere, especially when those same people are still employed by the successors of N–N, or are in other parts of the industry. However, I have noticed, over the years, how bus stations and garages have their 'hangers on' who, in their own, unofficial way, have added their 'two penn'orth' to the scene to make up the fascination of the bus station or garage.

Lower Mosley Street had more than its share of characters. Along Great Bridgewater Street, which divided the bus station, was a Salvation Army Hostel. This did an excellent job of looking after some of the wanderers of Manchester. Before it was time for them to book in at the hostel, a few of the wanderers would appear at the bus station and carry passengers' luggage to the taxi rank at Central Railway Station, or on the station itself.

One of the characters I came to know did similar work but was not one of the wanderers. He was well-known to the Ribble crews since he appeared to live in the Chorley area through which town most of the Ribble Manchester Garage services operated. Geoffrey had a flat cap and wore an overcoat, whatever the weather. He would often be found with the crews in the Golden Horse Cafe, supping tea, or helping to carry luggage. He was an oddity since, although he was generally considered to have 'a slate loose', he never seemed to miss a trick and seemed to know exactly what he was doing. Whenever I climbed out of a bus cab on the bus station when Geoffrey was around, he would stride across the bus station oblivious to all around him, including traffic, arm outstretched, and shake my hand heartily, addressing me as 'squire'. A most friendly and helpful character!

Apart from the London service, and the official one man operated Bradford service, conductors were carried on all the Company's express services from Manchester. We had one conductress who was famous for her knitting. Once fare collection was complete, she would find a spare seat or, if the coach was full, sit on her ticket box on the top step of the front entrance, and knit whilst talking to the driver.

She was a character who could charm a bus load of passengers, if she so wished. She did not believe in talking softly so everyone joined in the 'entertainment'. Once she had collected all the fares she would ask if everyone had a ticket and if they would like to pay again. When I was her driver, she knew that I preferred to drive without disturbance, so she used to find an empty seat down the bus, take out her knitting, and proceed to tell the passengers that I had fallen out with her, and she would talk to them instead. She was a character of the type that one man operation cannot fully replace, although some OMO drivers can be oddities in their own right!

Chapter Three ~ Driving Techniques and North Westerns 'Kick it in' Training

This chapter will, of necessity, light on many aspects of a driver's work, ranging from the fierceness of a clutch, to the way in which a 36 ft. bus or coach is handled in confined spaces of bus depots or bus stations which were designed for 27 ft. 6 in. long vehicles.

A driver can climb into his cab, or however one might describe entering the cab of a rear-engined double decker or underfloor-engined single decker, and immediately feel 'at home' in a comfortable seat or not, as the case may be! Initial impressions, particularly transferring from one bus to another, are not always correct.

On many occasions, I have climbed into another bus after a break from driving a similar type and reacted to a feeling of an uncomfortable seat or steering position only to find, after fifteen minutes driving, that I have adjusted to the new vehicle and find it as comfortable as one could hope for. I always considered the Mark 2 Lolines to be better, as far as the cab seat was concerned, than the later Mark 3, which had the more rectangular seat squab and cushion. To some extent, the inferior seat was offset by the improved gearbox and gear change lever arrangement of the Mark 3. Rarely, therefore, does one find a design that is perfect in all respects, even solely from a driver's point of view. When one has to consider perfection from the points of view of engineering and management, then overall efficiency often becomes a low percentage. For a bus to be reliable suggests simplicity of design, ease of access to components for servicing or eventual replacement, without excessive time off the road and out of revenue-earning service.

Daimler Fleetline No. 167 (DDB 167C), photographed on 20th August 1967, and one of the types of vehicles referred to in this chapter.

Taking this to what might now be considered the extreme, would call for the continuation of the crash or constant mesh gearbox in place of the pneumocyclic unit. For practical purposes, only the Bristol RE was fitted with a non-pneumocyclic type of unit, of the rear-engined variants, as far as my own experience is concerned. It is of interest to note, however, that the prototype Daimler Fleetline sported a preselector gearbox, in its early days but, by the time of its Commercial Motor Show appearance and subsequent demonstration, the pneumocyclic version had been fitted, together with the gearchange switch similar to the Leyland Atlantean fitment. Interestingly, the two gear switches varied, from the driver's point of view, only in the length of the gear-lever. The Atlantean edition was long enough to be moved by finger tips with the hand remaining on the steering wheel, whilst the Fleetline version was stubby and the driver's hand had to leave the steering wheel to change gear. Perhaps, since most of my driving was on Fleetline variants, I have never found the Daimler version inconvenient in comparison with the Leyland. On more modern machines of AN68 or Fleetline types, the offside position of the gear-lever is rationalized even more by the fitting of the same unit on both chassis types.

A Weymann bus-bodied Leyland Tiger Cub, No. 578A (FDB 578), fitted for one man operation and photographed in August 1965.

A driver will be required to spend much of his time behind the wheel of one or several buses or coaches during his spell of duty. A duty could be short, paying the minimum six hours and forty minutes, or one operating on express or 'limited stop' work, where more than ten hours could be called for. Not unnaturally, driving a vehicle which is of an acceptable standard will help the duty go down well and keep the driver happy enough to do his work efficiently and well. At the same time, the interior of the vehicle must satisfy the conductor's requirement for similar benefits in this area.

Since my own interest in the job, whilst following that of all employees to be able to make money, was important, my bus enthusiasm enabled me to take a little more than average interest in other directions; namely the vehicles.

With no disrespect to my colleagues, a general bus driver's attitude is: 'If it goes fast, it's a good bus'. This can be further qualified by . . . 'and if it's got a synchromesh gearbox'. Well down the list comes any thought of brakes, steering and handling. This attitude, in my opinion, was the basis of the success of the AEC Reliance of the late 1950s and early to mid-1960s. Compared to North Western's Tiger Cub buses, whose top speed was often no more than 36 m.p.h., the Reliances would do 50, 60 or even more, as a general rule, only the earlier Weymann and

Newly delivered at Stockport Garage, in February 1959, is No. 760 (LDB 760).

Burlingham-bodied examples being healthily disliked. But the majority of Reliances were dual-purpose vehicles and had light steering, too light I thought, and excellent brakes, although when later examples departed from the 'organ pedal' operation, the light braking effort required caused difficulties to the driver who was trying not to upset his passengers.

My interest in the Reliance would not have generated any rosy glow of satisfaction at Southall, but then you cannot please everyone. The synchromesh gearbox worked well until you needed a swift change when, whether going up or down the box, the gear-lever seemed to hit a brick wall when moving out of neutral. Presumably this was a selector fault but I wasn't terribly interested in this 'A E C rubbish' as I termed them at that time! Despite my prejudices, firms such as Yelloway of Rochdale concentrated on this type of chassis for their high mileage coach fleet with considerable, apparent, success.

It can be appreciated, therefore, that many and varied are the requirements expected by the crews who work them, these requirements not necessarily coinciding with those expected by the traffic and engineering departments of the Company. During his work on a bus, a driver will take note of the engine, gearbox, brakes, steering, handling and general accessibility of the controls, but the order of his assessment will depend on his personal attitude to his work. There will also be a tendency for a younger driver to criticize a good bus purely because its maximum speed may be 40 miles per hour, whilst an older driver will consider the bus perfect, with its maximum speed being quite acceptable. However, I enjoyed my years with North Western and was a bus enthusiast, and still am, during the years recalled in these writings. This does not mean that there was never a time when boredom set in but, happily, the variation in work and buses did much to keep this to a minimum. As a realistic enthusiast, I would like to think my feelings tended to notice the mechanisms of buses and coaches as follows. The order of priorities, was not always the same for each vehicle but tended to be comfort, engine power, gearbox, brakes, steering, handling and general accessibility of controls as

listed earlier, as far as I was concerned. The description of 'engine power' needs to be qualified since I was young enough to enjoy speed, and may well have been referred to as a young tearaway driver at some time or other during my early career. But, the nicest, and most pleasant vehicle I ever recall driving, even now, sixteen years and many, many, buses later, was a Northern General Leopard coach with a Harrington Cavalier body. This was on a winter's evening journey from Manchester to Leeds and back, possibly the 18.40 ex-Lower Mosley Street Bus Station. That vehicle, I estimated, was slow by comparison with many of the North Western's excellent Leopards, but the handling, comfort and generally well-maintained works, ensured an unforgettable run. This was in the days of operation on this X97 portion of route via the old roads through Oldham, over Standedge across the Pennines, through Huddersfield and Dewsbury, and on to Leeds. A good bus on the Pennines was a blessing and fully appreciated when it was necessary to overtake the slow, lumbering, 'heavies' on the winding A62. The power of No. 1955 enabled light work to be made of the hills, whilst the other, very important factor of passenger comfort was well to the fore.

Any lack of top speed was, to some extent, theoretical since the old roads to Yorkshire presented few opportunities for excessive speeds, assuming one wanted to attain them. The run with that Leopard could be contrasted with the stark Bristol LS vehicles of West Yorkshire Road Car Company Limited, who supplied machines from the CUG series in their coach fleet. CUG stood for Coach, Underfloor, Gardner, I believe, but the translations from drivers not appreciative of these well built, solid, vehicles had to be heard to be believed! I found these LS vehicles solid, slow machines with a five-speed constant mesh gearbox, the first four speeds of which were identical in maximum speed terms, to the Bristol K5G of 1939 vintage, in which I had an ownership interest. The fifth gear of the LS took the modern coach up to about 55 m.p.h., in favourable conditions. It seemed an injustice to the Manchester to Leeds section of X97 and X99 services that we North Western drivers

No. 828 (RDB 828) is one of five AEC Reliances with 41 seat Willowbrook bodywork in the N—N fleet, which was built in 1960. It is seen, on 20th August 1965, at Stockport.

should labour slowly up Standedge with a CUG, unable to overtake a heavy lorry, whilst drivers of West Yorkshire vehicles were able to wave, gaily, as they passed in the opposite direction with a beautiful Y type-bodied Leopard of our Company! A consoling thought on this service, whose other ramifications between Manchester and Liverpool came into our jurisdiction was that, at least, we had a varied menu of machines and this, to an interested driver, meant a lot.

To digress a little, my interest in gearboxes has developed over the years, especially since many of my cars have been fitted with the preselector type of epicyclic box. For the record, this refers to Crossley Regis and Armstrong Siddeley Sapphire cars. The Regis sparked off my interest in old cars, although the first Regis was purchased as cheap transport; cheap, clapped-out transport, as I later found! The interest must have been uppermost in my mind since I eventually owned seven of these cars, although only two concurrently. The Sapphire was a lovely car which, at the time of purchase, was old enough at thirteen years to be cheap, but in good enough condition to look very expensive. I still have it in daily use. Surprisingly, my PSV preselector experience has been relatively little, with crash and constant mesh gearboxes taking a greater part of my time, with

pneumocyclic variants probably vying with synchromesh for second place.

When I first went to work for North Western in their head office at Charles Street, Stockport, my bus enthusiasm needed only one thing to make it, for me, perfection; a PSV driver's licence and badge. Having served in the Royal Air Force for my two years of National Service, I had been happy to obtain a driving licence and experience on a variety of cars and commercial vehicles, many with a German flavour, since I served in Germany for most of my two years. On return to 'civvy street', I waited for a suitable period to forget having learnt to drive on the right with left-hand drive vehicles, took my British test and was fortunate enough to pass first time. That was my first step. Earlier opportunities to drive had been very intermittent occasions when I had managed to drive the odd old bus in scrap yards where I knew the scrap man reasonably well. My first attempt was due to the scrap man being unable to find reverse gear in a Regent I or II, I forget which; an ex-Crosville Motor Services Limited vehicle. Having taken a keen interest for many years, I knew the gear layouts although I had never had the chance to prove my knowledge in practice. I happily reversed the Regent down the yard to the scrap man's satisfaction and, particularly, my own!

No. 141 (AJA 141B), a 1964-built Leyland Leopard with Alexander bodywork, is seen, in 1965, at Manchester Garage.

In 1961, my turn came and I was allowed to use my lunch hour, plus a little working time, to go through the driver training course of North Western. No. 146, (BJA 446) was a Bristol L5G of 1948 with an Eastern Coachworks B35R body used by the training department at Charles Street when I started my driving. I was quite happy about this, but only a few months earlier would have found a Bristol JO5G with an Eastern Counties body as my steed. I did not, however, look the gift horse in the mouth! The initial introduction took place one Saturday morning when the instructor drove No. 146 to Hazel Grove and stopped on the Macclesfield Road just past the Rising Sun, adjacent to the present terminus layby of GMT service 192. I took the wheel and, having explained controls and technique, the instructor said, 'Off you go'. He sat behind me in the first offside seat of the saloon, with only a dual handbrake to arrest my progress if it became necessary. I was in my element as I trundled slowly towards Macclesfield at the wheel of a bus, on the open road, for the very first time.

The narrow, pleasant countryside roads of Poynton, Pott Shrigley and Bollington made an excellent training ground, not just in an exercise of manoeuvreability but in gear changing on the hills. The gearbox of a pre-war Bristol is what I now consider to be 'very crash'. This is my definition of a crash box which cannot be mis-used. Some vehicles, I later found, had crash boxes where, if the revs were not quite right, could be forced into gear, albeit noisily, without further revving. The Bristol was not of this type. Although it was years later that I found the full details of the clutch stop, the technique of gear changing was geared (!) to this, so I will mention it now.

Newcomers were told to 'kick it in' when changing gear upwards and this meant that the clutch pedal was only depressed a slight amount, possibly half an inch to one inch, rather than right to the full extent of its travel. This enabled the gear change to take place in a slow cycle of lever going to neutral, revs falling to the correct level and the lever being moved to the next gear, both clutch movements being of the 'kick it in' variety. Changing down tended to be similar, but the novice tended to be overawed by the noise of the Gardner 5 cylinder revving high, ready for the downward change. This led to a crashing and often missing of gears so that the revs had to be built up again and a further attempt made. On downward hills, such a situation could find the bus running faster so that the second attempt could never hope to succeed, due to the relatively excessive speed of the bus. A missed gear was always overcome by letting the revs fall to the level required to engage the next higher gear, the one that we were trying to change from in the first place, before the second try was made. At least the bus was in gear, in these cases, and, technically under control.

Practice in gear changing was obtained by the simple expedient of upsetting the residents of a local housing estate. The efficiency of this method was that the populus could be upset in two ways. One of the routes used to assess applicants for PSV driving work was from Charles Street Garage, via Wellington Road South to Nangreave Road, by which time the applicant would have indicated his ability to the instructor and the next applicant would take over. It was not unknown for an HGV driver, although HGV licences were not in existence at that time, to be softened by synchromesh gearboxes in his daily work and find the usual double deck K5G to be more than his nerves could stand. Having fumbled the Bristol gears as far as Nangreave Road, such an applicant would leap out of the cab, tell the instructor to 'stick the job' and disappear up the road. Continuing along Nangreave Road, the road became Hillcrest Road after crossing Dialstone Lane. Between here and Marple Road was a roundabout, where two estate roads joined Hillcrest Road. The technique was to drive round and round the roundabout which provided practice in steering as well as in changing from second gear to third gear and back to second gear, so gaining plenty of experience in getting the revs right for upwards or downward changes. The instructions to change through the gears, to first or top, would offset any possibility of one becoming too accustomed to the whole affair and, at times, would create complete confusion for the novice. What the local residents thought of this pantomime is not recorded.

More scenic frays, during my early hours of tuition, took place in the pleasant countryside to the east of the A523 Macclesfield Road, where narrow lanes, steep hills and blind bends, with the added hazard of the occasional service bus on route 8, Stockport to Macclesfield, via Bollington, contributed to the finer points of familiarization, particularly in the gearbox handling.

A favourite ploy was for the instructor to order the novice to stop near the bottom of an incline. Lessons in fast gearchanging then took place, so that by the time the bus had arrived at the top of the hill, the quick change from first to second, and on to third, if possible, had been attempted, if not actually achieved, several times. Without knowing why, we were told to change from first to second as quickly as possible in one movement with the clutch pedal hard to the floor. Normally, the slow change involved putting the gear lever in neutral and letting the clutch pedal return fully, before again pressing the pedal and putting the gear-lever in neutral and letting the clutch pedal return fully, before again pressing the pedal and putting the gear-lever into the next higher gear. This allowed the engine revs to fall and was the usual 'double de-clutching' system usually necessary on crash or constant mesh gearboxes.

The quick change system used the 'clutch stop' by the pedal being depressed to the extent of its travel, and was usually needed for hill climbing so that engine revs could be maintained and a reasonable speed ensured. Faster operation in traffic, usually in the peak hours, benefited from the use of the 'clutch stop'. Once the learner had the hang of the essentials, 'promotion' to double deck Bristol K5Gs took place. This part of familiarization took place, therefore, on selected service buses. The PSV test had to be taken on a fully operational and PSV-licensed bus. Since the instructor, and later the examiner, had to be able to direct the driver, two of North Western's K5G fleet of sixty four vehicles were specially adapted so that the window, behind the driver, could be removed very easily but could be made quickly secure for service operation. To the novice, the two chosen steeds were the most clapped-out and difficult of the fleet of sixty four. This is probably untrue since my

No. 146E (CDB 146) a Bristol L5G with an ECW body, converted for use as a training bus for drivers. It is pictured at Stockport in February 1960, probably recovering from the author's gearchanges!

personal opinion, from later experience, was that the whole fleet of K5Gs was designed and built to make life as difficult as possible for the driver, from new! No. 404 (JA 7720) and No. 423 (JA 7795) were the training service buses although, a little later, when the withdrawal of the K5Gs began, No. 408 (JA 7724) became the permanent double deck training bus alongside the single decker, No. 146.

More experience and familiarization was gained in No. 404 or No. 423 around the Stockport test route, which was obviously designed to include the nastier problems associated with cobbled streets, crash gearboxes and reckless motorists. The latter were probably hired by the Ministry of Transport to make the driving test more difficult!

Another regular route was to follow the service 28 road to Marple and sometimes Hayfield or the 27X Circular around New Mills. Cafés were suitably placed, in all cases, but the one at Marple was the most popular.

In order to prepare us, in some slight way, for the wilds of PSV driving, we were taught the 'racing change' from second to third, by our instructors, and in the late stages of our training we would be asked to drive from Charles Street Garage to Nangreave Road with a new applicant who was then to try his hand at a K5G. The instructor would see how we coped up Charles Street and, if all was well, he would lean

through into the cab and whisper instructions for a 'racing change' into third. This was guaranteed to draw comment from the new applicant who was invariably several shades whiter at Nangreave Road than he had been at Charles Street. A successful 'racing change' always went down well and when climbing from the cab on one such occasion, the new applicant commented 'That's not the first b. . . .y time you've driven one of these b. . . . .s!' It boosted one's ego until the test day came along!

There was a time when I went whiter than white and was lucky (!) to be the first one in to drive. North Western usually made the examiner's journey worthwhile by booking four or so test cases at a time. Those awaiting their turn sat upstairs with the instructor, leaving only the examiner directing the novice driver around the test route. Having found that mirror or seat adjustment made driving the K5G no easier, great play of checking these items was made since it was reputed to impress the examiner. I don't think it did.

The test route wandered down Hillgate and along some of Stockport's badly cobbled streets before the instruction to 'stop here' and the next novice took over, came as a welcome relief to battered nerves. Nerves remained taut, however, since all was not yet over. Back at Charles Street, each driver went downstairs to grapple with the sequence of traffic light operation and mandatory signs, as one's expertise in the Highway Code was tested. At the end of my own test, the welcome phrase, 'You have passed' resulted, some weeks later, in the issue of PSV driver's badge No. CC73644, in November 1961.

It is an interesting comparison to look at vehicle familiarization in 1961 and 1981. After my successful test, the roads of service 28 were again put to good use on the section from Charles Street to Marple as a variety of North Western's multitudinous fleet was tried. My first 'modern' bus, of underfloor variety, was No. 500 (FDB 500), one of the Company's Atkinson Alphas, the fastest coal lorries built, as they were termed by experienced drivers. When I later came to drive these buses in service, I realized that they were indeed fast, but this was somewhat offset by the fact that their newness had worn off. My familiarization continued with a PD2 of 1947 vintage and an AEC Reliance of 1956. The latter was used to demonstrate the brake efficiency of the Reliance when the instructor leaned over the steering wheel and pressed the brake pedal with his hand. The effect was staggering.

This bus was No. 725 (LDB 725), and operated from Manchester Garage before that location suffered the misfortune to employ me. No. 725 left garage one morning to take up service at Lower Mosley Street Bus Station and, en route, it slid across the road and through a parapet to decant itself into the canal. Fortunately, the driver fared tolerably well, the canal being shallow at this point. At Charles Street office, the tale came through that the garage foreman had telephoned the Canal Company with a view to obtaining some floating assistance to retrieve No. 725. On being told that a bus was in the canal, the Canal Company's official blasted, 'Well, get your b . . . . y bus out of my canal'. When, later that day, a soggy No. 725 arrived in Charles Street Garage, it was parked near the wash to enable the cleaners to render it usable for the fitters to do their work. The number of muddy beer bottles that was discovered left the mind boggling. One or two other items of nastiness were unearthed as well. I like to think that there was no connection between this occurrence and my initiation on the type!

The Bristol vehicles in the fleet boasted few switches. Apart from the usual comforts to control, such as a steering wheel, handbrake lever and three pedals, throttle, brake and clutch, electrical devices consisted only of a starter switch, side and tail lamp, headlamp and foglamp switches, and windscreen wiper, which were all guarded by the master switch under the control box. Interior lights and destination light switches were situated on the bulkhead over the driver's head. A luxury item was an on/off switch for a heater blower. Direction indicators were the driver's right arm.

Standing at Stockport Garage, in March 1959, is an Atkinson Alpha, No. 512 (FDB 512), with a Willowbrook body, showing the rear entrance and the older white-roof livery.

In April 1965, the 'office' No. 962 (VDB 962). The driver's seat is finished in moquette instead of the more usual vyanide or rexine found in buses. The two speed rear axle shift is conveniently placed below and to the left of the steering wheel, close to the manual gear lever. In front of the steering column is the container for fluid to serve the hydraulic clutch release mechanism.

The modern bus has a multitude of switches with one or two oddments thrown in to confuse the driver who was not used to the type, such as gears, which do not engage if the platform door is open, or the starter, which is inoperative until the gear-lever is placed in a special position. In many cases, drivers now receive several hours of training on different types of bus, many of which are basically pneumo-cyclic transmission types with switches for lights and accessories in different positions. This seems an excessive training period to one brought up to the requirements of the immediate pre-war and post-war buses, despite the increased complexity of the modern bus.

After the official training programme, I was able to gain further experience on other examples of the Company's fleet during lunch times so that life took on a most interesting and rosy glow. This experience and the odd service journey, that I was called upon to work, was supplemented by the operational requirements of North Western, since the large express and 'limited stop' service requirements at weekends called for the transfer of buses from Stockport Garage and Works, to Manchester Garage. Buses coming out of the repair and paint shops at Stockport had to be ferried to Manchester on a Friday evening, ready for service duplication on Saturday and Sunday. I would often ferry three buses or coaches on this run on Friday evenings, which suited my interests admirably. Moreover, the absence of passengers made it easier on the conscience to experiment with fast gear changes on crash boxes, since there was no one on the bus to be upset by any inadvertent crashing of the gear. In this way, I became more conversant with the 'clutch stop', although my early attempts on different types of vehicles, after the supervised training periods, left much to be desired.

The crash box requires a 'double de-clutching' technique for changes from one gear to the next, either up or down the box. When changing up the box, the engine revs are allowed to fall when the gear-lever is in neutral so that the gearbox shaft driven by the engine, through the clutch, is revving at the same speed as the other gearbox shaft, which is connected to the road wheels via the back axle. The gears on these two rotating shafts can then be engaged when the gear lever is moved into position. The clutch is pressed only a short way down. Changing down the box requires the engine to be speeded up, by revving it with the gears in neutral, before engaging the lower gear. This again matches the revs of the two sets of gears.

On a synchromesh gearbox, the synchronizing is effected by a mechanism on the gears themselves, and the clutch is depressed once, the gear-lever then moving from one gear to the next. When a fast upward change on a crash box is required, the 'clutch stop' is used by pushing the clutch pedal down, usually as far as it will go. This rapidly slows the input shaft to the gearbox to the correct speed for the next gear to be engaged, and the change is made in one movement, similar to the synchromesh system. The speed at which the 'clutch stop' slows the input shaft, controls the speed at which the upward change is made, but, in most cases, this is very fast indeed and the movement of the gear-lever from gear to neutral, and through to the higher gear, is virtually continuous, without the double clutch movement of the slow change. It is of interest to find that, for slow gear changes, the clutch need not be used. This is consistent with the general requirements of the PSV driver. He is not a lazy person, but, as in any trade, he believes in making the job as simple as possible and tries to expend as little energy as possible during his driving hours.

As an enthusiast/driver, I had my interest to keep my job going during otherwise dull periods, but even so, the energetic use of the 'clutch stop' on crash boxes tended to be restricted to peak hour operation, hill climbing and, regrettably, times when I was showing off! My companions tended to be equally restrictive of their energies and from an older ex-driver friend from Stockport Garage, I first received the advice to change gear without the clutch. This can be effective on slow, or normal, gear changes. The absence of clutch separation requires very precise judgement of the revs, to enable the subsequent gear to be engaged, and this system can be adopted for changes up or down the box.

Whilst, however, the upward changes can be made clutchless without too much concentration, down changes need total dedication for the successful, noiseless, swapping of cogs. The newness of the driver of one's bus could, in the days of front-engined, rear-entrance, buses, be determined by the way the driver's neck went red when he crashed his gears! I was particularly aware of this phenomenon when I worked my first duty after passing my P S V test.

This was a Stockport duty, No. 74, worked on 3rd January 1962, and, to the novice, it was full of pitfalls. From Stockport Garage, the double deck bus allocated to this duty went to Mersey Square to operate the first of two trips to Wilmslow. The first return trip to Wilmslow was outward, via Woodford, as service 77, returning via Handforth and Grove Lane as service 78. This was my first trip in service and I quickly realized something that I had taken for granted and that no one had ever mentioned to me, that it is useful to know where the bus stops are!

The second trip was again with services 77/78 and the same bus was used for both trips. This was one of the twenty strong fleet of Guy Arabs, in this case No. 30 (BJA 186), supplied as utility-bodied vehicles. The

chassis were re-conditioned and re-bodied with Willowbrook bodies around 1951, the bodies being similar to those on the re-bodied Bristol K5Gs. With trials and tribulations of the Wilmslow route over, a short mealbreak was followed by a Mellor to Denton trip. This was part of the interworking of service 81 to Denton and service 83 to Mellor, Devonshire Arms. Fortunately both routes were reasonably well-known to me, but the Mellor route was renowned for its hills and this was my first attempt to drive a Bristol K5G in service; No. 420 (JA 7792), complete with audience. A small bonus was that it was dark, so that passengers could not identify their driver! Even so, my gear changing was such that, on the hills, there must have been some ribald comments! Fortunately for my peace of mind, the conductor was most tactful. Since that inauguration, I put in as much practice as possible and tried to improve my gearchanging, particularly on the Bristol marques. I like to think that I succeeded.

The evolution of the bus since those old-fashioned times of the early 1960s has brought us rear-engined buses with pneumocyclic gearboxes, a type of gearbox which quickly became available on the longer established underfloor-engined single deckers and the variants on that theme, where the engine is placed at the rear of the chassis. It is most regrettable that, in view of the vast improvement that this gearbox has made to the drivers' conditions, it is often badly abused and, sometimes due to this, and at other times because it is incorrectly adjusted, the driver who

Bristol K5G, No. 420 (JA 7792) was our original choice of vehicle in this class for preservation. It is seen at Marple in April 1961.

wants to change gear smoothly and efficiently is faced with many difficulties before he can be sure of achieving his objective.

The pneumocyclic gearbox has a remote gearchange by the driver's hand, usually on his left, the traditional gearchange position, but now often found on his right to avoid getting in his way when working a one man operated bus. The change is either electric or air, the former operating pistons on the gearbox under air pressure to change the gears themselves. The air change, identified by the large unit on a pedestal mounted from the cab floor operates directly from the gearchange to the pistons by air. In practice, this type is not as positive as the electric over-air system and I much prefer the electric types.

The vagaries of the pneumocyclic gearchange make smooth changes very difficult to achieve, particularly when fast driving, and, therefore, fast gearchanges are required.

The general instruction to drivers being trained on these types of bus are for drivers to pause in neutral before engaging a higher gear, so that the engine revs will drop to match the higher gear being engaged. This is, in effect, the normal crash box technique except that engagement of a gear at the wrong moment produces a jerk, felt by passengers and driver, but no noise from the gearbox. Whilst some manufacturers have approved 'straight-through' gearchanging in the upward direction, the use of this method, with the throttle wide open, has not been

altogether compatible with long gearbox life and was quietly abandoned officially! It does seem odd to me, however, that a crash box, which had been in existence since the beginning of the century, is capable of performing quick upward gearchanges in the hands of a skilled driver, whilst the modern unit suffers a reduction in its working life if subjected to such changes. As I see it, abuse will ruin the pneumocyclic unit whereas abuse on a crash box will sometimes damage the driver, rather than the box. Of modern gearboxes, the synchromesh probably has the least 'driver damaging' properties.

The introduction, therefore, of the pnemocyclic gearbox quickly, and most unfortunately, led to driver abuse and shorter life expectancy than the gearbox deserved. The pneumocyclic gearbox is based on the epicyclic type of gearbox which used to have the preselector gearchange. These latter gearboxes were introduced in the early years of motor cars and were used on Lanchesters and Ford Model Ts. The preselector gearbox, as we now recognize it, was first used, in 1928, by Armstrong Siddeley Motors Limted, then by Daimler, including Lanchester when taken over by Daimler in 1931, Crossley, Riley and the celebrated racing marque ERA, some of whose gearboxes were made by Armstrong Siddeley.

Other makers used the preselector gearbox in some of their models, at one time or another, but, for many years, the Daimler buses were famous for their addiction to this system.

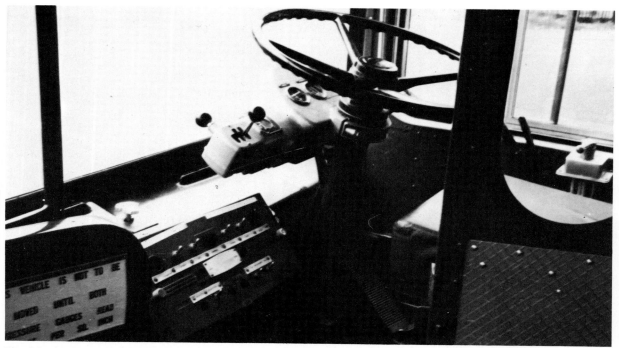

The driver's cab of the Daimler Fleetline, No. 102 (AJA 102B), which was fitted with an Alexander body. The notice on the inside of the door warns the driver not to move the bus 'until both pressure gauges read 80 lbs. per sq. inch'.

Up to the mid-1930s, when the Americans had adopted the synchromesh gearbox, and it began to be used in Britain, cars had crash gearboxes. This did not mean that all drivers liked them. They most definitely did not and it was because of this, and the fact that many drivers of the time had difficulty changing gear, that an alternative, easier gearchange, was required. The preselector was introduced and used in quite large numbers but its main drawback was its weight. The relatively light synchromesh gearboxes were later to become established without this drawback. From the bus operators' point of view, the relatively easy preselector gearbox also meant that the tram to bus conversions could be accomplished more easily, since the tramcar motormen could be trained to become bus drivers if the easier gearchange was used. Daimler did well out of this, and justifiably so.

The preselector gearbox worked by putting the gear-lever, usually in a quadrant working in an almost horizontal plane under the steering wheel, into the gear required. A pedal on the floor, in the position of what would normally be a clutch pedal, but was, in fact, a gear change pedal, was pressed to the floor and then released under control of the left foot and the gear was engaged. And that was it! The connection between engine and gearbox was via a fluid flywheel, as on modern rear-engined buses, so that engagement of first gear or any gear, in fact, was possible without the engine stalling. Pressure on the accelerator then started the bus from rest and subsequent gearchanges made as necessary. Downward changes would benefit from a 'blip' on the throttle whilst the gear change pedal was at the bottom end of its travel. The beauty of the system was that whilst moving in a gear, the next gear required could be selected on the gear quadrant ready for its engagement. A seasoned driver will drive in top gear with third selected ready for use when traffic, or other reasons, require the lower gear to be engaged.

This remarkable gearbox was as reliable as the modern synchromesh gearbox, giving 400,000 miles between overhauls. Its detractors said it was too complicated, but this was hardly a problem if the company's fitters were trained to adjust and generally maintain these units until the full overhaul was necessary. Based on this working life, the modern penumocyclic unit must be a disappointment to its manufacturers and operators, particularly so, since the units themselves are capable of the long life of the preselector predecessors. Mileages of 90,000 from new units with 45,000 from reconditioned pneumocyclic gearboxes are the norm. That the basic design is right is borne out by the fact that owner/operators and small independents, using this type of gearbox, can claim much more optimistic long unit lives due, I feel, to their control over the driver or choice of drivers, which is only possible in small companies.

The driver wishing to take an interest in his driving, faces many difficulties on the pneumocylic gearbox. The electric change is more positive. If, however, the actual gearchange pistons at the gearbox itself work slowly, then it is possible that two gears could be engaged simultaneously and, even though it may be for a few seconds only, added wear on the gearbox bands will take place, and be multiplied every time that gear is engaged. An engine that is slow to drop its revs will mean that, when changing up, the time needed to let the revs drop sufficiently for a smooth change will be overtaken by the bus slowing down, whilst in neutral, so that the bus will stagger along in the higher gear, so the change will have to be made earlier than is desirable and then the revving engine will cause gear slippage with its attendant wear.

These points must all be taken in account when driving. The apparently simple upward change must take into account the engine's characteristics, how quickly it revs or the revs fall, what 'lag' there is between moving the gear-lever from a gear to neutral, and again to another gear, and the 'lag' is invariably different for each gear. The complication of hydraulic accelerators sometimes causes a delay in engine response to the movement of the pedal, so that the accelerator may be released a second before the gear-lever moves to neutral to compensate for these delays. If the gear change delay is the longer, then the gear-lever is moved from the gear position before the accelerator pedal is released. All in all, a complicated business, which does not lend itself to total dedication in city traffic, and also when the driver is devoting a lot of his efforts to fare collection.

I have mentioned the absence of 'quick change' training. The gearbox changes should be made with no load, or drive, being transmitted through the bands, in order to ensure that no slip takes place and, therefore, excessive wear. A quick change, which must be made when hill climbing, for example, will require the gear-lever to move in one movement from the lower gear position, through neutral, to the higher gear position. Bearing in mind the above comments on the 'lag' of gearchange and/or accelerator pedal, practice is necessary and each vehicle is, indeed, an individual!

The air change system, with its large gearchange, usually by the left side of the driver, has a few peculiarities of its own. Assuming the gearbox to be a traditional four-speed type, with the gearchange of the 'H' pattern, it is often found that moving the gear-lever across the neutral position, will engage third gear when the lever is only on the threshold of the gear opening and still, apparently, in neutral. This is no doubt due to incorrect adjustment in the system but the effect on the driver can be frustrating since he may be trying to ensure a smooth change when suddenly, third gear is engaged whether he likes it or not!

Since drivers rarely seem to use first gear on pneumocyclic gearboxes, for starting from rest, when the gear is used, it tends to drag and take its time in releasing. Having used it on a hill start, therefore, the bus is virtually going backwards before the gear releases. Something of an exaggeration, perhaps, but

North Western had only ten Leyland Titans with concealed radiators of the type introduced by Midland Red. One of these is No. 661 (KDB 661) which displays its Weymann lowbridge body, complete with platform doors.

it seems like that. The answer is to move the lever straight from first to second and accept the lurch, the gearbox band slippage and wear. This little idiosyncrasy applies to the electric pneumocyclic shift as well. It has been suggested that the lack of use of first gear, in itself, renders the operating mechanism for this gear more liable to sticking, or lagging. No doubt there is a technical explanation, but the fact is that the reluctant gear is, indeed, a source of frustration.

The first gear band is built to take the strain, or torque, of starting from rest. Drivers trained on manual gearboxes, where second gear starts are accepted, find the need to start in first gear on the pneumocyclic variety unbelievable. It would appear that training on manual boxes covers clutch control so that the second gear start does not have the devastating life-shortening that is found when employed on the modern boxes, but there appears to be no easy way out on the modern unit other than to start in first gear.

It is because of these difficulties, and the fact that many operators consider that they get good value from drivers on one man operation, that the search is on for a good, reliable automatic gearbox, whose life will be back in the 400,000 mile region, but which will ensure passenger comfort into the bargain.

It is probably true to say that gearchanging, an aspect of the driver's job which is so important to passenger comfort and to the life of units, forms a relatively small part of the driver's work now that the conductor is being phased out of the industry. The automatic gearbox gives the driver an even easier time when driving, and leaves him free to devote his energies to fare collection at bus stops. Unfortunately, the perfect automatic gearbox seems a long way off and, from my own experience, restricted to Atlanteans, Nationals and Metrobuses, the automatic car gearbox is superior to the bus unit. It seems unfortunate that some automatic gearboxes insist on changing down through the gears as the bus brakes to a halt! The absence of engine rev sychronization with road speed makes the bus lurch

as each change down occurs. This has its effect on passengers walking to the exit, ready to alight, and no self-respecting PSV driving instructor would dream of teaching pupils to change down through the gearbox from top to first gear on the approach to a bus stop! The instructor certainly ensures that trainee drivers are taught to be able to change down correctly if the conditions demand this, but even so, a manual box, be it crash or synchromesh, or the semi-automatic and preselector types, still allow the engine revs and road speed to be correctly synchronized at each change, to avert the lurching effect of what is, technically, a bad gear change.

North Western's training ground for gearchanging covered some of the steeper hills on the Stockport Depot routes, including Brabyns Brow, between Marple and Marple Bridge, handily placed for cups of tea in the Bridge Cafe, Marple, whilst service 28, which travelled to Marple and then on to New Mills and Hayfield was well used and suited to driver training with its narrow roads, sharp corners and hills. There is, to some extent, a repetitive aspect to driver training since numerous runs around the variations of the test course (so that at least most of the routes will be familiar to the driver when the examiner directs him round the test course) do lead to the habit of changing down to third at a particular spot, such as a shop or lamp-post, ready for a descent or corner. This is a useful anchor for the early days of training, but should be ignored as quickly as possible since a sudden onslaught of traffic can lead to one not being in top gear at that spot in the first place, and if the trainee has come to rely on this system, if he is stopped in mid-stream, so to speak, he may be completely disorientated and fail his test.

Whilst North Western certainly ensured that possible test routes were fully covered, such was the variation of bus routes that were followed in training, that traffic conditions themselves removed possible repetition and the instructors, themselves, were well competent in keeping their charges on their toes.

North Western has always included Leylands in its fleet from the earliest days, Tiger TS type coaches being used when the Bristol J and L types formed a goodly proportion of the bus fleet. Post-war years brought the inevitable influx of Titans to the double deck fleet, although Bristol Ks had a good foothold, with sixty four in the Willowbrook rebodied guise, until the early 1960s when withdrawals commenced.

A number of PD1 chassis, with the ECW bodies, were withdrawn just before I began to take a serious driving interest in them, by which time it was too late. They had a reputation for slowness which, I feel, could not have been much worse than some of their PD2/1 successors.

The PD2/1s, numbered 223–236 (CDB 223 etc), at one stage were the mainstay of Manchester Garage's allocation, others of this batch being allocated to several other locations including Oldham and Urmston. No. 224, one of the currently preserved PD2s of the fleet, was one of Manchester's fleet which later graduated to the training fleet at Charles Street. Nos. 224–228, 234 and 235 worked from Manchester during my period at the garage.

My interpretation of an uninteresting day's work was to have one of these vehicles as my steed for a full 'Nags and Lions' duty. A top speed of, generally, 36 m.p.h., with often no more than 32 m.p.h. available, gave the driver no sense of achievement or satisfaction during his work. The driver's seat was of the older type where a side adjusting handle moved the seat up, and away from the steering wheel or down and closer to the wheel! If your preference was to be high, but close to the wheel; hard luck. It was, however, usually possible to find a reasonable position as an 'average' man, but others were not so lucky.

Whilst I never drove Manchester Corporation buses at that time, I seem to recall that the performance of both the Corporation's Daimler CVGs and the Company's PD2s was evenly matched, or pathetic, whichever way one cared to view them! These PD2s spent most of their time on the Urmston/Flixton route, services 3, 5, 11, 11X, 23 and 23X. About

1965, when North Western took over one bus on service 12, this became part of their work as well.

Service 3 terminated at Cannon Street, Manchester, by the Corn Exchange Building, alone, amidst the Corporation services. Services 5, 11 and 23 with their variations and service 12, all went from Piccadilly where it was possible to find another North Western Manchester crew to chat to. With service 11, it was usual for peak hour variations of this service for a PD2 to appear at Carrington, Moss Lane, since Partington services, which went past this point, were the domain of the Loline. The later PD2s, usually Nos. 241 or 243, were the mainstay of Manchester Garage's one bus on the Airport service; route 64 from Piccadilly to the Airport, Moss Nook or Styal. Styal later became service 63 when the old Heywood route had been extended to Darn Hill Estate and been renumbered to 163. Moss Nook was a 'short' on the Airport service, turning about one mile earlier in the middle of nowhere! These PD2s were of 1949 vintage and fitted with constant mesh gearboxes. As a result, they were not universally liked but as an incentive, perhaps, they could go faster than the earlier PD2s.

On a slightly better level, the PD2s, Nos, 251-260, (DDB 251 etc), which carried MCW bodies, tended to be slightly faster and have a generally 'tighter' feel about the controls; altogether, a better type. These would be found on the Urmston/Flixton services like the 223 batch but would sometimes appear on the Chorlton Street to Alderley 52 service, although this was usually a Loline stronghold. The later PD2/21s, Nos. 661-670(KDB 661 etc), appeared on service 52 reasonably often, as well as on service 64 and on the usual Urmston/Flixton services. These were the only 'tin front' Leylands in the fleet and tended to bounce around, due to their lightweight Weymann bodywork. Their lowbridge seating layout, upstairs, was different to the other lowbridge Leylands since the seats were in pairs, with the pair against the side of the gangway set slightly back from those against the nearside windows. This arrangement was supposed to increase passenger elbow space but I always thought this was

No. 667 (KDB 667), a Leyland PD2/21 with a Weymann body, arrives, in April 1962, at Preston Coach Station from Manchester.

psychological rather than an actual benefit. The PD2/21s were fitted with platform doors, a rare feature on North Western's double deck fleet at that time, although Nos. 246-250 had jack-knife doors fitted from new on their Leyland bodies for use on the celebrated X60 service to Blackpool.

The air-operated doors on the PD2/21s had all sorts of idiosyncrasies and it was necessary to discover the particular quirk on the vehicle being driven at the time, before successful operation could be achieved. The easier problems to overcome were those where the cab-operating handle had to be moved only part way through its travel. Should it be moved further, the doors would stay firmly shut (or open). In some cases, the door lever would be moved to 'close' and as the bus arrived at the next stop the doors would slam in the faces of the passengers awaiting to alight!

On one occasion I was driving No. 668 on service 64 to the Airport. Past the Heald Green Hotel, the road is particularly narrow. The winter evening was dark and a BMC 1100 car came rushing round the bend towards me over the white line. I had just pulled away from the hotel stop and the car caught the offside rear wing of the bus. I stopped, almost as the car hit, but the car kept going and disappeared into the night! The only damage turned out to be slight bruising of the paintwork on the rear wing, and a small hole out of which stuck a chrome strip from the side of the car. It was all rather like a cowboy film, with the wagons bowling along with arrows sticking out of the sides. I pulled the strip out and put it in the cab as evidence to go with my report of the incident.

It was No. 668 which retained an oddity in its livery whilst I was at Manchester. The upper deck window surrounds were painted cream as on all the double decks, but the front corner panels, between the front windows and first side windows, were completely cream. All other double deckers had the red brought down from the roof line to join the red panels below the upper deck windows. This quirk enabled the knowledgeable to identify No. 668 from afar, to the surprise of other staff whose interest in buses was less than enthusiastic! A nonchalant glance down the road, to see No. 668, was invariably accompanied by much finger-crossing in case the Works had done a re-paint on traditional lines to make one's prophesy a complete shambles. These PD2/21s tended to appear on express service duplicates at times and I have driven them on Bradford, Liverpool and Blackpool services. What the passengers thought of them can only be guessed!

Of the earlier PD2s, No. 259 was one which I had driven on a full Alderley duty one Saturday; four journeys on service 52 with no meal break as such. No. 259, at that time, was just recovering from accident repairs and the Company fleetname was not yet applied to its flanks. One of our summer part-time conductors, with whom I was friendly, was my mate on that day so we concentrated on being friendly and helpful to passengers, pretending that we were an independent operator. It kept us amused for the eight and a half hours or so.

Before I worked at Manchester, the allocation of Leyland double deckers included Nos. 552 and 554. These were the smartest double deckers in the fleet, to my eye, being Weymann-bodied PD2/21s, although perhaps the single Leyland-bodied PD2/10, No. 464 (EDB 325) was an equal.

No. 464 was a solitary Leyland-bodied PD2/10 which had the 'Farrington' style body, with a well-finished interior, where panels were lined in brown vyanide or rexine. Originally destined for an independent operator, the order was cancelled and it was sold to North Western. Its performance was on a par with its looks; superior by far to the usual PD2 batch numbered 223-239.

A batch of six Leyland PD2/12 vehicles in the N—N fleet, which were fitted with Weymann bodywork, was built in 1953, and No. 552 (FDB 552) is seen on service 128 in August 1965.

Photographed at Manchester Garage in May 1958, No. 555 (FDB 555), a Leyland PD2 with a Weymann body, is seen in its original state, prior to experiments with a Ruston & Hornsby air-cooled engine, which altered its appearance by frontal modifications.

With conversion completed, having had the Leyland 0600 engine replaced by a Ruston & Hornsby air-cooled unit, No. 555 (FDB 555), a Leyland PD2/12 is seen in Stockport on 20th August 1965.

Nos. 550—555 (FBD 550 etc.), were handsome-looking buses, and since they left Manchester before I joined the garage, I had to wait a long time before I had the opportunity to sample them. The first occasion was when I called for a changeover, whilst in the Stockport area, on service 20 to Woodford. Out came No. 555 to Longshut Lane from Charles Street Garage. This was a famous bus in the fleet having had the 0600 Leyland engine replaced by a Ruston & Hornsby air-cooled unit. The bus was fast, gearchange was good, but on arrival at Woodford, the conductor's remarks showed that the Company's interest had evaporated before the heaters had been fitted. The original water heaters were useless with an air-cooled engine. Unfortunately, the heaters had been removed and the resultant holes left empty. The bus tended to be draughty! However, the driver could not complain since the cab side was well heated by the engine. Whether or not I would have been as impressed on a hot summer's day will never be known.

Of the double deck fleet, the PD2/21s were the last examples. Later orders brought Dennis Lolines into the fleet, with the improvement for passengers of a centre gangway upstairs, but still retaining a low-bridge overall height. These were in turn succeeded by Daimler Fleetlines.

However, the Leyland single deck fleet went from strength to strength, the standard Leopard forming the backbone of the coach fleet right to the end of the Company's days. The earliest examples, during my driving days, were the two Olympics; the integral-bodied buses with MCW bodies. These were Nos. 396 and 397 (EDB 323/324) of 1951. Whilst not particularly fast, they were pleasant enough to drive. The front platform doors were electrically-operated so that if the door was closed before the engine was started, the power drain, from the well-used batteries, would enable the doors to spring open. Having started the engine, the doors would have to be closed again by use of the appropriate button. If this occurred at a bus stop, where a full load had boarded, then stalling the engine on take off would lead to the doors opening whilst a re-start was made, so leading to argument, with passengers trying to board the full bus! The Olympics were usually found on service 32 to Higher Poynton, a route generally supplied with Tiger Cubs but which, at various periods, revelled in a Royal Tiger allocation.

These buses, Nos. 514—549 (FDB 514 etc.) were again of the standard BET/MCW style of 1953. Like the Olympics, they were not over-endowed with performance, whilst the vacuum brakes varied, one from the other. The intriguing position of an offside gear-lever, as well as one to the driver's nearside, confused the novice. The right-hand lever actually operated the door, it was found. Moving the lever forward closed the doors, which was of the usual jack-knife type. A feature not always explained to the uninitiated, was that the driver had no need to thump the lever hard to push it forward. Slight pressure on the knob, on top of the lever, would move it down and unlock the catch and enable it to be moved with the minimum of effort.

One of the two solitary Leyland Olympics in the fleet, with Weymann bodywork, No. 396 (EDB 323), is seen at Poynton Church on service 32, en route to Higher Poyngton, in May 1964.

One interesting journey to Higher Poynton is remembered because the Royal Tiger, which we had, ran out of water. At Southfield House bus stop, just south of Bramhall, a motorist pulled in front and then came to tell me that there was something hanging down underneath the bus. After the appropriate thanks, I alighted and peered underneath to find that what appeared to be fan belts were, indeed, taking a rest. Taking the bus slowly to Poynton Station, I requested water at the local shop whilst the conductor made contact with the garage at Stockport for back up service! Having been told to keep going after watering, we did just that. Almost at the terminus, we noticed that what turned out to be a hole drilled in the top of the filler cap, was throwing hot water over the pavement as the bus pulled up at bus stops. This did not seem a desirable feature and it was probably fortunate that passengers were alighting, rather than queueing to board, since the queue would have been in line for the water from our boiling engine.

At Higher Poynton terminus, instead of the usual reverse over the crossroad, I took the bus over the railway and on to the canal bank. The local boatyard sociably loaned a bucket and the next ten minutes were spent emptying several gallons of Macclesfield Canal into the radiator. Further representation to the garage brought a changeover out to Bramhall, on the way back to Manchester. Royal Tigers Nos. 537 and 530 (FDB 537/530) were the stars of this episode.

Bramhall was also the scene of a changeover involving Royal Tigers on another occasion. This time the brakes seemed bad, so a changeover was called for.

Another Royal Tiger was supplied by Stockport which was found to have good brakes but had heavy steering. I continued to use it and on return to Manchester's canteen, was told, by another driver, that the bus I had just brought in had been changed over by him earlier in the day for heavy steering! This did tend to happen when other garages were involved or when there was a bus shortage. Heavy steering is often dependent on the whims of the driver and, whilst the same can be said of brake efficiency, this is, indeed, a more important area and cause for concern.

Heavy steering was never, ever, to the best of my knowledge, a cause for complaint with the Tiger Cubs, either bus or coach, used by North Western. With 89 buses, 15 dual-purpose vehicles and 28 coach versions in the fleet at one time, 132 was a good percentage out of the fleet of almost 600.

The Tiger Cubs had the usual Leyland air brake, hard pedal feel, but they worked. Steering was always light but positive whilst the constant mesh gearbox was a delight to use. Very often, a top speed of 36—38 m.p.h. spoiled the overall effect but I used to enjoy them generally. Doors, on the bus and dual-purpose versions, were worked by air pressure and controlled by a lever. The bus versions had a normal four-speed gearbox whilst later examples of dual-purpose vehicles and coaches had a five-speed unit, still constant mesh. Some of the early Burlingham Seagull coach-bodied examples were getting well worn and had only four gears, but later Willowbrook examples would do a genuine 60 m.p.h. plus.

In February 1960, No. 603 (FDB 603), a refurbished Leyland Royal Tiger coach with a Leyland body, is seen at Stockport.

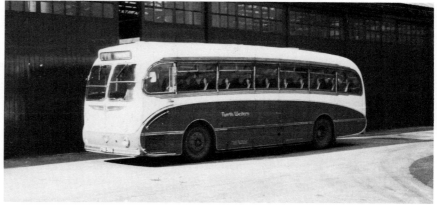

In March 1959, a Leyland Tiger Cub with Burlingham Seagull coachwork, stands at Stockport prior to its transfer to the fleet of Melba Motors.

No. 633 (KDB 633), a Leyland Tiger Cub, with a 44 seat Weymann body, passes through Bakewell on a Derby service, on 30th June 1967.

The 631—700 series (KDB 631 etc.) were used on all types of services, from the lowly Higher Poynton to the lengthy Scarborough express service. When used on the holiday express and 'limited stop' services, the rear pairs of seats were reserved for luggage, and were usually loaded through the rear emergency exit. At the height of the summer season, Tiger Cubs would be seen in many of the holiday resorts served by the Company's route. Their day to day venues would be the less exotic meanderings from Lower Mosley Street, Manchester. Although not the fastest buses, I always appreciated the ease with which they could be driven, although they tended to be taken for granted from a maintenance point of view, as I once found out.

This was on the celebrated Higher Poynton route when, surprise, surprise, Manchester brought forth a modicum of its rainy weather. At Cheadle Hulme, I decided that the wiper was useless. It worked well, but the rubber insert in the blade had perished and had certainly seen better days. Like a knight in shining armour, I leapt from the cab to rectify the matter, full of confidence. As an amateur mechanic I have, over the years, tended lovingly to the vagaries of my motor cars. At this stage, most of my attentions had been bestowed on my Crossley Regis and

more practical hints and assistance had to be culled from the pages of *Car Mechanics Magazine*. I make no apology for the unsolicited testimonial! In the 'Readers' Tips' section, I had recently read of a car owner faced with wiper blades in this condition. I failed, at the time, to appreciate that such an owner must have been unsociably careless to let his wipers reach this stage in the first place. Our unknown hero advised that the infallible, quick and instant, solution was to cut slits in the rubber along the length of the blade. I could just reach the wiper blade on the driver's side and rapidly carried out the instant repair. Equally rapidly, I was disillusioned. The improvement being of the extreme negative kind, I struggled on and obtained a replacement when we returned to Manchester. Despite this, I still read the magazine!

A more interesting and acceptable incident took place on the X39 service, during one summer Saturday, whilst using a Tiger Cub, No. 652 (KDB 652) on this service to Sheffield. We rarely had the opportunity to work the X39 service and, therefore, tended to find that it was a pleasant change from better-known routes. Even so, the generous running time, even after an extended stop at Snake Inn, did tend to offset the interest to some extent. On this occasion, No. 652 seemed lively. On the A57 to

Glossop, no great opportunity presented itself for any benefits to be gained from this liveliness. Climbing Snake Pass itself, however, showed a most unusual trait with 38m.p.h. coming up with third gear, and a promise of more to come. Since this was close to normal top speed in fourth gear, it was reasonable to assume that something had 'slipped'. After some slow running, the speed past Ladybower Reservoir was maintained well into the forties without the governor showing signs of chipping in, so it became my best Tiger Cub of that batch and made the journey most enjoyable. I never did find out why it went so fast but having found a bus that does go fast, one rarely complains, in case some fitter in the garage discovers its power and does something to curb it. Given luck, and a fast left-hand, it was possible to change gear quickly on the Tiger Cub, despite the absence of a 'clutch stop' and this, together with the light steering and well-placed controls, generally made up a very pleasant package. It was a pity that the low speed tended to frustrate the driver, on many of the examples, but this was the Company's economy measure rather than a fault of the vehicle.

The speed, or rather the lack of it, of the Tiger Cubs and Royal Tigers in particular, tended to make some drivers ambitious to try to improve their lot. On some models it was found that by pressing the 'stop' button, with the throttle open, the bus would suddenly discover added power. The success of the attempt was usually indicated by the emission from the exhaust of an illegal amount of black smoke as the rack on the fuel pump opened up. It was illegal to be able to operate the rack whilst the vehicle was in motion, so the makers quickly modified their controls! Also, once the accelerator pedal was released, after operating the 'stop' button, the improvement in power was lost and one went back to square one.

Presumably, something had slipped in this department on No. 652, I'm delighted to say!

The coach examples had Burlingham Seagull bodies, a very smart looker, I thought. Those in the 700 series, Nos. 701–702 (LDB 701 etc.) had two-speed rear axles, which provided useful ratios for various occasions. Unfortunately, I must leave two-speed axles to the Leopards, on which I must base most of my experience.

Last of the Tiger Cub intake were Nos. 761–775 and 782–796, all appropriately registered in the LDB series. Of the first fifteen, ten were delivered in a cream livery with red band, and were fitted with better seats for use on express and 'limited stop' services, including London. I was working in the Charles Street offices when they were delivered and well remember the consternation when the engineers found that the ten coach variants were scattered ad lib throughout the batch. A few telephone calls and negotiations enabled the registration and fleet numbers to be transferred so that they formed a batch numbered 766–775.

No. 786 (LDB 786), a Leyland Tiger Cub with a Willowbrook dual-purpose body, is seen, in April 1965, on service 32 at Boars Head Hotel, Higher Poynton.

Of the fifteen vehicles in the batch, six needed to be renumbered, including the transfer of their numberplates. These were as follows:

No. 762 became 770 : chassis No. 585919
No. 764 became 773 : chassis No. 585920
No. 765 became 774 : chassis No. 585937
No. 770 became 762 : chassis No. 585992
No. 773 became 764 : chassis No. 586034
No. 774 became 765 : chassis No. 586038

The whole batch of vehicles was North Western Contract No. 818.

Basically, these coaches did well. With the diversion of some of the London express journeys, via the newly-opened M1 motorway, seizures of engines sometimes occurred, but experienced drivers found that ten minutes at, say, 50 m.p.h. would enable the engine to 'rest' so that the remainder of the run would be possible at 65 m.p.h.

I liked these later Cubs and have used them on Blackpool and Nottingham services and have enjoyed the run on both these routes. Relatively uneventful journeys were made to Blackpool, the route being reasonably flat, with the Ribble Valley, on the approach to Preston, being the major depression on the route. Preston, itself, was served by the 'temporary' coach station in North Road which was built for about a ten year life span. It was situated round the corner from the bus station. After my departure from the Company in 1967, the present impressive bus station and multi-storey car-park was built. I assume that this was inevitable and not a direct result of my having left the Company!

This, like Lower Mosley Street, Manchester, was another example of the demise of a bus station with character, although the potential passengers at Preston seem to have received slightly pleasanter facilities than those at Chorlton Street, Manchester, which replaced Lower Mosley Street.

In the other direction, Nottingham was a route full of hills, valleys and tight bends. The famous Long Hill, at that time part of the A6 trunk road, prior to the Chapel-en-le-Frith road to Buxton taking over this role, was part of the route and it was along this section that X2, as the Nottingham service was numbered, operated as a stage carriage service. The rural aspect of the area meant that this facility was rarely used although I have used some of the stops to set down passengers from further afield. From Buxton, the route continued along the A6 to Bakewell, via Monsall Dale and Taddington. After wending through the dales, the approach to Taddington called for an energetic climb up from Topley Pike Quarry. The use of a two-speed rear axle on the Leopards was an added benefit but the five-speed Cubs would end up in second gear when not well-loaded; mind you, the gradient was severe. Once at the top, a more or less flat road, for a mile or so, brought us to the Taddington Bypass, a dual carriageway bypassing the village of Taddington but,

seemingly, going from nowhere to nowhere. This down gradient needed care in its descent since the bottom of the hill was the end of the bypass and the road returned to its not over-generous width with a further, more gentle, descent through the dales. Bakewell to Matlock was less complicated but with the usual impressive scenery of the Peak District. Beyond Ambergate, where the A6 was left, the approach to Heanor was by a particularly steep and uneven hill, where, as is often the case with awkward ascents, the gradient increased just prior to the summit and, depending on the particular Cub and its load, would depend on whether or not first gear was necessary. Mostly, second gear would suffice, but only just. Later on, as more Leopards came into service, these became my firm favourites on this and other routes.

The Leyland Leopard came into North Western's fleet in 1962. The first ten examples were the 'elongated Highlanders', as we, in the traffic office, termed them. Highlanders were the Alexander-bodied AEC Reliance coaches of 30 ft. length, the Leopards being 36 ft. Fitted with the 0600 engine, these Leopards remained the fastest buses in the fleet until 1967 when I was no longer in a position to be sure of the situation. Four-speed gearboxes were fitted and the bodies of the last two of the batch, Nos. 915 and 916, had forced air ventilation systems. The batch, itself, was numbered 907 to 916 (VDB 907 etc.). No. 912 was reputedly the fastest, and most London service drivers agreed on this point. The four gears were supplemented by a two-speed rear axle which, in my opinion, made for interesting and enjoyable driving.

My first introduction to these coaches was on a delivery trip between Stockport and Manchester garages, when a London driver from Stockport was taking one to operate the London night service, and I had been working late in the office. I was impressed by the vehicle and its handling characteristics. With later experience thrown in, I can describe these vehicles as good performers, with good brakes, if a little hard on the pedal pressure as were other Leylands at this time, with steering that was steady at speed and positive, but with a tendency to heaviness when loaded. As time went on, each of the ten adopted different characteristics so that some became extremely heavy on the steering. This never seemed to apply to Tiger Cubs which stayed reasonably light on steering throughout their lives. When using one of these Leopards on the Nottingham service, or, indeed, any steep hill climb, I adopted the system of engaging top gear and high ratio or, at least, high ratio with a lower gear, whenever possible on the approach, so that a change from high to low axle ratio could be instantly achieved and aid the upward surge. The downward axle change was made by putting the steering column control switch to the low ratio position and dipping the clutch pedal quickly, leaving the throttle open to compensate for the higher revs required. If one was climbing a hill in low ratio, and

In February 1959, No. 765 is in the process of being renumbered to 774. The numberplate (LDB 774) is now fitted.

In May 1964, No. 912 (VDB 912), one of the early 36ft. Leyland Leopards with Alexander coachwork, is seen at Coliseum Bus Station, Blackpool, on an X70 working.

the gear was, for example, in second, third gear would possibly be too high to maintain speed without having to revert to second. At the same time, high second might be acceptable except that to change into high ratio meant that the engine revs had to drop, so that by the time high ratio was engaged, there would be insufficient speed to maintain the gear; so back you went to low again! Upward changes of ratio were made by moving the switch to the high ratio position, then dipping the clutch and easing off the accelerator and waiting for the axle to change. A golden rule was to never move the two-speed axle switch from one ratio to another after easing off the accelerator. This would give rise to a series of clankings from the axle which, apart from doing the said axle no good over a period of time, did not enhance one's reputation as a professional PSV driver with the passengers, especially those seated close to the offending axle!

The 1962 Commercial Motor Show brought forth a prototype of the North Western Leopard coaching fleet with a body deserving of a Leopard chassis. This was No. 952 (VDB 952), again a PSU3/3RT with an Alexander Y type body which had, in my opinion, timeless, elegant looks to attract passengers to the services. No. 952 perpetuated the earlier Leopards with the two switch panels at the base of the windscreen, where it was sometimes necessary to reach switches by going through the spokes of the steering wheel. 'Production' versions, No. 953 onwards, had a much-improved layout with all switches to the driver's right, with only the speedometer and air gauges on the dash in the usual, rather austere, but readable, Leyland style.

(Above) At the 1962 Commercial Motor Show held in September, No. 952 (VDB 952) is seen on the Alexander stand. No. 952 was the only Leopard in the N–N fleet ever to carry the Leyland Leopard badge. This was removed at Charles Street, prior to the coach entering service.

(Below) A Leyland Leopard, No. 960 (VDB 960), fitted with an Alexander Y type body, is seen at Manchester Garage in September 1963.

Crosville took over No. 218 (FJA 218D) in addition to others of this batch when N—N was broken up in 1972. This Leyland Leopard is seen at Blackpool, in July 1973, in the Crosville green livery.

In my own opinion, these were coaches the Company could be proud of. The Highlander style on A E C and Leyland chassis seemed rather austere and after the Burlingham Seagull and Weymann Fanfare designs, only small batches of Willowbrook Viking and Harrington Contender coaches had been delivered, prior to twenty Highlanders. The Y type became the standard coach body for North Western for many years to come, all fitted on the excellent Leopard chassis of varying designations. It was only after these coaches had been in service for a year or so, that the name Travelmaster was used by the Company to describe this type. As more batches came into the fleet, certain controls differed between batches, which, incidentally, usually comprised ten vehicles. This necessitated the Company issuing a double-sided sheet, showing a plan view of each batch, with the positions of heater, demister and rack ventilation controls and water taps to ensure that drivers could supply warm or cold air to passengers and themselves at the appropriate times. This broad sheet also included advice on the operation of the roof vents.

The manual gearbox Y type-bodied Leopards quickly established themselves with the Company and appeared on London and other express services, together with the inevitable peak hour duplicate journeys. This operation of new coaches on service work invariably followed hard on the heels of the chief engineer and garage engineer's comment that a new coach would not be used on service work until the newness had worn off. Peak vehicle availability meant that, with the best will in the world, only a few days would elapse before such usage occurred.

Fleet Nos. 215—224 (FJA 215D etc.) were the first pneumocyclic Leopards to be delivered (PSU3/4R) and I well remember that as I had graduated to 'C' sheet by this time, a good percentage of my work involved the express journeys such as Nottingham, on which this class of coach was used. I had decided that I should look to the future and progress my career. Having been offered a job in the Civil Service, the attraction of pneumocyclic Leopards was too strong to resist, so I threw caution to the wind and stayed on 'C' sheet. It was an enjoyable experience and a wise decision!

Pleasant though these coaches were to drive, they did suffer from the annoying faults that seemed to be the lot of the big pedestal air gear change, aspects of which have been mentioned in the pages of this book covering 'driving techniques'.

Flagships of the Leopard coaching fleet, for a time,

were Nos. 962 and 963 (VDB 962/3). These were Plaxton Panorama-bodied examples of quite luxuriously high standards. Allocated to Stockport, within easy reach of most depots for high-class private hires, they would be temporarily allocated to another depot in order to perform such duties. This happened once when No. 962 went to Buxton Garage for a weekend. I had ferried a bus from Stockport Garage whilst on a spare duty at Manchester. Stockport, being short staffed on this occasion, asked whether I would be prepared to work a three hour 'call out' for them to collect No. 962 from Buxton on its return from its private hire operation. I leapt at the chance and returned to Manchester where I signed-off at 22.00. I then drove to Stockport Garage in my car and left it in their car-park so that I could catch the 22.25 service 27 to Buxton. On arrival in Buxton Garage, at about 23.45 I ended up by waiting until almost 01.30 before the coach in question appeared. The wait had been worthwhile. No. 962, and her sister No. 963, were well-insulated for passenger comfort so that the splendid Leopard engine roar was an impressive, subdued hum. The journey to Stockport, in those early hours of the morning, was via Long Hill and was a most satisfying drive. It left me favourably impressed with the Plaxton coachwork and even more so with the chassis. Later on, when the Company was chopped into pieces, Crosville took over the Northwich Garage and, for a time, had the two Panoramas, which were painted in the Crosville coach livery, based there.

Later intakes of the Leopard coach fleet were Nos. 140—149 (AJA 140B etc.) still PSU3/3RTs with Y type coachwork. In 1965, a further ten, Nos. 155—164 (DDB 155C etc.) again with similar chassis and body specification, were delivered. The 1966 deliveries were the aforementioned pneumocyclic versions, and later additions of the Alexander types arrived after I had left the Company in 1967.

Other Leopard deliveries, in between, consisted of small batches of vehicles to improve the Company's coaching image. These were Nos. 150 and 151 (AJA 150B/151B) of the L2T type, with Harrington C41F coachwork, and slightly later deliveries, Nos. 152—154 (DDB 152C etc.) were to the same chassis and bodywork specification. These were delivered in 1965 whilst the 1966 delivery was five PSU4/4Rs with coachwork by Duple (C41F) and numbered 225—229 (FJA 225D etc.). I note from my diaries that No. 226 and 229 were the only vehicles of these small batches that I drove and this was on short journeys between Manchester and Stockport garages, rather than in service. The impression was of a nicely laid out cab with controls in good condition and with the right feel about them. Whilst this is indicative of a well-designed vehicle, their relative newness of no more than eighteen months hardly allows for excessive wear or deterioration.

Of the Y type Alexander-bodied Leopards, I had, on one occasion, No. 148 allocated for me for a Nottingham journey. This was a normal allocation for this service but, on boarding the bus in the garage, I was intrigued to find a box-like fitment on the edge of the dash, below the steering wheel. This turned out to be a line of four warning lights which indicated the state of the following systems:

WATER LEVEL	WATER TEMPERATURE	EMERGENCY DOOR	AIR PRESSURE

To the best of my knowledge, no other vehicle in the fleet had this attachment added, although more sophistication came later as warning lights became more popular, and useful, and were incorporated by chassis manufacturers as a matter of course. But that is ahead of my driving time.

One modification to the Leopards, which I, unfortunately, failed to record, where fleet numbers are concerned, was the fitment of a thermostatic engine cooling fan. In order to ensure that engines operated at the correct temperature, these fans were fitted so that they came into operation electrically only when the temperature rose above the running temperature. The fan would then bring the excessive heat down and so switch itself off until the process was repeated. Correct operating temperature was important, since, apart from reducing engine wear and fuel economy, the more heat there was, the better it was for passenger comfort through the heater blowers. Except in traffic delays, long hill climbs or, occasionally in this country, hot summer weather, the fan was rarely in operation.

The predecessor of this system on the North Western's Leopard coaches was a switch which was situated to the driver's right between the two dash switch panels, which manually operated the fan. A red warning light informed the driver when the fan was switched on. I always felt that this was a risky business, since the fan had to be worked by the driver after the usual temperature gauge had registered that the coolant heat was excessive. I never heard of upsets caused by drivers ignoring the gauge so, presumably, the cooling capacity was adequate in the first place.

My liking for the Leyland marque stems from my early contact with the make when following the fortunes of the Ribble Company. The designs produced by Leyland Motors Limited were, I thought, well planned and up to the early 1960s, the Leyland customer seemed to be able to choose a Leyland bus to suit his requirements. The days of car-type production of Leyland Nationals were in the future and North Western was never subjected to this model.

Memories of Leyland Tiger TS types remain happily in my mind, operating out of Lower Mosley Street Bus Station for both Ribble and North Western. Regrettably, driving experience, certainly during my 'professional' days, was never attained on the pre-war types.

No. 962 (VDB 962), one of the Plaxton Panorama-bodied Leyland Leopards, parked round the corner from the garage office at Manchester Garage in April 1965.

A Leyland Leopard with Harrington Cavalier coachwork, No. 154 (DDB 154C), stands parked at Lower Mosley Street Bus Station in June 1965.

Chapter Five ~ 'If it's fast, it's a good bus' - The AECs

A good selection of North Western's single deck fleet comprised AEC Reliances in various forms. The Reliance was generally well liked by the road staff and, judging by the comments of drivers, the light steering and brakes, together with a fully synchromesh gearbox, were the foundation of this appeal. It was rare for a driver to condemn Reliances out of hand although, naturally, particular examples would be the subject of the inevitable criticism.

One of the main reasons for this general appeal seemed to be found in the thread running through tales of runs in Reliances, when mention of a speed over 60 m.p.h. would be made. With certain exceptions, the 616 and 720 batches in particular, many of the Reliances would 'motor' as the saying goes, so that once this was established, something would have to be seriously wrong before a driver would condemn his steed. In effect, 'if it's fast, it's a good bus'.

The first of the Reliances were the Weymann bus-bodied examples, Nos. 556–559 (FDB 556–559) of 1954. These had the AH410 engine, unlike No. 570 (FDB 570) the prototype Weymann Fanfare coach in the North Western fleet, which had the AH740 version. This latter vehicle was unusual in being fitted with 37 coach seats at a time when N–Ns norm was 41.

Another early batch of Reliances was Nos. 616–625 (HJA 616 etc.) of 1955. These were Burlingham-bodied bus examples with AH410 engines. Some, if not all of this batch, were delivered with single rear wheels but were relatively quickly converted to standard twin rears. The normal bus livery was used. The next batch of Reliances were 'firsts' in the fleet being Weymann bus-bodied vehicles finished in a livery of black and red with a cream waistband. Again featuring the AH410 engine, these vehicles were dubbed 'Black Tops' and despite normal bus seats, were considered suitable for express and 'limited stop' holiday work. Their outward appearance, at least, gave the impression of something better than a bus. These were Nos. 720–739 (LDB 720 etc.) of 1957.

Of all of the Reliances, by the time I drove at Manchester, these were the ones that bore the brunt of criticism. When the newness had worn off, both these batches were renowned for lack of top speed and pulling power. The Weymann-bodied class was among the first of the Company's vehicles to be converted for one man operation when an 'A' suffix was added to the fleet number. By the mid-1960s, this suffix was abandoned as most single deck buses were one man vehicles (OMV) by this time. As such, these early 700s were used on the X12, Manchester to Bradford service by Manchester Garage and the inevitable lack of heat from the heater units denoted a blown cylinder head gasket.

I never operated as a 'one man' driver but I drove these Reliances on various services operated from Manchester Garage, and detested them. Just as nasty were the Burlingham-bodied examples, but this was mainly due to an uncomfortable driving seat and a low top speed.

Generally, buses turned out by garage staff for service are deemed, by them, to be perfect. An apology for any shortcomings is never made by the fitters, except in the case of the 720–739 batch, when apologies were made that several new cylinder head gaskets had been fitted but had not made the slightest improvement to the heaters and, more important to the driver, to the demisters.

On one occasion, I had an enjoyable and most unusual day's use out of No. 734. This was not due to any herculean effort by the garage staff to render the bus perfect, but was due to the fact that I was allocated to two journeys on service X39, Manchester to Sheffield, via Snake Inn. The rarity with which Manchester Garage operated this service made even two journeys a flag day to the beneficiary. I enjoyed the day, particularly since, it being summer, I was independent of the heating/demisting system! Perhaps it was due to these early Reliances or, possibly, the excellence of the Tiger Cubs and Leopards, but I began to nurse a distinct dislike, even hatred, for those Southall products.

One of the batch had given cause for some hilarity during my career in head office. The private hire department, in which I was working at the time, shared its office space with the representatives of the charting office and also excursions and tours. The incumbent of charting office was on holiday. His job entailed totalling the numbers of passengers booked on express services and ensuring that coaches were available to carry them. His stand-in was in the hot seat and telephoning details of the morning's London departure from Lower Mosley Street. Not being a bus enthusiast, he came upon a problem. Looking up from the telephone he asked the more knowledgeable members of the office 'What type of coach is No. 736?' It is best to summarize the answers by saying that he was told that it was not a coach, in most unmistakable terms. It appeared that London had 'burst', needed another vehicle, and Manchester's answer was to field No. 736. No doubt it was all they had and had been dredged from the innermost recesses of the garage to cover the deficiency.

The charting office was recommended to ensure that the next stop for the London service, Altrincham, be the terminal point of No. 736's journey. I gather that Altrincham did, indeed, save the day by finding something better, but the rest of the day seemed tame compared to the excitement of the morning.

The coach equivalent of the time, Nos. 626–630 (KDB 626 etc.) were 1956 examples with the Weymann Fanfare coachwork which actually looked like coaches and were appropriately equipped. These had the AH740 engine with more power and performance, but retained the tendencies to devour cylinder head gaskets. No. 713 (LDB 713) was a Burlingham Seagull example, similar to the twelve Tiger Cubs, and

In March 1959, the first N—N AEC Reliance with Weymann Fanfare coachwork, No. 570 (FDB 570), is seen at Stockport Garage. This coach featured in many adverts in the technical press of the period.

One of the 1955-built AEC Reliances of the N—N fleet, No. 620 (HJA 620) is pictured in Stockport, in August 1965. These Reliances were fitted with 44 seat Burlingham bodies.

No. 734 (LDB 734), an AEC Reliance with Weymann bodywork, stands outside Snake Inn, in May 1966. on a return working to Manchester.

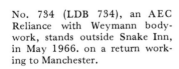

An AEC Reliance, No. 738A (LDB 738), fitted with Weymann bodywork, is seen at Matlock on 30th June 1967. This vehicle was built in 1957 and the 'A' suffix to the number denotes that the vehicle has been converted to one man operation.

reasonably fast. The next batch, consecutive to the Weymann 'Black Tops' were Nos. 740–745 (LDB 740 etc.) which were again Weymann Fanfare coaches, but with a destination and numeral indicator display over the windscreen. I thought these were quite acceptable machines and was pleased when one was allocated to me.

Prior to my arrival at Manchester, it was these later Fanfares that had been equipped with high ratio axles to operate the London services, via the newly opened M1 motorway. Despite the higher gearing, a certain amount of trouble had been experienced with engines seizing, due to the prolonged high speed running that was new to this country at the time. Since the water cooling system of the Reliance was full of bends, it was notoriously easy to get an air lock in it when filling at the garage, so that less than the appropriate, and very necessary, quantity was available for cooling. Very often, drivers were warned, when signing-on at Manchester Garage that, having been allocated a Reliance, they should ensure that it was full of water. This was usually achieved by filling up with the engine running and then, when apparently full to overflowing, the engine was revved, after which another two gallons could often be taken by the system. No doubt the tendency to consume cylinder head gaskets did nothing to help the cooling system either.

Consecutive to the Fanfares were the first of the AH470 Reliance 'Black Tops', which were to prove so popular with drivers whilst retaining their idiosyncrasies where cooling systems and gaskets were concerned. The remaining 'Black Tops' were Nos. 746–760, (LDB 746 etc.), 797–811 (LDB 797–800 and RDB 801–811), and 852–871 (RDB 852 etc.). In between, Nos. 776–781 were delivered also, being AH470s but with rather nice Harrington Contender bodies. Registered in the LDB series, two of these six coaches, Nos. 776 and 777, went straight to Altrincham Coachways, a North Western subsidiary, so that with the 'small operator' tendency, these two always looked in better condition than their North Western counterparts.

North Western, looking forward to an improvement in its coach fleet due to increasing private hire commitments, looked in vain when Reliance AH470s were delivered in 1960 in the batch numbered 827–831 (RDB 827 etc.). These carried the rare Willowbrook Viking coachwork and North Western took only one; No. 831. This was, again, due to the requirement of the subsidiary coaching operations, with Nos. 827 and 828 going to Altrincham Coachways whilst Nos. 829 and 830 went to Melba Motors of Reddish, to boost its ailing fleet of 564 type Seagull-bodied Tiger Cubs which were acceptable on contract works journeys, but were not really up to tour work, as far as their bodywork was concerned.

Once forming an important part of the North Western single deck fleet were Willowbrook-bodied AEC Reliances. One of these, No. 752 (LDB 752), looks particularly handsome in its red, black and cream dual-purpose livery.

The solitary N–N AEC Reliance with Willowbrook Viking coachwork, No. 831 (RDB 831). The remaining four examples were used by subsidiary companies, Altrincham Coachways and Melba Motors. No. 831 is on the X60 route, in May 1964, at Preston's North Road Coach Station.

No. 830 (RDB 830). One of the few AEC Reliances with Willowbrook Viking bodywork, is seen at Marple Church, in July 1960, conveying guests to the wedding of the Manager of Melba Motors Limited.

No. 834 (RDB 834), seen at Marple, in April 1961, when new; one of a batch of twenty. The Alexander-bodied Reliance was heralded as 'the coach of the future' by the then Traffic Manager. Nevertheless, they filled the gaps in North Western's coaching requirements on express and private hire work.

In May 1962 AEC Reliances, No. 778, fitted with a Harrington body, and No. 837 with an Alexander body, pose for photographs above Mellor.

With the railway viaduct in the background, No. 920 (VDB 920), a 53 seat Willowbrook-bodied AEC Reliance, stands, in August 1965, in Stockport.

In 1960, North Western's 'Coach of the Future' delivery, as the Traffic Manager described them, was twenty AH470 Reliances with Alexander bodywork. These were austere coaches with rather thin-looking semi-coach seats, albeit comfortable, and were bought with the intention of eventual down-grading to stage carriage duties, which is what actually happened to them. They soon established themselves in true tradition with water and gasket problems.

I remember one grateful episode, with one of this batch, on the X12 service to Bradford. There being no one man driver available, I operated an evening journey with a conductor. All was fine, with the coach running well, until Halifax Bus Station was reached on the return journey. It was then found that the interior lights were useless. The local BET Company was the diminutive, but very interesting, Hebble concern. A Royal Tiger PSU1/13 bus, No. 164 (CJX 65) was fielded as a changeover and, whilst not particularly thrilling to drive, was an interesting change for an enthusiast driver, for which I was suitably grateful. Regrettably, Manchester Garage fitters were not as impressed when I appeared 'on the pumps' that night with a strange vehicle and somehow, they had to get their own back.

These twenty Highlanders, as the Company called them, were numbered 832—851 in the RDB series. While they were, indeed, sparse as coaches when compared to Fanfares, Contenders or Vikings, they acquitted themselves well and must have appeared on all types of express, 'limited stop' and stage carriage services which North Western operated, as well as on excursions and tours. As new vehicles, they were infinitely more acceptable to the public than six or more year old Seagull-bodied Cubs.

I have cause to remember another member of this batch, from my office days rather than from a driving point of view. No. 845 was used as a directors' coach during the annual visit of the Company's directors. This was probably during 1962, when the batch was relatively new. The reason for choosing No. 845 was due to the experiments at that time being carried

out with publicity material and a new coach fleet-name style. No. 845 carried the symbol for approximately one year and it consisted of a circle with the compass points 'N' and 'W' marked boldly on the appropriate lines with the North-West line marked in as well. Later on, a Company neck tie was produced with this symbol in more detail, including some of the compass rose degree markings in addition to the 'N' and 'W'. Designs were also produced showing the 'N' and 'W' compass markings superimposed on a tyre; shades of Midland Red symbols, with a Harrington Contender coach in a three-quarter view in the centre of the tyre. This, I remember, since I still have the original sketch, being the artist of the first designs!

My impressions, so far, of the Reliances delivered to the fleet are not good, as I think the reader may have gathered! The synchromesh gearbox, usually of the five forward speed variety, needed a knock to operate properly. Being synchromesh, it was liked by most drivers but most would admit to a certain awkwardness at times. The times were invariably the most inconvenient from the driver's point of view. When changing down at speed on an upward gradient to ensure that maximum speed was held for as long as possible, the gear-lever would often come from the higher gear and, in neutral, seem to be hitting a brick wall! This baulked the nicely-planned quick change-down so that, by the time successful engagement of the lower gear had been achieved, speed had fallen, and the long run down through the gears was necessary for a long slog up the hill. It would be found that relative movements of the clutch pedal and the gear-lever were crucial to a clean change and experimentation was necessary, since each vehicle was different. Since the problem was not always apparent, a sense of security would be banished at the most awkward time. Such shortcomings did not crop up too often, but the occasions when they did, made up for this in timing. I, therefore, preferred the constant mesh offerings of the Tiger Cubs, even if it was necessary to think about every gear change.

VPM 898 was a 36ft. Harrington Cavalier demonstrator coach with a Reliance chassis. Not actually used in service by N—N, it is seen in January 1962, at Charles Street offices.

Of the dual-purpose 'Black Tops' No. 867 (RDB 867) seemed to be a particularly unkempt and miserable example. Allocated to me, on one occasion, for a Nottingham 'duplicate', we took few passengers to Nottingham but were fully loaded with passengers and luggage on the way back to Manchester. By the time we arrived in Matlock, I had identified the banging at the rear end, as the nearside wheel arch being thumped by the wheels. This seemed to be due to a weak or broken spring, so changeover was required. Matlock allocated No. 845, their sole Highlander and after swapping luggage over (the passengers swapped themselves) off we went. By this time, of course, No. 845 had reverted to the standard fleetname styling. For once, Manchester Garage was pleased with a coach as a changeover for No. 867. That could not be said for a friend of mine within the Charles Street offices who was responsible for coach allocation. When later contacting Manchester about their allocation, he was told they had also got No. 845. Knowing No. 845's home garage, his query was something along the lines of 'How the flipping heck did you get that?' On being told, I received a few choice comments when I next saw him.

Some sort of criticism or rude comment from the fitters was generally forthcoming when a foreign bus was brought into garage after a changeover had been necessary. I was, therefore, somewhat surprised at the reaction I received when, yet again, one of my favourite clapped-out Reliances gave trouble en route to Higher Poynton. I forget now, which it was, but at Parrs Wood, near the Manchester Corporation garage, I decided that the engine was rattling. This was in my early years as an amateur mechanic so my knowledge, to say the least, left something to be desired. By way of example, I can quote nothing better to illustrate this lack of expertise other than stating that I sometimes drove my Crossley Regis car of those days at 60 m.p.h., with an oil pressure reading of barely 5 p.s.i. One could argue that, providing there is some pressure, why worry. I didn't, but the more I have learned about cars, the more I think I should have done! Anyway, my Reliance sounded ill and it seemed wrong to roar off until it would not go any further. I telephoned Manchester Garage for help and they told me to leave the bus where it was and await a changeover. We transferred passengers and waited. To my surprise, the chargehand appeared, and after listening to my bus said that I had done the right thing and saved the engine from going 'bang'. I was somewhat relieved to hear this and it remains a rare occasion where praise was received after a changeover was called for.

One particular trip with a Highlander was memorable for its length, rather than for the vehicle. On early spare, I was called upon to work a Leeds 'duplicate', the through service to Newcastle having 'burst'. Unfortunately, it was late when I was called and even later by the time I had topped up my coach with water, and driven to Lower Mosley Street.

Instructions were to go to Leeds where another bus would take the through passengers further. It was fortunate that I had an experienced conductor who had done the Newcastle journeys for years, although nowadays, North Western staff rarely went beyond Leeds. The weather was pleasant, but cold, until we began the climb over the Pennines on Standedge. Here we entered a blizzard, or freak hurricane, since we had to stop and put the locking bar across the folding entrance doors to stop them blowing open. Once down into Marsden, the weather eased up and improved, eventually, to sunshine. At Leeds, a shortage of crews and buses brought forward the request for us to continue to Harrogate where the situation would be better. Needless to say, Harrogate had no warning about us and we continued north. I enjoyed the run tremendously and under the direction of my experienced conductor, I was able to operate into the official refreshment stop at Leeming Bar and then proceed to Durham Bus Station. So we wandered through the afternoon, arriving about 5p.m. at Newcastle (Haymarket). We sought refreshment and instructions. A rather surprised inspector told us to return home 'private', which we did. This part of the day was spoilt by the nearside driving mirror swinging loose into the side of the coachwork. Some string and a modicum of ingenuity sorted it out and we arrived home late in the evening, without the aid of the modern motorways which, at that time, were only in the planning stage. A long, but rather enjoyable, day!

The first batch of Reliances in the 900 series, Nos. 917–951 (VDB 917 etc.) were divided into four and six-gear batches and, again, into bus and dual-purpose types. The bodywork was the smart Willowbrook 36 ft. length, Nos. 917–951 being 53 seat buses, the remainder being 53 seat dual-purpose. Instead of the previous 'Black Top' livery, these dual-purpose vehicles were red with a broad cream band which earned them the inevitable title of 'banana splits'. Needless to say, some of the dual-purpose vehicles were four-speed gearbox types, as were all the buses.

This batch of Reliances was a great improvement on earlier deliveries but suffered one particularly annoying design feature. All Reliances I have driven have had good brakes. The keenness could be carefully regulated by the driver, since an organ-type brake pedal was used, so that with the heel of the foot firmly anchored, the pedal pressure could be maintained as appropriate by the driver, except in an emergency situation where full retardation would, in any case, be needed. Alas, these new deliveries had pedals of the normal type issuing from the floor. There was no heel rest and the pedal height did not allow the heel to be held against the floor. With the usual sensitive AEC brakes, a driver had to take the greatest of care when stopping, since a pot-hole could jerk his foot, so that an almost dead stop could be achieved, to the detriment of the standing passengers who would be waiting to alight. But at least the four-speed gearbox was all right!

No. 121 (AJA 121B), an AEC Renown with Park Royal bodywork, stands in Lower Mosley Street and is ready to leave for Macclesfield on service 29 in April 1965.

The six-speed gearbox was good but one had to get used to the rather close layout of the gate. Second gear starts, at first, tended to end up with a change from second straight through to fifth gear! Practice tended to reduce this unfortunate trait, and at least these were fast vehicles, even if speed dropped when the overdrive sixth gear was engaged. With these vehicles, on the 27 Manchester to Buxton service, the timetable prevented sixth gear being used and, if the truth was known, even fifth was too high for the timetable until the last stage, between Dove Holes and Buxton, when it was the norm to bat across Fairfield Common like the clappers. The anticipation of sixth gear's top speed was better than its actual performance since the winds that blow around Buxton are always against you, (try cycling in the area for proof!) and a change into sixth gear at, would you believe, 55 m.p.h. would achieve a startling reduction to 45 m.p.h. within a couple of hundred yards. I never drove one of these machines on a motorway so I never found out how fast I could manage flat out in sixth with these North Western variants.

These were the last single deck deliveries of AEC made to North Western. They had, incidentally, the AH590 engine which seemed less temperamental with gaskets than the earlier types. No. 936 dispensed with even this engine after a while, being fitted with a Ruston & Hornsby air-cooled unit, which necessitated a separate saloon heater and demister system, unlike the double deck experiments using No. 555! I never drove this bus so can make no comment on its behaviour.

The 590 engine features in the last AEC orders that entered the North Western fleet. This was the AV590 fitted to the AEC Renowns, Nos. 964–981 (VDB 964 etc.) of 1963, which were fitted with Park Royal LD74F bodywork. The bodywork was another 'first' for North Western in its modern fleet. A further fifteen Renowns were delivered in 1964, being Nos. 115–129 (AJA 115B etc.) of which No. 129 was on the Park Royal stand at the Commercial Motor Show of 1964. These latter buses were, however, seated only for 72.

First driving contact with these buses was achieved when Macclesfield Garage received an allocation and promptly put one to work on the 29, Lower Mosley Street to Macclesfield, service. Manchester's No. 20 duty operated the 16.10 service 29 and then the 19.10 journey. At 22.10, the same service was started by the Manchester crew, but at the Blue Bell Hotel, Handforth, a change to the inward-bound Macclesfield car was made, both crews changing over buses in order to end up at their home garage. This way, I came to try one of the new Renowns on the 'Blue Bell changeover', as it was called. There was no vehicle for familiarization training but situations of North Western drivers driving unknown buses for the first time, in service, were found across its empire, particularly on express work.

North Western had two batches of AEC Renowns prior to deciding to standardize on the Daimler Fleetline for double deck purposes. No. 125 (AJA 125B) is of the second batch, and is fitted with Park Royal bodywork. It was photographed, in August 1965, in Stockport.

The gearbox was the usual synchromesh and being new, all was nice and clean and shiny within the cab. I liked the bus and, as a bus, I still consider the Renown to have been a good product. As usual, however, it had its share of oddities. Unfairly, I came to criticize the curved window between cab and front entrance platform since, for night driving, a rather 'sissy' sort of curtain was used to overcome interior light distraction. No doubt, I should really have blamed Park Royal, the body builders! The other points were AEC responsibilities, but were niggling, rather than serious, handicaps to the operation of a Renown. At anything over 35 m.p.h. (perhaps one shouldn't grumble at being able to exceed this speed), the gear-lever vibrated to give an annoying whirring noise, unless it was held by the driver's left-hand. That was a cure which would be frowned upon by driving examiners. Also at speed, the compressor on the engine made a constant 'flup, flup' noise which, on service X60 to Blackpool, could be most distracting. As well as these insignificant niceties, the first batch of eighteen had no heater blowers, relying on the ram effect for heat flow, which, as I found out on one Christmas Day at Hayfield, was non-existent at the speed necessary to maintain time on that service. After the first trip, I assumed it to be a typical AEC water malady, so I pulled across the almost empty bus station at Manchester to top up with water at the Ribble Garage. At last, some heat seemed to be reaching the parts hitherto unheated. Regrettably, the heater's enthusiasm died before Stockport and our second three hour round trip was as cold as the first. The two trips to Hayfield constituted our Christmas Day's work and we left the bus, after warning our relieving crew, and searched elsewhere for Christmas spirit.

When I first began to work full-time as a driver at Manchester Garage, I had already sampled my first Leopards and found them more than interesting. So I assume that my lack of feeling for the AEC fleet was due to this love of the Leopard. My early enthusiasm for the bus industry had stemmed from Ribble's all-Leyland (almost!) fleet which, no doubt, impressed the finer points of the Leyland range upon me. Having said that, the fact that so many supporters exist for the products of Southwall would seem to indicate that I was not altogether a majority voice! My old car interest tends to leave me with little tolerance of more modern machinery. Reliable though the modern car may be, I find that having to lean forward to reach switches in certain cars is annoying. It doesn't happen in my old car, so it shouldn't in a more modern design, I argue. Such relatively slight faults tend to annoy on even a reliable vehicle which will, otherwise, do its job efficiently, but without driver interest to me.

Such is the Reliance. The universal system in the PSV/Heavy Goods Industry of flashing headlights as a means of signalling should mean that switches are placed easily to hand. The Reliance's high driver position required the driver to bend almost double to reach the light switches on some vehicles, the Highlanders being an example, which was a constant source of annoyance to me. The intermittent 'stone walling' when gear changing, together with a woolly feel to the steering, did little to add to my enjoyment when driving these vehicles.

One final aspect of these motors was the centre of the steering wheel which carried a pressed metal circular cover for the securing nut depicting the AEC badge, not surprisingly. These covers were a push fit, so that when waiting to depart from a timing point, a driver would inevitably pull the cover off. This was not an act of vandalism or even interest to see what was under the cover. It was something to occupy the time! However, having pulled the cover off, it was always worth while turning it over since some wag would have written a suitable comment; the most usual one being 'Put it back, you nosey b . . . . . d.' I preferred the one that said 'Help, I am a prisoner in a steering wheel factory.'

Chapter Six ~ Fun with the Lolines

Our depot had a good supply of the Company's fleet of Mark II and Mark III Dennis Lolines. These machines were the result of a test period with Aldershot & District's No. 351, a Mark I Loline, which operated on N–N's usual test route, service 28, Lower Mosley Street, Manchester to Hayfield. This service passed close to Charles Street Works and Depot, which shared operation with Manchester Depot, so Stockport could easily field a foreigner on their share of service 28 as necessary. Apart from observing this demonstration bus, I had no other contact with it.

The earlier N–N machines were East Lancs-bodied and of the batch of fifteen, twelve had Leyland 0600 engines. The first three, however, used the Gardner 6LX.

We had one of the latter vehicles, No. 813 (RDB 813), an unpopular bus at the best of times. We also had several of the 0600-fitted examples, including Nos. 817–822 (RDB 817 etc.). The solitary Gardner example, No. 813, confirmed something that I had heard about in bus fleets. If a batch of buses is delivered and one of the batch seems to be a 'bad un', then no matter how much maintenance or how many overhauls it has, it seems to remain bad! In the case of No. 813, its clutch tended to spin, making gear engagement difficult, when stationary. Despite several adjustments, renewals and curses, it remained like this all the time that I knew the bus. It also gave lie to my own suspicions that if a bus is fast, it is considered to be a good bus. No. 813 went fast, very fast, but it was still disliked.

To some extent, this was due to its constant mesh gearbox, but all other Lolines had the same box but not the reputation of No. 813. These buses I found pleasant to drive, with the comfortable cab seat and a steering wheel tilted like a car, or a pre-war Crossley Condor, which, I hasten to add, I knew only in name and from photographs; not being that old.

The Mark II model had reasonable brakes although it did have a tendency to sometimes stop working the harder the pedal was pressed, and this fact did not endear it to all, and probably accounts for my white hair. On one occasion, in a relatively empty, wide main road, a bang and sudden bumping made me think that I had a puncture, until I noted that the air gauges were rushing towards 'empty'. I stopped within half a mile, on the handbrake! Apparently, some insignificant washer had failed and allowed me the thrill of a lifetime and a few more white hairs.

My favourites were Nos. 818 and 819, whose engines seemed to have a beautifully tuned sound, as though some loving fitter had spent a day fiddling with tappet adjustments and timings for my benefit. Needless to say, there was little love lost between fitters and Lolines; or any engine. It was a piece of work and that was that. Nos. 818 and 819 went nicely for a long time and the run to Partington 'limited stop', until turning off the main road at Ashton-on-Mersey, was delightful. Beyond Manor Avenue, open country allowed the most impressive engine sound to reach a crescendo so that it was with difficulty that passengers could entice me to stop for them. One winter's day, this section of road was almost my downfall.

No. 818 (RDB 818) stands parked at The Green, Partington, prior to moving on to The Greyhound inward bus stop in April 1964.

Arriving at depot for an 05.30 start, I worked the first Partington, 05.50 from Piccadilly Bus Station. On my way to work, it rained hard and it began to turn to snow. By the time I had sorted my bus out, a Mark II Loline, No. 820, it was snowing hard and sticking, so all looked most impressive and picturesque in town before traffic had reached sufficient density to make the usual slushy mess. By the time we arrived at Manor Avenue, snow was well over an inch deep, with very few tyre marks from other traffic. I approached a long right-hand bend with fields on either side and leafless hedges, at about 20—25 m.p.h. Almost through the bend the front wheels went right across the road, and embedded themselves in the grass verge, leaving the rest of the bus to pivot round so that as the bus became parallel again to the verge, the front wheels were drawn out and I was left sitting in my cab with a beautifully parked bus facing back towards Manor Avenue. During its turn, the bus swayed alarmingly and I recall thinking 'What a b . . . . y fool; it's going to turn over.' The movement was similar to the way ships turn in narrow channels; by dropping anchor and swinging round through 180 degrees. This method was used, at one time, by Isle of Man boats arriving at Fleetwood on the River Wyre. I stopped the engine, climbed down, and opened the saloon door. Fortunately, no one was hurt, just surprised. I apologized for the inconvenience and explained that I would go back to Manor Avenue and turn round there, hopefull to get to Partington on the next attempt. Happily, we did just that and had no further snow troubles.

I was proud of my expertise in handling a crash gearbox or a constant mesh gearbox and attendant 'clutch stop', or clutch brake as it is sometimes called. One of my 'tuned' Lolines, No. 819, knocked the cockiness out of me when I was showing off to a friend who was travelling to Lower Mosley Street Bus Station from Piccadilly with me on No. 819. A quick move across the gear gate from second to third, should have sent the bus off at a high rate of acceleration. Unfortunately, I muffed the change so badly, that the lever went from second to first and acceleration was, in fact, retardation. My face went red even though I was well out of sight of most passengers in my half cab, but I think I became a little more careful about my driving when carrying passengers on subsequent occasions.

Not all the idiosyncrasies were the monopoly of the Mark II Loline. The Alexander-bodied Mark III machines had their fair share. This was a batch of thirty five vehicles numbered 872—906 (RDB 872—900 and VDB 901—906). Some of the earlier members of this batch had four-speed gearboxes, the remainder having five-speed boxes. The gear-lever had a more positive movement than those on the Mark IIs, but the practice of starting in second gear on five-speed boxes became fraught with danger after the newness had worn off. I recall several occasions when taking over a bus in service and slipping into second gear, after which the bus would leap backwards! This was due to wear in the gate between the forward gears of second, third, fourth and fifth, and the two gears on the extreme left of the gate, first and reverse. The gate was spring-loaded for a downward push to pass the gate so that wear on the gate and spring meant that the gate ceased to exist. Most gearboxes require a pull upwards on the gear-lever to pass the gate, so that spring wear is not as crucial to the longevity of the driver's nerves. Happily, I know of no occasions when this lapse caused any damage, although it put the fear of God into the 'Corpo' 47 that was pushing you!

One incident which raised a laugh and, fortunately, caused no personal injury, I missed, but I did see the results. It was normal practice for drivers to sign on early duties at the depot and drive to Lower Mosley Street Bus Station to collect their conductors. The early hour meant that the bus station was empty except for these few parked buses. One chap parked his Loline on the Buxton stand, which was on the front of the station at the Bridgewater Street end, across the street from the Golden Horse Café. Most crews met in the cafe and had a 'cuppa' before setting out on service. It is natural that both driver and conductor like a warm bus, so, on this occasion, the driver left his engine running with the handbrake on. Being on private property, this act was not against the law of the land but was against Company rules.

The driver, and all his fellow drivers, was surprised when the Loline decided to join them for a drink! The handbrake had slipped and the bus rolled across the road and came to rest in the window of the café. Two passengers, who were standing outside the café, leapt for their lives, leaving the Loline to make mince-meat out of their suitcases. I forget which Loline was involved but I was sorry that I had missed the incident since I generally carried my camera with me.

Another incident involving a Loline, and on the in-famous Partington route, took place on Sunday morning. Unfortunately, I was scheduled elsewhere and was, again, unable to take advantage of the situation and record the scenes with my camera.

One of the newly-trained drivers had discovered the turn of speed of a Loline and was, no doubt, aided by the virtually non-existent patronage, on the outward journey to Partington, of the early Sunday morning. On the bends between Shell Chemical's West Gate and the low railway bridge, the Loline left the road and toppled over. I later received an eyewitness account from the conductor who threw himself to the floor when he realized what was happening. Happily, only the conductor's watch suffered in the incident. After this accident, No. 813 received the attentions of Charles Street Works and bodyshop and appeared in service again little the worse for wear, complete with its spinning clutch and heavy steering! It went as fast as ever, as I found when driving it on the X60 service to Blackpool one summer's day.

(VDB 905) No. 905, a Mark III Dennis Loline with Alexander bodywork, is seen in the Ribble Works yard behind Frenchwood, Preston, parked up during an X60 'duplicate' working on a football match day in January 1962. The author drove this bus back from Preston to Manchester, on service X60.

A Dennis Loline, No. 813 (RDB 813), with East Lancs bodywork, is pictured, when new, at Marple, in April 1960.

No. 892 (RDB 892) a Dennis Loline Mark III with Alexander bodywork, is seen at Canning Place, Liverpool, in August 1964, duplicating an LUT coach on service X97.

N–N were joint operators with MCTD on service 11X, Davyhulme, Nags Head and on service 23, Flixton, Red Lion, both leaving Manchester from Piccadilly Bus Station. These services were scheduled alternatively as 11, 23, 11, 23 etc., so that our duty schedule contained Nos. 31 and 33 duty, both early turns, which went on to 'Nags and Lions' after the meal break of twenty four minutes. Alas, I detested 'Nags and Lions' and two 'Nags' and two 'Lions' together were made bearable when a good or interesting bus was the tool for the job. On one such occasion, when No. 33 duty was my lot, I had a five-speed Mark III, No. 889. Although generally a good solid bus, on this occasion the gear-lever must have been out of adjustment. Every gear change was made with a slight 'snick' as the gear was engaged. To make matters worse, a friend decided to choose this day to record the Loline's sounds on his tape recorder for posterity. Neither of us was amused. Nevertheless, it was still better than 'Nags and Lions' with a clapped-out PD2.

Partington seems to figure prominently in my memory. We operated all the service until about 1965 when the Corporation became joint operators. Until then, Manchester Corporation had operated short working as service 91 Manor Avenue to Ashton-on-Mersey. Friends were travelling on my bus to Ashton and, just prior to leaving the main Chester Road, I negotiated the roundabout which used to be the end of the Stretford to Worsley motorway, M62 (now M63). To this day, I swear that I was not driving more than 20 m.p.h. and the curve of the roundabout was not severe. Despite my care, the large, one-piece, air-operated sliding door fell off into the road! A changeover was requested, not without accusations of vandalism from the depot staff. Anyway, I had a sit down and chat with my friends for half an hour or so after explaining our difficulties to the passengers. For safety reasons, we could not continue in service without a door on a front entrance vehicle which was something which was highlighted, tragically, on another occasion.

This was an incident where a driver opened the door at some traffic lights where the Partington route came on to Chester Road. The lights were notoriously biased in favour of Chester Road, which was not surprising. Unfortunately, one passenger stumbled against the bus when the lights had changed, with fatal results. Notices, warning drivers against the practice of opening doors at unofficial bus stops, were hurriedly renewed in the depot. Despite the fact that passengers discussed the regrettable incident whilst travelling on the Partington route, they continued to get upset when the driver, quite rightly, refused to open the door at these same lights! This is a problem which continues to this day, even more so since almost all buses now have a front entrance.

Lolines were to be found on most of Manchester Depot's route network where double deckers were required. Services 3, 5, 11, 11A, 11X, 12 and 23, on the Flixton/Urmston side, used them, although the old CDB-registered PD2s were well-used on services 3 and 5 with a good proportion on services 11 and 23. Due to their seating capacity, the Lolines were favourite vehicles for working to Partington. This service operated as 222 or 223, the latter operating via the works road of Petrochemical Limited. Service 223 would leave the 222 route at Carrington Moss Lane, also the terminus of service 11, and proceed via the works road to return to the 222 route close to the road which went to Partington coaling basin. Since all the N–N fleet of double deckers were low-bridge examples, the low bridge, prior to the Partington housing estate, held no terrors for us. The operation of two routes to Partington led to the inevitable sight of brake lights suddenly appearing on a Loline as it passed the works road. The conductor would appear at the back of the bus which would then reverse so that the correct route could be taken.

Partington held a place of high esteem in my eyes since, as a car enthusiast and owner of Crossley and Armstrong Siddeley cars, a Crossley Regis was to be seen in Partington in my early years on the road, and examples of Armstrong Siddeley appeared in Wood Lane Estate and at a Carrington farmyard a year or two later. I regret to admit that on the inward journey to Partington, a Crossley Regis passed across the traffic lights going towards Manchester. I gave chase, silently cursing passengers wanting to board or

alight and making me stop at bus stops. Luck was on my side and I caught the Regis at King Street traffic lights, Stretford, where my conductor was able to run ahead to pass my address to the owner, with whom I was able to speak some weeks later. Needless to say, the bus on that occasion was my favourite, No. 818, with its tuned engine.

I was always sorry that I had been unable to drive a Loline, such as those which were owned by Halifax Corporation, which were fitted with a pneumocyclic gearbox and a centrifugal clutch. My Armstrong Siddeley car has this type of clutch but it is allied to a preselector gearbox. If I over-rev the engine when at slow speed, the clutch will go together with a hefty thump, and I often wonder how such a clutch on an eight ton, or over, bus will react. Presumably, they were similar to Leyland PD3s, which use a centrifugal clutch. These didn't thump, but after a little service, rattled at idling speed.

By way of a change, the 29 service to Macclesfield gave rise to a contretemps between myself and the shift foreman at Manchester Garage. I was allocated No. 813 on the late duty which started with the 16.10 to Macclesfield from Lower Mosley Street. The three hour round trip returned at 19.05 for the 19.10 to Macclesfield so that whilst a cup of tea could be disposed of at Lower Mosley Street, more ambitious refreshments had to await the ten to fifteen minute layover at Macclesfield. At 22.10, the last journey

Lower Mosley Street, in March 1962, with services 29 and 32 with their usual vehicle allocation, Mark III Dennis Loline, No. 886 and a Leyland Tiger Cub of the KDB series, No. 656.

of the duty went only as far as the Blue Bell Hotel, Handforth, where it was necessary to change buses with Macclesfield Garage's inbound 29 service. The crews crossed the road, drove back in the direction from which they had come and ended up back at the home garage. The following day, the Manchester Garage working would field a Macclesfield bus, and vice versa, until the Blue Bell changeover took both buses back to their home base.

Unfortunately for some, No. 813 was on a fuel consumption test, or so I was led to believe by the garage staff when I returned to garage later that night. On the 19.10 journey, the air-operated door on No. 813 decided to go on the blink! Lolines often suffered this defect and No. 813, with its reputation, was no exception. By the time we arrived at Wilmslow, both my conductor and myself were showing irritation, which is probably a polite under-statement of the situation, and requested a changeover. We promptly received Wilmslow Garge's worst Loline Mark II, which could not possible be worse than No. 813, and off we went, leaving No. 813 in the hands of Wilmslow Garage. This posed a jolly problem for Manchester and Wilmslow garages, since Manchester ended up with a Macclesfield car, Wilmslow had Manchester's No. 813, whose reputation needed no explaining, and Macclesfield had a Wilmslow car that they hadn't expected, but probably preferred to No. 813 for the next day's 29 service anyway!

The door of No. 813 had been the source of the problem. Considering the number of operations that a door would make during an eighteen hour working day, (bus, not driver, I hasten to add!), I suppose it did remarkably well. Whilst a door could fail to operate completely, it was more often the case that the door would become sluggish in its operation, and the time wasted would be a source of annoyance to both crew and passengers. Sometimes, when the operating handle was turned, nothing would happen for a few seconds; a long time to a waiting passenger who would then cast a disgruntled glance at the driver. All the Lolines had an angled window between the cab and the platform, to improve visibility, but the glass prevented any explanations to passengers on such occasions. Eventually, the door would open and the passengers would rush off on their way.

Intending passengers would suffer similar delays, and less observant passengers would assume that the door was at the rear and wander off towards the back of the bus, only to stare at a similar bus side panel whilst the gaping hole of the doorway awaited them at the front. This was all very jolly outside the peak periods, when a little light entertainment would go down well to ease the boredom.

Somewhat more dangerous were the idiosyncra-sies of the Loline Mark III doors. The door that fell off has been mentioned. That was not an isolated case and seemed to be preceded by the door closing very quickly. This does not really describe, adequate-ly, the speed at which the door closed or the terror that it inspired in those around it. What happened was that the door would be open and the driver would move the lever to the 'closed' position. For a couple of seconds nothing would happen, then the doors would close like lightning and would knock hell out of the front corner pillar of the bodywork. Any passenger running for a bus, and boarding it at that moment, would probably have been maimed for life! When the door was opened, it often moved sedately and correctly as though trying to inspire passengers with its genteel behaviour. The fact that it almost pushed the front off the bus when it closed was neither here nor there.

An early morning journey to Woodford Church on service No. 20, is remembered for a totally different reason. This was a Sunday working, Mark III Loline No. 889 (RDB 889) being the vehicle; not that it matters, since the bus and the journey went without a hitch. However, on the outward journey we stopped at Poynton Station to pick up passengers there, and parked at the roadside facing the opposite way was a Crossley Alpha being towed by a Landrover. The Crossley was one of the old Manchester Corporation buses and was in a relatively complete, but tatty, state.

To my lasting regret, I assumed that the tow would be delayed for some time and having church-goers aboard, I continued to the terminus. On returning to the site, fifteen minutes or so later, both the Crossley and the Landrover had vanished. Again, I assumed that the bus was to be restored, its radiator being in-tact, complete with 'Crossley' script and badge, so that one of the bus magazines would carry some information sooner or later. Alas, this, to my know-ledge, never happened, and I have never heard about this most desirable preservation project since. It is a horrible thought to think that it may have been en route to a scrapyard.

Dennis Loline Mark III, No. 890 leaves Lower Mosley Street Bus Station on service 28 for Hayfield.

Chapter Seven ~ The last days of the Bristol Tradition - and No. 432

When my 'Manchester' career began, in 1963, the marque 'Bristol' had two years and two months to run in the North Western fleet. This was certainly not due, initially, to the Company's lack of interest in the vehicles, but was mainly due to the fact that Bristol Commercial Vehicles Limited were part of the British Transport Commission empire, and the Company's output was absorbed by the BTC-allied bus companies after 1950 or so. The coachwork on the Bristol chassis was generally built by Eastern Coachworks Limited of Lowestoft, similarly owned and tied to the BTC outlets. In 1942, North Western was involved in an exchange deal with Crosville Motor Services Limited, Chester, and each company changed sides! After the 1950 embargo, therefore, no new Bristol vehicles entered the North Western fleet until 1968 when sales controls were eased by the interest that British Leyland obtained in the Bristol Company.

In 1963, the remnants of the once-vast North Western Bristol fleet comprised L5G buses and K5G double decks. The latter were all 1938 or 1939 models, refurbished, but with their original high radiators, and rebodied in 1951 or 1952 by Willowbrook of Loughborough. The single decks were MCW or Burlingham-bodied examples, the latter being on rebodied 1938 chassis, the MCW buses being amongst the last of the 1950 intake. Some of the 1946 L5G chassis, carrying the 1952/3 Willowbrook bodies, also remained in service at this time although their operation, by Manchester Garage, as with other older single decks, was restricted to temporary allocation for weekend work to release large capacity single decks for express and 'limited stop' service duplication.

In February 1960, a Bristol L5G with Burlingham bodywork, No. 366, stands over the pits at Stockport Works.

The beautifully-designed Bristol L5G, with 32 seat Weymann body was, for many years, a familiar sight in the North Western fleet. No. 301 (DDB 294) is pictured just outside Matlock, on 21st August 1962, working into the town. This vehicle was one of a batch, with Weymann bodies, which was built in 1950.

Another fine example of the Bristol L5G, No. 363 (AJA 117) is this Burlingham-bodied version. It is, in fact, a 1938 vehicle having had the Burlingham body fitted in 1950, and it was photographed, in August 1962, at Stockport.

My initial attempts at driving these buses was described elsewhere, but after the initial success of gaining a PSV driver's badge came the moment of truth! Now was the time to find out exactly what the 'clutch stop' did for gearchanging, and how it differed from bus to bus. This was not made easier by the presence of passengers to listen to one's wildly inaccurate gear changes which sometimes resulted. Although these vehicles were close to the end of their lives with North Western, gearchanges were, in most cases, remarkably positive; a compliment not always earned by some newer models of other makes. With the L types, the layout was also unusual in the provision of a fifth 'overdrive' gear. The gear gate was of a normal 'H' pattern with fifth gear being reached by the lever moving from fourth, at the bottom right of the 'H', to the right and forward, when revs would fall dramatically and speed would increase most satisfyingly! It was impressed on the novice that fifth gear must be abandoned before stopping, since it was impossible to move the gear-lever when the bus was stationary. This was achieved by simply reversing procedure and moving from fifth, backward to fourth gear, giving the appropriate number of revs prior to the final movement to the left into fourth. Perhaps 'simply' is the wrong word. The use of fifth was often ignored by many of the more recent intake of staff, except on long open roads.

Prior to my full-time driving, I drove part-time whilst fully employed at head office. On one of the occasions when I ferried the Friday night intake to supplement Manchester's weekend fleet, I drove one of the L5Gs. As I drove towards Mersey Square traffic lights at Stockport, I remained in fourth gear on Wellington Road South until the lights had changed, and I was able to go through them and up the hill towards Manchester. In order to maintain speed up the hill, I changed down to third. Alas, my newness to these buses gave me no experience to draw on and I failed to observe the rule that, when in fourth gear, I should ensure that the lever is held to the left before changing down. The gear-lever had moved to the right and my valiant double-de clutch changedown ended up with a most leisurely 'plodding' from the engine, as overdrive engaged on the uphill gradient. No doubt Stockport Corporation crews fell about laughing as I passed the 92 service relief point! I then had to extricate myself from fifth, by which time road speed dictated second gear being engaged for a much slower ascent of Wellington Road North than had been intended. These were the occasions where lessons were learned, which helped later on. Slow gearchanges up and down the gears could be achieved without the use of the clutch pedal and the Bristols tended to be the training ground. After the Bristols had been mastered, Leyland and Dennis gearboxes were simple, by comparison.

A post-war Bristol L5G, with Weymann bodywork, stands in Warrington Bus Station in May 1958.

No. 290 (DDB 290), a Bristol L5G with Windover coachwork, photographed, in March 1959, at Stockport Garage.

A Bristol K5G, No. 411 (JA 7727), with Willowbrook bodywork, leaves Mersey Square, Stockport, for Denton, in April 1958.

The last eight K5G deckers were not withdrawn until 31st July 1965, our own No. 432 being one of them, of which more will be said later. Manchester had no permanent allocation of either single or double deck Bristols but, during the summer weekends, everything with wheels was needed, to allow larger capacity and more modern machinery to cover express and 'limited stop' duplication. On such occasions, a spare duty had been allocated a Bristol K5G and then been called upon to run as a 'duplicate' to Blackpool or Liverpool. It was as an X97 'duplicate' to Liverpool that I remember taking No. 406 (JA 7722) on a Saturday, in its last year of operation. With a top speed of about 38m.p.h., there seemed little difference in the vibration of the engine and bodywork at that speed, than at 30m.p.h. so full speed was the order of the day. The X97 route was from Manchester, via Altrincham, Lymm and Warrington and despite its rather limited performance, compared to the more usual dual-purpose vehicles used on this service, the journey was completed within the official running time. That was the 'service' route. The return as service X99, was to Warrington, and then directly via the A57, through Irlam and Eccles; not quite up to the same standard of view, but shorter and speedier. On that occasion, one Liverpool service was the limit of my day's work, but this was not always the case.

The single deck Bristols, usually sent for the weekend from Stockport, tended to be used on the Higher Poynton or Middlewood routes; service 32. At that time, Manchester Garage had no permanent operation on service 31 to Bramhall other than the morning and evening weekday duplicate workings, otherwise, no doubt, the Bristols would have been used on that route as well, in contrast to the coaches that were allocated to the peak work. By way of variation, the L5Gs would sometimes operate on service 12A to the Greyhound Hotel, Partington, on the rather rare Saturday morning journeys of this timetable.

It was on Sundays where they came into their own at Manchester. Service 32 would operate virtually full to the gunwales of fishermen and their accoutrements, as they headed to the Macclesfield Canal at Higher Poynton. It was often necessary to pass stops beyond Barlow Moor Road/Princess Parkway with a full load, so that not until well beyond Poynton Church could space be found for intending passengers, as the fishermen, complete with rods, baskets and lunchtime butties, left the bus at different stops to head for their favourite spots. The rods could easily be stowed on the luggage racks but some of the baskets seemed built to most optimistic fishing proportion and were balanced precariously on their owners' knees in an already crowded bus.

The Bristol tradition of North Western ended in 1965. After the fame of the Tillings in the fleet, the Bristol was an admirable successor. The reorganization of Bristol Commercial Vehicles Limited, in 1967, led to the delivery of the first modern Bristols, the RE type, in 1968, when all single deck bus deliveries were of this chassis type, in long or short lengths, until the final dissolution of the Company in 1972, when 104 examples had been delivered, with 14 still outstanding. Twenty five VR double deckers were also on order at this time; certainly a case of making up for lost time where the Bristol marque was concerned!

It was during my career at Manchester Garage that an event occurred that produced some amusing incidents. A colleague at the Charles Street offices mentioned an idea to me of purchasing a Bristol K5G, the remnants of the batch of sixty four rebodied examples having entered, what turned out to be, their last year in service. As has been said elsewhere, the name of 'Bristol' was synonymous with North Western Road Car Company Limited and in the case of these double deck examples, they, to me at least, personified North Western in their rebodied, Willowbrook form, rather than in their original ECW forms.

Rebodied in 1951, No. 432 (AJA 152) was latterly allocated to Northwich Depot and was looked after very well indeed. During its final year, it was used, with No. 420, on a PSV Circle tour which included a trip via Snake Pass to Sheffield. The originator of the preservation idea was present on this tour and remembers that No. 432 behaved well, apart from a hot exhaust pipe scorching some floor-boards on the long climb over Snake.

Needless to say, I joined my colleagues in the preservation idea, along with two other friends and, on 1st August 1965, we took delivery.

A slight hiccup in the system occurred when someone painted over the 'Travel by Bus' advertisements which were to be found on many BET group vehicles at that time. A painter had been told to paint out the advertisements on the last K5Gs and included No. 432, despite it having been parked in a completely different part of Stockport Garage. Whilst not a serious calamity, it did test our patience and limited resources a couple of years later when we had to strip the advertisements and paint, in order to repaint the whole vehicle.

At first we were fortunate in obtaining parking accommodation at the side of the Reddish Garage of Melba Motors Limited, a North Western subsidiary company. Although in the open, it had three distinct advantages. It kept the bus off the road when not in use; it provided some shelter with the bus being alongside the Melba garage; and, most importantly, a slight slope allowed us to roll-start No. 432 if our non-too-clever batteries were feeling too frail! The careful use of the Gardner engine cold-start mechanism saved us on numerous occasions and quickly became a fully appreciated facility on the bus.

As an initial deterrent, light-framed timber doors were fitted across the rear platform, which performed well, two wing nuts allowing the units to be removed as necessary. These lasted for some years and survived several gale force winds until eventually succumbing to Pembrokeshire gales after the transfer of No. 432 from its Rochdale mill to the more pleasant country-

On 27th August 1962, a Bristol K5G, No. 400 (JA 7716) is seen at Stockport, on service 28.

side of South Wales. The temporary accommodation at Reddish lasted for about ten months when a more permanent and secluded site was found under cover in a cotton mill yard. The open aspect of Reddish meant that no extensive work could be undertaken and, fortunately, was not required, but the return of the original North Western livery to No. 432 was, therefore, delayed.

The move to Rochdale was made with mixed feelings. One of our number had gone to South Wales to live and work, and the mill looked uninviting and difficult for access to the newcomers. The mill yard was gated, and generally secure, but access through the gate was between buildings approximately 30 ft. long by 11 ft. wide, after which a hard left turn required a reverse to place the bus under cover. The timing of turning left and reversing was gained by experience and could, eventually, be undertaken in the dark. On further acquaintance, the mill became a 'home from home' and later we were joined by an ex-Hales Cakes staff transport, ex-East Midland Motor Services TS7 which was then put through the restoration process.

During the first year or so in the mill, brake linings were renewed, as was one front wheel bearing, an exhaust silencer and the fuel filter housing. Fuel filters were also cleaned and the chassis received a general clean up and grease. The brake servo benefited particularly from a clean out and fill up with fresh oil although, mechanically, the bus was in remarkably sound condition.

At that time, we also thought that the body was in a similar condition. The main consideration for the bodywork, from both a practical and aesthetical point of view, was to return the bus to the earlier, famous North Western livery of cream roof and upper deck windows, with red between the decks, and cream lower deck windows with red lower panels. The colour change, at upper and lower deck waist positions, was picked out with black beading and all wings were black. At this juncture, even a lowbridge double decker seems high when the roof is to be painted. The final livery, prior to withdrawal, was red, with cream round the windows. The radiator was scraped of its red paint and the roof was undercoated ready for its first cream colour coat. These were relatively early days and the prolonged scraping, leaving and general fighting to remove the upper deck advertisements, which had been overpainted at Stockport, was a sore trial of patience and an excellent source of swear words. Several weekends and other spare time was taken with this work before we were able to put some sort of colour on to these panels. In the event, a delightful shade of pink undercoat was used, made up of red undercoat plus the remnants of a gallon of upset white undercoat which, unfortunately, burst open on the platform during a run around town. The paint which was not saved for the pink tin was spread generously over the platform before being covered in black gloss. As the gloss wore off, the white came

back into view! The re-covering problem solved itself years later when the platform timbers decided they had taken enough abuse and, having rotted, fell out. The new platform has no illusions of grandeur and should stay reasonably black.

The pink eventually gave way to the appropriate Dulux 'North Western' red, although the interim livery did not preclude the use of No. 432 in North Western territory on a number of jaunts, including the wedding of a colleague at head office. Much fuss was made of No. 432 by road staff on the Mersey Square bus park who would, no doubt, curse the bus if it had been offered to them for service! The attention bestowed on our pride and joy, despite the untoward livery, acted as a spur to complete the paintwork to its 1951 style, which was the year of rebodying.

Work proceeded apace and although the upper deck advertisement panels did not reflect the finish that we would have liked, the overall effect was a vast improvement, and psychologically useful to our efforts to keep the bus in good condition. The appearance of the bus in the full North Western livery of the 1950s was further enhanced by the fact that one of our first, and somewhat easier tasks, involved cleaning the paint that masked the destination blind glass, so that we could show a full three line blind display instead of the single line of later service days. As it happened, a Stockport Depot single deck blind was used. I seem to remember that it was obtained from a fellow enthusiast in exchange for an 'East Midland' radiator plate. In this guise, No. 432 took part in several rallies and runs in addition to running a fair mileage around the North Western area for the sheer pleasure of driving it. To ensure our priorities were maintained, the chassis was steam-cleaned and sprayed silver, which pleased all those who had to check the underneath for the annual MOT test, and which anticipated the requirements of the current Class 5 test.

Most of this work took place whilst the writer was driving PSVs as a full-time job with the celebrated North Western, so that excursions were, indeed, part of a busman's holiday! The bus was used as transport to and from work on several occasions, including a Christmas holiday period when the writer's Crossley Regis (car not bus!) was undergoing heavy repairs. On these occasions, early duties found No. 432 arriving at Manchester Depot when everyone else was driving buses away from the depot. Since a number of drivers converged on the depot via Chester Road, No. 432 often gave the impression of being an official staff bus, on arrival at Hulme Hall Road. Only the most careful parking ensured that some hapless soul did not end up with a late-out-of-depot 'Nags and Lions' working with No. 432 as his steed.

On one occasion, after working a split duty, where the morning part of the duty operated to Buxton on service 27, (07.30–09.11: Lower Mosley Street, Manchester to Buxton; 09.15–10.56: Buxton to Lower Mosley Street, Manchester), I wandered off to

No. 432 covers old ground and is seen at the Hayfield stop in New Mills in March 1966.

No. 432, now preserved and seen in the Mill, near Rochdale, in August 1966. The roof, except for the front dome, has received its first coat of paint. The exit of the premises is to the right, by the rear of the car. It was necessary to reverse through the narrow entrance. Accommodation for buses, especially double deckers, has always been difficult to find and we were delighted with the Mill.

Reddish, climbed aboard No. 432, and drove to Buxton for lunch in the canteen. Since Buxton was, and still is, a single deck area, the appearance of a double decker in the area which I then parked on Market Place, set many people staring, although this was probably an outstanding situation. Generally, No. 432 remained incognito, other than being a bus for which people put out their hands, despite our efforts to ensure that 'Private' was displayed on the blind unless in a rally, where our appearance as a non-local bus was accepted. Often, though, the bus would be beckoned to stop, even if the area which we were in had green, blue, or any colour other than red, for its own buses.

On another occasion, I operated a journey from Lower Mosley Street, Manchester to Hayfield on service 28 and, jogging steadily along between Marple and New Mills with my Mark II Loline, I discovered a 'duplicate' behind me, with the fleet number 432. On the stop at New Mills, the few passengers for Hayfield were unsure whether to board the relatively new-fangled Loline, or No. 432, which had parked behind us. During its early career as a preserved bus, it became necessary to convert the headlights to the double dip system. Originally, like many pre-war vehicles, the offside headlight was extinguished when the headlights were dipped, the nearside unit alone having a dipping mechanism or filament. Measurements, for wiring, were made and the cab switch box was opened. A harness of what appeared to be unused wires was noted, since the insulation had been removed, or burnt off. On testing, all the wires turned out to be live, but in terrible condition, so that the end product of re-wiring the sidelights, headlights, fog lamp and horn called for about 200 ft. of wire to be used. The result was well worth the effort, and worked well.

On one occasion, in the early years, the nearside mirror came loose and had to be secured. When carrying out this work, it was found that the canopy over the engine slightly needed tidying, where the mirror bracket was mounted. This was due to the timber frame rotting slightly but, fortunately, the repair was easily done and the job was soon finished.

The tax was due to expire at the end of November 1968, so on the last day of the month, I took the bus out to 'blow the cobwebs out' with a run to Altrincham where it was photographed outside the depot to which it had, at one time, been allocated. The following day was to be spent checking softness in the corner fillets of the rear window on the platform stair panel. Apparent rot had been noticed here during the rally season and the winter months were to be spent checking this point. The mill at Rochdale could hardly be described as inviting, but the winter months soon found us putting a ten hour day's work, usually Sundays, into the back of No. 432. A paraffin heater, in the lower saloon, enabled tea and lunch breaks to be rather pleasant occasions, and made the work tolerable. As experienced owners of any old vehicles, from bikes to buses, will know, in areas where slight attention is apparently needed, often, dismantling will reveal the full, frightening scale of the damage. No. 432 was no exception. The beading around the rear window on the platform was removed and the window was taken out. The surrounding timber was rotten. Further removal of body panels was necessary to confirm the extent of the damage until, after several weeks, it was found that the whole rear of the bus, from the emergency window sill down to the platform, was rotten. The upper deck corner panels were also removed to reveal the curved timbers to be rotten, so that solid 'bus' was only reached after the first side panel had been removed. Approximately 100 ft. of best ash was eventually found and bought to allow the repair to commence. During the dismantling process, it was found that in using the rear of the upper saloon for carrying spare wheels on a long run, only the handrail on the staircase had held the structure together and probably prevented the spares from going through the rear of the bus! The construction of the bus had helped where panels butted together and where beading covered the joint. The screws passed through the beading and panels before entering the wood and were offset in the beading, so that alternate screws passed through each panel and 'knitted' the whole together, despite the fact that, prior to the repair, the wood was almost too weak to be of use.

During dismantling, the lower half of the staircase was removed and then a pair of step-ladders was used as upper saloon access, since the new timber was located there. Once the rotten frame had been uncovered, it was left in place until measurements had been taken ready for rebuilding. On one occasion I slipped on the step-ladder, but I fortunately managed to grab a handrail, but not before I had bumped the timber and found the whole rear end falling out. It never ceases to amaze me when looking at photographs of No. 432, just prior to its rear end rebuild, where the bus looks really magnificent in its full North Western livery, how bad the structure was under the paintwork.

The lower part of the staircase was badly corroded and a replacement was made, professionally, at a reasonable price. The remainder of the work was carried out with our own resources, except for the construction of the curved corner sections which we were fortunate enough to have cut to shape by North Western's Stockport Works. The work of constructing the new framework was easy enough, since joints in such work are halving joints rather than the more complicated dovetail joints. Nevertheless, dimensions had to be carefully followed so that the original panels and platform window would fit the new structure. The emergency window, on the upper deck, was solid except for the sill, a 6 in. by 2 in. section of about 5 ft. in length. To avoid stripping the corner and roof panel from the rear of the dome, the lazy way out, of bending the panels away from the joints to allow the new window sill to be spliced in, was taken, and then the panelling was bent back into

No. 432, at Manchester, waiting to be steam cleaned, in April 1968. The initial return to the 1951 livery has been made. The extremely tidy rear gave no indication that all the wood framing behind the panels was absolutely rotten!

place. This left slight creases in the panels which, at a later stage, were filled and smoothed.

A sense of achievement was experienced as timbers were cut and placed in position, without screws, whilst checks were made that panels fitted correctly. The new framing made the rear end most impressive so that after many weeks of work, it was almost a disappointment to have to cover the new framing with panels! Needless to say, the bus was driven into the open yard of the mill so that photographs could be taken.

With panels back in place, the beading was refitted with mastic sealing compound underneath to prevent water reaching the new timber. The 'knitting' effect of the screws, alternating through beading to adjoining panels, was retained to give a strong and lasting repair.

It was only towards the end of the rebuild that a target date for completion was established. We had previously agreed to let our partner in South Wales have the bus for a few years, since he was a 'moving light' in the scheme, and he wished to use the bus in December 1969. Work continued apace, therefore, but did not prevent us from including the arrangement of a rear indicator box in the new framing and panelling. The original state of the 1951 design had this facility and its removal, by North Western, some years prior to the 1965 withdrawal, had followed a change in the Company's policy of indicator displays. Our main problem was to ensure

delivery of the rebuilt staircase in time. Two weeks prior to delivery to Wales, No. 432 was driven to the Rochdale Corporation Transport Garage for its MOT test, having been groomed and suitably prepared beforehand. Its only blemish was the lack of stairs but, since this did not inhibit the test arrangements, we were not worried. The test went well and a new certificate was obtained.

It was at this time that an incident occurred which slightly marred the final rebuild. I did, as always, photograph the bus on its MOT trip, without stairs. When, during evenings in the ensuing week, the stairs were fitted, more photographs were taken.

On the appropriate Friday evening in December we watched out favourite TV programme and then set off at 11.30 p.m. for South Wales. One of us drove the bus for the first one hundred miles, the other followed in the Mini. In the middle of mid-Wales, my turn came to continue to Pembrokeshire. The weather was crisp and cold, with a thick frost. This had been anticipated and I was suitably attired in my North Western driver's uniform, including cap, greatcoat and gauntlet gloves. All these items turned out to be needed in the weather of that night. On the A40, just outside Fishguard, a shower of rain fell and turned to ice, so that on a long descent further on, I had to cautiously steer for the grass verge and then park up with a long line of traffic whilst the ice melted, or the gritters came. It was 8 a.m., and we eventually made our move at 11 a.m., even though

73

there was no sign of the gritter. A few miles down the road, the ice had gone and we reached our destination safely. Whilst we were waiting for the ice to melt, I took some more photographs, together with views of the completed rear-end, and sent them to illustrate a magazine article. Before I could print more views, I lost the film and this interesting few weeks in the career of No. 432 has not been recorded in the photograph album.

Having delivered No. 432 to its new home, its history, although less detailed than during its career in Northern parts, continued to be an interesting record of attendance at local events and, in some cases, not so local. It has attended a Bristol Vehicle Rally at Bristol, its city of building, and quickly entered the ranks of the Pembrokeshire Vintage Car Club. On the occasion of the Pembrokeshire Agricultural Show, No. 432 attended on two days and towered over the exhibition of excellently-restored cars of the PVCC.

Another electrical interlude in the history of No. 432 took place when flashing trafficators became necessary for the continued well-being of the bus. Up to this time, No. 432 had boasted no indicators, other than the driver's right arm, and the length of the bus, and the growing apathy of other drivers to look for hand signals, rendered some sort of illuminated signal essential.

My successful involvement in the mysteries of the electrical system of No. 432, on the headlight front, made me an obvious choice as the source of a set of flashing trafficators. The appropriate units and switch were purchased, and measurements for wiring were calculated from a general arrangement chassis drawing for a wiring harness to be made up. Since the bus is 26 ft. long, the amount of wire required was considerable but, nevertheless, the harness was made up,

and all parts were conveyed to Pembrokeshire at the earliest opportunity. Once on site, the harness and lamps were fitted by a local electrician and all was well. Most unfortunately, business commitments in recent years have led to a decline in the fortunes of No. 432 or at least in attention being given to her, since a period of two years or so inaction, other than general attention to ensure that the 'works' had not seized up, have left the paintwork in a rather unkempt condition and, in parts, covered in green 'fall out' from nearby trees. For all that, No. 432 remains sound in wind and limb for new owners to tidy up the appearance and restore to rallying condition.

On Saturday, 14th November 1981, No. 432 made the journey north from Pembrokeshire, now Dyfed, and arrived at the Transport Museum, Boyle Street, Manchester, with relatively little trouble. Apparently, its new owners suffered only a few engine stalls, due to possible fuel problems, together with some wiring difficulties, which seemed to stem from dirty switch contacts. Laying up a vehicle invariably causes electrical problems when it is restored to use, so that cleaning of contacts is necessary for full operation of lights and accessories. This highlights the difficulty of moving a vehicle from a point over two hundred miles from the ultimate destination. If time is available, all the necessary checks can be made and all should be well, but this is rarely the case. Fortunately, the difficulties, on this occasion, were relatively easy to overcome so that No. 432 returned, albeit a trifle dilapidated, to its native heath.

Work is now well in hand to restore No. 432's N—N livery and I wish her new owners well with their endeavours. It is not always appreciated by the spectators at bus rallies, how much work has to be put into a vehicle to just keep it clean. To maintain it in working condition requires dedication as well.

No. 432, photographed at the famous Potteries Motor Traction café at Newcastle under Lyme, whilst en route to the Midland Festival of Steam, in July 1967, at Bellamour Hall. North Western, Ribble and Standerwick service coaches share the parking space.

Chapter Eight ~ Oddments: Albion, Atkinson, Guy and Daimler

This chapter deals briefly with types of buses that tended to rarely feature at Manchester. The Albions never worked from Manchester, as allocated vehicles, but that is not to say that they never appeared at Manchester. The one example I mention proves this point and I doubt that was the only one!

The Guy Arab double deckers were in a similar position, although service 28, Manchester to Hayfield, was certainly worked by Guys which were fielded by Stockport Garage, so, no doubt, changeovers would upset the organized workings at times. Otherwise, my Guy experiences are drawn from the period just after training when odd bits of Stockport duties came my way. For this reason alone, my lack of experience makes it difficult for me to assess the machines as everything I drove at first was good! The Atkinsons did feature at Manchester and I had good mileages out of several of them, sloppy gearchange and all. They operated on the Torkington and the Higher Poynton services alongside the Royal Tigers, Tiger Cubs and various other types of Reliance.

Of the 'oddments' however, the Daimler Fleetlines deserved the title only for a few years since they gradually became a good percentage of the double deck fleet, running on services that had been the habitat of the early PD2s which they replaced.

North Western's fleet of Albion Aberdonians totalled six vehicles. These were Nos. 714–719 (LDB 714–719), all being saloons fitted with the standard BET-style MCW B44F bodywork. All were allocated to Oldham Garage where I had little contact with them, although I observed them on service 159, Middleton to Woodhouses, when in that area.

My only contact, as a driver, came when I had wiper trouble on a PD2/21 that was allocated to me for X12, the Bradford service. On my return, the windscreen wiper gave up and I called at Oldham Garage for assistance. They were unable to sort out the problem so they allocated me an Albion. Not having driven one before, I took my time on the way back to Manchester, which was just as well. The gearbox gate was right to left, instead of the more usual layout, and any fast second to third changes would have resulted in a noisy reception from both gearbox and passengers, if I had tried a fast change, since I was, at that stage, unaware of the quirk. Having discovered the layout, the journey was uneventful and I recall nothing outstanding about the performance.

A more interesting aspect of the Albion tradition, I thought, was to be found at Old Trafford, Manchester. On the corner of Stretford Road and Warwick Road North was the Leyland Service Depot. As well as the appropriate Leyland sign at the side of the entrance, was an old brass plate stating 'Albion Motor Company Limited'. The title was erased by a line stamped through the lettering but this did nothing to hide the old title. Many years later, well after my bus driving career was ended, at least as a full-time occupation, the sign disappeared. No doubt someone had managed to catch up with history!

Atkinson

One of the early underfloor-engined designs of the 1950s was a joint effort by Atkinsons of Preston in conjunction with N–N engineers. Eventually, a total of sixteen vehicles was supplied, of which two were lightweight examples with single rear wheels.

The 1951 deliveries were Nos. 394 and 395 (EDB 321 and 322) which were fitted with Weymann B42R bodies. In 1952 the main batch was delivered, Nos. 500–513 (FDB 500–513) with Weymann bodies except for Nos. 512 and 513 which carried the Willowbrook B44R bodies and were also delivered with single rear wheels. Within a short time these two vehicles were fitted with normal twin rear wheels. When I first came into the driving seats of these motors, they were still solid, and sound in wind and limb, but a trifle worn in gear linkages. Their reputations as the fastest buses on the job was probably close to the truth, despite AEC Reliances in the fleet being capable of 65 m.p.h. and more. This, of course, was a reputation gained prior to the delivery of Leyland Leopards, the first batch of which were extremely fast machines.

The Atkinsons, however, had heavy steering and brakes, and needed a strong arm on the gear lever. The accelerator was not without interest. As delivered, the accelerator pedal of the organ-type pointed downwards below the horizontal plane, when the throttle was half open; not a popular situation with the drivers who overcame this problem by using wedges tied to the top of the pedal. This was later overcome by re-adjusting the pedals but they were still not the most comfortable for drivers. The five-speed gearbox was right to left, opposite to the more usual layout, with fifth speed overdrive being over to the left, and forward. This was a unique gear when I knew these buses. It was easy to engage providing any gear, other than fifth, was the one you wanted at that moment. Changing from second was a doddle, even if the third gear you wanted was in the completely opposite direction! Nevertheless the 'Atkis' went well with their Gardner engines and Manchester Depot's service 51, Chorlton Street to Torkington, provided opportunities for speed on the Kingsway extension. The success of this section of road was spoilt by the reluctance of the vacuum brakes to brake, and the wanderings of the rest of the route through Cheadle Hulme and Bramhall, and so on, to the Torkington Estate. For scheduling purposes, a service 51 arrived at Torkington, became service 165, rushed into Mersey Square, Stockport and, after a quick cuppa, rushed back to Torkington, reverted to service 51 and meandered back to Manchester. The twists and turns in the Torkington Estate were designed to give 'Atki' drivers super biceps. Royal Tiger buses and Tiger Cubs were often to be found on these journeys, with a little less wear and tear on one's arms and feet.

One of the 1952-built Weymann-bodied Atkinson Alphas, No. 511 (FDB 511), seen working, in August 1965, in Stockport.

After passing my PSV driving test with the Company, No. 500 (FDB 500) of the Atkinson fleet was one of my first underfloor-engined conquests, but my impressions were more than a little rosy in view of my delight at having passed the test. The rear entrance design of the batch was particularly welcomed by small boys who delighted in watching the driver from their corresponding nearside front seat. I joined the ranks of drivers who have stared at the blank offside wall of the cab wondering how to get in; later finding that the entrance was through the rear passenger door to the saloon and then through the cab door. This was the case with Nos. 394 and 395 and was a peculiarity shared by some underfloor-engined Guy Arab single deckers used by joint operators on the Leeds to Liverpool service.

At one time, service 32, to Higher Poynton and Middlewood, was another mainstay of the Atkinsons, but Manchester's allocation of the type was not great, intermittent, perhaps, so that peak hour work made up most of their work and took them over many areas served by Manchester Depot.

Guy

Not surprisingly with a BET operator, Guy was a marque represented in the fleet in relatively small numbers, although there were more Guys than Albions.

Experience was to be drawn from two distinct ends of the vehicle scale, since my initial driving impressions were gained on wartime Arab double deckers which, like North Western Bristol Ks, had been rebodied in 1951 with Willowbrook L53R bodywork. Later, at Manchester, LUT and Northern General underfloor-engined single deck Arabs were the new generation of Guys which were experienced.

The North Western Arabs were of momentus memory for two reasons. The first duty out on the open road, that I worked, led to me taking No. 30 (BJA 186) out of Stockport Garage, during my Charles Street career. A Guy was, therefore, the first type of bus I officially drove in full passenger service. Secondly, the gearbox was the 'wrong' way round, that is, in the normal 'H' layout, first and second were on the right-hand side of the gate, rather than on the left.

Since all the other gearboxes in the fleet, except for the Albion and Atkinson single decks, had a normal 'left to right' movement, this caused some upset to one's organized driving approach, when concentration tended to wander! When driving the Guy Arab on service, I was relatively inexperienced so that I probably had less trouble with the gear layout than a driver who was used to driving the remainder of the fleet. That is not to say I was better at gear-changing! This first duty has been mentioned elsewhere so that my driving abilities were only a

No. 22, (BJA 107), a Guy Arab with post-war Willowbrook bodywork, at Stockport Garage in March 1959.

small portion of my problems that day. The correct route to take and the positions of bus stops hidden in hedges were all problems that ensured that that duty remains a vivid memory.

Such memories include the return to Mersey Square, Stockport, after the first Wilmslow trip. Leaving a gap between my bus and the traffic ahead, when descending the hill from Stockport Town Hall to the right turn, as it then was, into St. Petersgate, commensurate with the Arabs vacuum brakes and my newness to the job seemed sensible. Unfortunately, the impatient driver of a Ford van decided to advance his place in the queue and nipped into the rather generous gap in front of me. The brakes on No. 30 worked to capacity, whilst I had the fright of my life, but all worked out in the end with the narrowest of gaps appearing between the Guy's radiator and the rear bumper of the van. My modest grasp of Anglo-Saxon gained rapid proficiency with this incident!

Oddly enough, my next contact with another variety of the make is illustrated by another incident although my rather sketchy notes of the time are not clear in identifying the actual bus. It was a Guy underfloor bus on a Liverpool to Leeds service, on the stand in Lower Mosley Street, ready to depart for Leeds. I jauntily leapt aboard at the usual front entrance for access to the cab, only to find a blank wall; a metal and glass partition, to be correct. One does feel foolish, as an apparently sane, fully licensed

PSV driver, when one does not know where the cab door is! On this bus, as with some of the North Western's Atkinsons, the door was on the outside, in the traditional 'half cab' position. Early underfloor examples, which were not designed directly with one man operation in mind, had the outside cab access, even where the front entrance would automatically qualify the vehicle for one man operation. This was basically the limit of outstanding memories of the Guy Arab. I associated the Arab single decks with Bristol and, later Seddon underfloor and rear-engined models, in that the construction seemed to be more than adequately solid, giving a heavy feel to the vehicles, rather than designed to be sufficient for the job in hand, as was the impression with the Leyland and AEC product.

Daimler

Apart from the early years of the Company, North Western's first Daimlers were wartime editions, later swapped, with Potteries Motor Traction Limited, for Bristols. When North Western next bought Daimlers, they found themselves well-pleased and, eventually, operators of a fleet of 95 Fleetlines, with only two batches of AEC Renowns intruding, in 1963 and 1964. The Daimler supremacy lasted until the swansong order for 25 Bristol VRs which reached Charles Street only in time for its SELNEC days.

In December 1963, No. 1 (YJA 1) is pictured at Woodford Church, on the Wilmslow to Stockport service 75. This first batch of the Alexander-bodied Fleetlines had very small number indicators.

A Birmingham Corporation (City Transport) Daimler Fleetline, No. 3246 (246 DOC), on hire, leaves Mersey Square, Stockport for Manchester whilst being operated on service 28, Manchester to Hayfield.

No. 1 (YJA 1) arrived about the middle of 1963. My first introduction to the rear-engined decker, professionally, was when I returned to garage at about 20.45 one evening on a part-day duty. As the bus was being refuelled, the fitter asked whether or not I had tried a Fleetline. I had not, so after running through the wash and parking up, I was told to take the Fleetline down to the garage, into the yard, round, and back into the garage. The fitter stood on the platform to answer any queries, and that was that. There was no extra training on the type, no extra pay, and, when the time came, I was considered competent to drive a Fleetline. This generous and comprehensive training was deemed necessary, since Stockport had taken the first examples of the new buses, but the remaining buses having been delivered, Macclesfield Garage had been given an allocation. It was arranged that service 29 would be operated by Fleetlines so that although Manchester had no allocation, the 'Blue Bell' changeover was going to provide us with

the opportunity to drive them. This had happened when the Renowns had arrived, so Manchester men felt put out that none of the new buses, either Renown or Fleetline, had so far been allocated to their garage.

My own introduction to the Fleetline model came when the Company borrowed No. 3246 (246 DOC) from Birmingham Corporation, and operated it from Stockport Garage, as was the usual policy with demonstration vehicles. No. 3246 operated on the test route, service 28, Lower Mosley Street, Manchester to Hayfield. On one occasion, I managed to drive the bus for a full round trip of three hours and found the experience most enjoyable. I think the Stockport driver was delighted to be able to sit back and rest from the usual slow run, necessary to maintain time at Hayfield. This was before I had received any formal, if that is the word, training on the type.

No. 3246 was with the Company for several weeks and I recall that at about the same time, a Lancashire United Fleetline was tried as well. Of the 'opposition', Leyland Atlanteans had been tried when a Trent vehicle had been used, one of the N–N Lolines being borrowed by Trent in return. Unfortunately, I never managed to drive the Atlantean.

We had not long to wait before the 1964 deliveries brought Nos. 100, 101 and 102 to the Manchester fleet. Five more in 1965 were Nos. 175 to 179 (DDB 175C etc.). With the delivery of No. 100 and its followers (incidentally, these were AJA 100B etc.), Manchester found that life was not all rosy with these new buses.

No. 101 was an impressive piece of engineering from its early days. Presumably the jack-knife door adjustments were unknown at the time, since opening the air-operated door would render closing it impossible, unless the conductor was available to give one of the door panels a thump. Someone had a think and the next time I drove it, the door worked without a hitch. Unfortunately, the method of overcoming the problem, was to insert a brick, as used in the building trade, behind the offending door leaf to stop it going 'over centre' on its pivot, which was the cause of the stoppage. It would have been better to have adjusted the doors in the slides, one would have thought, as a permanent solution. No doubt this was a temporary 'repair' intended to keep the bus available in the busy peak periods when everything on wheels was needed. As a temporary 'repair', the brick lasted an awfully long time!

Apart from such incidents, it was a novelty to drive these new buses, but tales from other drivers, already experienced on rear-engined buses with other operators, were found to be true where heavy steering was concerned. A full load on a Fleetline led to a greater deterioration on ease of steering, than on a front-engined bus, where the steering was geared to cope with a heavy engine at the front, from the outset. It was certainly necessary, when turning in congested areas at low speed, with a fully loaded Fleetline, to stand up, in order to pull the steering wheel round more easily. Fortunately, the absence of a clutch, in the transmission layout, helped.

My notes of the times do not make it clear whether it was the 100 batch or the 175 batch, but another moan was caused by the accelerator pedal. This was a hydraulic system, and quite acceptable in operation. After a time, however, I understand that a filter in the system had to be cleaned or changed. If this was not done, the pedal was hard to operate and led, on one occasion, to an unusual remedy. Taking over a Fleetline at Lower Mosley Street Bus Station, I found a piece of string tied to the accelerator pedal with the other end secured to the base of the door-operating handle. When the pedal was pressed, it was loathe to return to the 'off' position and judicious use of the string did the necessary. When operating on full throttle, which usually meant 42 m.p.h., a gradual fall off in speed would need the throttle to be lifted

and pressed down again to maintain the maximum, which was very necessary when on service X60 to Blackpool.

Whilst the Alexander bodies on the Fleetlines were, in my view, the smartest of the rear-engined designs, the craze for forced ventilation meant that there were insufficient opening windows to cater for the warmer weather. This had its effect on the stomachs of passengers travelling by Fleetline to Blackpool, when it was often necessary to have floors cleaned on arrival in the Coliseum Bus Station.

The arrival of the next batch of Fleetlines brought another craze to Manchester Garage. Nos. 194, 195 and 196 (FJA 194D etc.) were Manchester's allocation from a delivery of 25 CRG6LXs, with standard Alexander LD75F bodies numbered 190–214. No. 194 had an advertisement for the *Sunday Express*, with white lettering on a blue background, on its roof! It was thought that, with the number of tall buildings coming into use, it was a useful direction into which one's advertising could be diverted. To my knowledge, No. 194 remained the sole example to use this type of advert. Incidentally, I saw more of this advert after I left the Company to work in the fourteenth floor office of the Department of Employment, when I would look down on No. 194 at the Flixton or Partington stand and regret leaving 'the road'. This was partly compensated by weekend work with a local operator, driving Bedford VAL14s. At least the engine was a Leyland!

These three Fleetlines were the last that I drove prior to leaving North Western. The later deliveries of what, in the event, were the last of North Western's Fleetlines, did not arrive until mid-1967. For the record, these were Nos. 245–254 (JDB 245F etc.).

With the arrival of Fleetlines in the Company fleet, double deck allocation on X60 or X70 services to Blackpool inevitably boasted one of these machines. Dennis Lolines continued to be used for 'duplicates' as did Bristol K5Gs, even in their last year of operation. The Daimlers tended to have a maximum speed of 42 m.p.h., but odd ones would show slight improvement to 45 or even 46 m.p.h. They drove well and handled acceptably except in crosswinds when the lighter loading on the front wheel made them yaw from side to side, similar to a Manchester 'Pilcher' tramcar at speed, which, in the case of the tram, would be 25–30 m.p.h. I remember, but only vaguely, the 'Pilcher' cars on Oldham Road, Manchester, when travelling on the service 36 trolley bus from Moston to Stevenson Square, during the war.

Oddly enough, after leaving North Western, my double deck driving experience continued, three years later, whilst I worked part-time for Lancashire United Transport Limited, on Fleetlines. My Atlantean experience in any depth had to wait until a further four years had passed.

Chapter Nine ~ Other Operators

North Western's service network on the express and 'limited stop' side involved much joint operation with neighbouring BET and BTC companies. Varied driving experience was gained when a scheduled duty used a joint operator's bus or coach as well as occasions where it was necessary to obtain a change-over at a 'foreign' garage. This latter course was never popular with the garage staff due to the problems of retrieving the vehicle after repair.

The majority of North Western's express services were jointly-operated with other companies but the interchange of drivers and buses was confined to the following services:

X2 Manchester to Nottingham
North Western; Ribble; Trent

X60 Manchester to Blackpool
North Western; Ribble; Trent

Lancashire United Transport Limited were joint operators but did not take part in any exchange of drivers except in emergency situations (i.e. vehicle failure, etc.) on the X60 or X70 services.

X97/X98/X99 Tyne-Tees to Liverpool
North Western; Lancashire United Transport Ltd.
Yorkshire Woollen District Transport Co. Ltd.
West Yorkshire Road Car Co. Ltd.
United Automobile Co. Ltd.
Northern General Transport Co. Ltd.

Coaches on these services, including Lancashire United examples, were constantly interchanged between drivers so that on arrival, say, at Leeds with a North Western car, it would not be unusual to return with a coach from one of the other operators. These 'foreign' vehicles would end up in North Western's Manchester Garage overnight so that a driver who was scheduled for a Liverpool service journey, could take a Northern General vehicle to Liverpool and return to Manchester. He could then either leave the vehicle, and take another operator's vehicle for another journey to Liverpool and back, or proceed to Leeds before changing vehicles for the journey back to Manchester. The permutations were endless on the Leeds to Liverpool, as the X97/98/99 services tended to be called.

The X60 service tended to be restricted to through journeys of X1 (Derby) or X2 (Nottingham) which, on arrival in Manchester, operated as X60 to Blackpool. Through coaches from any operator could be driven during the period of a North Western duty. On service X2, any of the three operators' coaches (N–N, Ribble or Trent) could be used by the North Western duty driver between Manchester and Nottingham. Summer service variation on X2 led to duties such as the one I once worked on a Saturday.

I signed-on at 05.30, when I took a coach to Liverpool 'private'. At 07.00 showing the destination

Northern General No. 2507 enters Wellington Street Coach Station, Leeds, in February 1966, whilst en route to Liverpool.

Ribble's No. 1077 (FFR 360) is a Leyland Royal Tiger with Leyland coachwork, renumbered from the Standerwick fleet to release fleet numbers for new deliveries. It is seen at Lower Mosley Street, in August 1965, on service X1 to Derby.

'Lowestoft', I proceeded to Manchester, and on to Nottingham, where another driver took over. I returned to Manchester with a Trent coach on service X2. The Trent service to Lowestoft was numbered X7 and this was sometimes to be seen, incorrectly, on vehicles north of Nottingham.

The London service was jointly-operated with Midland Red but even vehicle failures did not guarantee a coach replacement, Midland Red being very wary at lending their home-made coaching stock to other operators. On a few occasions, North Western drivers have arrived in Lower Mosley Street Bus Station at the helm of a Midland Red bus, to the chagrin of the passengers. However, other operators were more co-operative, so a vehicle failure would normally result in a vehicle of reasonable comfort as a replacement. Such goodwill went by the board, however, when the request was made at a time when there was a peak vehicle demand, such as a summer Saturday, when one accepted whatever

serviceable vehicle was available.

In such circumstances, it was normal to request a changeover by telephoning the nearest garage of the joint operator, or sometimes, the home North Western garage. If a vehicle on a journey to North Wales failed in Llandudno, Crosville would either repair one's motor or provide a replacement, but the preference on the other operator's part was to repair rather than replace. Replacement could lead to difficulties in getting your own coach back, if repair was out of the question.

On one Nottingham journey, I drove an excellent Trent Leopard. It gave up at High Lane, on the journey from Manchester. This was a Saturday afternoon when buses and coaches were at a premium, so I pulled up an engine cover in the floor and repaired the offending accelerator linkage with an elastic band from the conductor's waybill board, and carried on to Buxton. Two more temporary repairs were

A stranger on service X97. A West Yorkshire Bristol L type, (KWU 393), works a 'duplicate' on the Leeds to Liverpool service at Lower Mosley Street in March 1966.

necessary before we reached Buxton, where we deposited the majority of the passengers at the Market Place refreshment halt whilst we popped into Buxton Garage for a more permanent linkage repair. Happily, all went well from Buxton.

Many vehicles from other operators' garages were of similar types to those operated by North Western. AEC Reliances of Yorkshire Woollen District were slightly different in having, in some examples, vacuum brakes which were far more efficient than the Leyland variety.

Leopards and Tiger Cubs were common to many of the joint operators, Northern General having a very high standard in all its vehicles which I encountered, as my comments on one of their Leopards, elsewhere, will confirm.

Yorkshire Woollen District stood alone with their Commer TS3 two strokes. 'WD' vehicles tended to seem in well-kept condition, as far as the examples on the Leeds to Liverpool service were concerned, and the Commers were no exception. These being the only examples of the TS3 model, comparison with other operators was not possible but they compared favourably with other makes which I drove. I recall the staccato exhaust note which resulted from the need to keep the revs up and, like the Leyland Leopards, encouraged me to open the driver's side window or the signalling window (a sign of the times, no pun intended) to listen to the exhaust. To digress a little, mention of the signalling window tends to make me realize that almost twenty years have passed since the mid-1960s and hand signals generally tend to be given only on rare occasions, nowadays. Perhaps the wave to overtake a stationary vehicle is the most often-used variation.

However, the need to rev the engine high on the TS3 was reflected in the provision of a rev-counter with its red 'danger' segment to remind the over-enthusiastic driver. I regret that the uninterested driver would probably pay little heed to such an instrument although he would, no doubt, try to get the engine to slog up a hill with rather poor results! Apart from the TS3 model, I cannot recall any other examples of vehicles with Beadle coachwork that I have driven.

The Bristol coaches which I drove were, generally, those of the West Yorkshire Road Car Company, although I did sample the odd United Automobile example; but this was a rare event. The underfloor-engined Bristols were solid and, to me, uninteresting machines, the gearchange lacking the precision of the Ls and Ks that I had driven. Slogging over Standedge with a West Yorkshire CUG did nothing to inspire me and even my anti-Reliance bias tended to be overlooked when I could hand over a CUG at Leeds and return with an AEC Reliance. Anyone's Reliance was more welcome than the Bristol! The weight of the CUG's coachwork tended to overtax the usually efficient Bristol vacuum brakes, whilst the heavy steering was not appreciated even though it was at least positive and direct.

By comparison, the only independent operator on the service was Lancashire United Transport Limited, who fielded Reliances and Tiger Cubs during the period in question. They all seemed to be in a reasonable state of repair without leading me into the same realms of praise as the Northern General Leopard. The more recent additions to the LUT coaching fleet at the time were six-speed examples, similar to North Western's aforementioned 'banana splits' (see the AEC chapter). The same comments applied to the LUT machines where sixth gear was high enough to be affected by wind pressure, to the detriment of top speed!

A more devastating situation arose one day when I was allocated an LUT Tiger Cub for a round trip, Manchester to Liverpool and return. Opportunities for high speed tended to be restricted to the section of route common to both X97 and X99 services, between Bold and Whiston. The X97s winding lanes, in the Lymm area and in the congested Chester Road between Manchester and Altrincham, compared with the A57, Manchester-Irlam-Warrington road for delays.

On the outward trip nothing untoward occurred but on the return, I recalled that the Cub had a six-speed box. Engagement into the appropriate slot brought nothing but a high-pitched grinding of teeth! I returned to fifth gear and then tried again with the same result. On arrival in Warrington, I stopped at traffic lights which gave me the opportunity to peer down at the gear layout diagram which was placed down the side panelling in a spot impossible to see whilst actually driving. The explanation was simple. I had been 'rubbing' into reverse; not sixth! I shudder to think what could have happened if reverse had engaged.

Other services where an interchange of vehicles took place gave North Western drivers the chance of trying the delights of Ribble and Trent machinery. Both of these companies' vehicles could be driven by North Western men between Manchester and Blackpool whilst, between Manchester and Nottingham, Trent was in the majority, naturally enough, but a few Ribble vehicles were operated on this section.

Ribble's operations were worked by Leopards with Harrington Cavalier coachwork as well as the more angular semi-coach Marshall-bodied Leopards. Leyland Tiger Cubs with several varieties of Burlingham Seagull coachwork were also allocated to these routes. Examples from Ribbles's famous Leyland coach-bodied Royal Tiger fleet could be seen, with, in the later days of the fleet's life, transfers from the Standerwick fleet, renumbered into the 1,000 series, to make way for new deliveries to Ribble's coaching subsidiary. For this reason, itself, renumbered some of its Royal Tiger coaches.

Tales of heavy steering on the Royal Tigers, and my own experience of North Western's bus fleet, made me feel fortunate to find that the examples of Ribble's fleet, which I drove to Blackpool, were quite light to steer. Unfortunately, the brakes were still not

Working an X66 service to Blackburn, Lancashire United's No. 521 (STF 206), a Weymann-bodied 1954-built Guy Arab, waits at Lower Mosley Street Bus Station on 30th August 1962.

Two Leyland Tiger Cub buses, with Weymann bodies, were added to the Lancashire United fleet in 1956. One of these was No. 563 (WTB 72) seen here on 19th August 1965.

man enough for these coaches, which weighed almost as much as some of the vehicles in the double deck fleet.

The Ribble Tiger Cubs were similar to North Western's, with the top speed being as high as 60 m.p.h., like North Western's 770-type coaches, depending, generally, on the age of the vehicle. Trent's input of Leopards, between Nottingham and Blackpool, tended to comprise Willowbrook-bodied examples that were nice to drive, with full instructions on the use of the two-speed axles that were fitted to them all. The operation of the axle shift was usually good, although occasional mistaken identity of switches on the steering column, dipped the headlights instead! Trent's Tiger Cubs ranged from the older HRC-registered Willowbrook-bodied class, which were quite nippy, to the rather smart Alexander Y type examples, which seemed equally speedy.

Apart from vehicles, other operators also controlled some of the bus stations used by N–N on the joint services. Omnibus Stations Limited controlled Lower Mosley Street, Manchester and also the Coliseum Bus Station at Blackpool, which was adjacent to the Corporation bus and tram sheds. Arrival at Blackpool on services X60 or X70, with nothing more generous than time for a quick brew, enabled one to make a speedy visit to the sheds in order to see what the latest concoction was for the illuminations.

The Ribble subsidary, W.C. Standerwick Limited, was based at Blackpool at Devonshire Road Garage, and it was to this garage that we went for any small repair or changeover. It was always an interesting place, due to the visiting BET coaches that could be seen parked up there on tour or on long distance service lay-over. The other Ribble depot at Blackpool was Talbot Road but, to the best of my knowledge, was never used for changeovers on X60 services, so is outside the scope of these comments.

When operating into Blackpool with any reasonable length of 'stand down', (i.e. time when the bus would be parked at Blackpool), it was customary to park at a bus park off Bloomfield Road, from where one would be called by the bus station inspector when required. Otherwise, a driver would unload at the bus station and, on his way to the parking area, would be told to return at a specific time. The Coliseum would swarm with homeward-bound trippers and holiday-makers, on busy summer weekends, and I always felt that it was best to be a 'service car' with time for a quick cuppa and then off, out of the bedlam with a full load, to leave others to worry about the crowds.

A Ribble Leyland Leopard with a Harrington Cavalier body. No. 1049 (PCK 631) waits at Blackpool, Coliseum Bus Station, in May 1964. Vehicles of this type were sometimes worked by N–N crews on Nottingham and Blackpool through journeys.

Preston Coach Station was the official stop in Preston for the Blackpool services on which N—N operated, and this was a relatively small station which was situated round the corner from the main Tithebarn Street Bus Station. North Road seemed a trifle grand for the actual coach station, but I felt it had a good share of atmosphere, like Lower Mosley Street, Manchester, that the later, large Preston Bus Station lacked. The new bus station could never appeal in the same way, since I no longer drove buses for N—N when it came into operation. In my driving days, it was always interesting to have a look at the old Ribble Park Road Garage on the way to the coach station, to see what old Ribble vehicles one could spy during the brief moment in passing the entrance.

The Ribble bus stations, at both Chorley and Bolton, were to succumb to modernization. It does at least show, perhaps, that both Councils and Company were aware of the need to make the surroundings for waiting passengers more attractive. In the case of the old Chorley Bus Station, with its two lane system, fraught with traffic delays when buses were unable to pass those parked at the front of a line, the traditional Ribble 'head-on' system was introduced, and seemed to work well. It did not seem to lose too much of its former appeal once the newness had worn off. Granted, one seemed to see few of Corless and Hart's buses in later years, but this was due to their take-over by Ribble, rather than a disastrous fault in the design of the bus station! Perhaps I am leaning towards old memories here, since the well-remembered Leyland Royal Tiger buses of Hart's of Coppull and the Corless pre-war Leyland Titans disappeared in the mid-1950s, well before I drove either at Charles Street or Manchester. The famous Ribble 'ABC' featured a sketch on the cover of one edition showing Chorley Bus Station (old style) with a PD1 type 'White Lady' to the fore.

Bolton was of the usual 'head-on' layout with Ribble and other express operators, at one end of the concourse, and the Ribble stage carriage and Corporation services interspersed along the remaining area. The later design separated the Ribble and Bolton Corporation's successor, SELNEC/GMT services, and abandoned the 'head-on' system as well.

These were the bus stations that created an impression with me over the years, although my original Ribble interest, no doubt, contributed to the bias of my interest on the Blackpool service bus stations.

Most of the other bus stations used by N—N on its 'limited stop' services were of the 'run-through' type, such as Nottingham, Derby and Dewsbury.

The Leeds Bus Station, at Wellington Street, had another system where buses reversed on to the stand. Inadequate in the off peak periods, Leeds was a shambles on a summer Saturday. In this respect, all the bus stations shared this one common bond. They were inadequate for the numbers travelling at the weekends. Whilst this is no doubt, to some extent, a matter of economics, the degree of inadequacy did seem to be somewhat extreme. However, it is prob-

ably true to say that of all the bus stations, Lower Mosley Street, Manchester, seemed the most overworked during the summer weekends.

Lastly, on Leeds to Liverpool routes, bus stations were owned by the Company at Oldham and Altrincham. Oldham's 'on-street' stops gave way to a modern garage which doubled as a bus station which seemed an improvement over the 'on-street' facility. However, to me, it never seemed to create a great deal of interest.

Altrincham Bus Station was a combination of 'head-on' loading bays and the 'run through' design, and later became a 'head-on' system completely.

At the Liverpool end, Lancashire United Transport's facilities at Canning Place were insignificant, by comparison, having the appearance of an old wartime air raid shelter, which housed an inspector's office and toilet facilities. The mobile café around the corner dealt with the mandatory cuppa. Even the road was cobblestone in parts.

More important to the Liverpool Terminal was the LUT inspector, George Crofts. George was a friendly and efficient gentleman who would always receive full co-operation from the crews under his control. When the LUT terminal office was closed a few years later, George went to Hindley Depot, where he eventually became District Superintendent. I was fortunate enough to meet George later in my career when he was just as cheerful and helpful to everyone. Most regrettably, he died just as he was due to retire.

In other directions, bus stations were used of varying sizes in towns throughout the N—N empire. The Nottingham Service called at the few stands alongside the market sites at both Buxton and Matlock, the latter deserving more the title of bus station. Northwich, home of the large ICI Limited complexes, needed a large bus station and garage, far larger than one would expect for the size of the town, and the North Wales services called here. More impressive was Macclesfield Garage and bus station where the bus station was built on the garage forecourt with an 'island' fronting the main road which housed office and passenger enquiry facilities. Services 29 and 30, from Manchester, terminated here whilst the X1 Manchester to Derby service also called at this location.

Manchester's 27 and 28 services, to Buxton and Hayfield, in addition to the many express services, including certain London variants, used Mersey Square, Stockport, as that town's bus station. Plans for a central bus station in the town materialized, in part, only a few years ago. The mid-1960s, therefore, saw Mersey Square in much the same guise as it was when Stockport's trams were running. A small office and enquiry facility was situated adjacent to the arch carrying the A6 trunk road over the Square, with the staff canteen actually situated under the arch. A narrow street, alongside, carried stops for certain services whilst the remaining services parked in front of the office or the adjacent pub! For this reason the area was named 'The Scilly Isles', although I feel that

Lancashire United's No. 97 (561 TD), a Daimler Fleetline with Northern Counties bodywork, on hire to N—N in July 1962, is seen at Marple on service 28, Manchester to Hayfield.

the 'c' was omitted by most of its users. Odd lengths of kerb provided very basic stops for both Company and Corporation buses, whilst the departure for Manchester wandered round a positive obstacle course to reach the A6.

A final point in the Stockport story is that on the Manchester side of the traffic lights guarding the entrance to Mersey Square, were two bus stops on the A6 which were situated about 30 yards apart. Here, local travellers would wait for the local 89 or 92 service buses. Some, however, would be travelling to stops further along the road, served by services 27 and 28 of N—N. Since the Corporation services were more frequent, travellers would usually wait at the local bus stop, leaving the 'limited stop' position empty.

Especially on last journeys into Manchester, but at other times as well, departure from the Square would be carefully regulated, to try and coincide with the green phase of the traffic lights, in order to present the waiting locals with as little chance as possible to recognize a bus which they could catch other than their 89 or 92, and so prevent them from running to the N—N stop. It was in these situations that fast gearchanges on non-synchromesh gearboxes came into their own, without fear of being called a show-off. To miss a crowd of 'runners' was a guarantee of praise from the conductor, even if the gentlemen at head office would have frowned on the procedure.

Chapter Ten ~ Manchester Garage: Services and Schedules

The two lists of services shown in Appendix 'C' cover the period during which the writer drove at Manchester Depot. Although for example, service 91, Piccadilly to Ashton-on-Mersey, was operated by N—N's Manchester Depot, this operation had been replaced by the new service 222 to Partington, with its 223 variation operating through the works of Shell Chemicals Limited. All service 91 operations were carried out by Manchester Corporation, during the period in question, with the main alteration in this corridor being the introduction of Manchester Corporation workings on services 222 and 223.

Service 11 operated in the peak hour to Carrington Road, Flixton or, for works purposes, to Moss Lane, Carrington. Most of the daily operation was as service 11X to the Nags Head, Davyhulme, working, in effect, as shorts of service 23 to the Red Lion, Flixton. One variation of service 23 was the 23X, which operated from the Red Lion in the morning peak, via Woodsend Road, past the Union Inn (which gave the service its popular name, since most crews referred to it as 'The Union Inn') then on to Davyhulme Road to the Nags Head, and via the normal route to Picaddily.

Unfortunately, my records of the period do not reveal which of the Urmston local services were operated by Manchester Depot, but I remember operating to Nags Head from Piccadilly, then via Barton Road, Broadway, Woodhouse Road, Union Inn, Woodsend Road, Woodsend Crescent Road and Irlam Road to the Red Lion. This was a school journey which conveniently fitted into an available gap in Manchester's schedules.

The 11/23 network was prominent in the 'newcomers' sheets at Manchester, so that new drivers were inevitably told by depot staff that the buses knew the way if the drivers didn't; 'and anyway, follow the white line from the Nags Head.' This latter comment was more useful than it appeared on first hearing, since on leaving Nags Head, the white line in the middle of Davyhulme Road continued without a break to Urmston Baths roundabout, guiding the 23 through the curvaceous Cornhill Road. Granted, one still had a splendid choice of exits from the Baths roundabout, but once there, the rest was reasonably easy.

One last quirk of service 23 was lying in wait for the unwary driver from Manchester. One journey, in the evening, terminated at Park Hospital, just past the Urmston Baths. Turning a bus into the hospital lay-by needed care, as the deterioration of the low wall, dividing the lay-by from the footpath, testified, together with a general tattiness of the offside panel edges, especially on Daimler Fleetlines.

A favourite Dennis Loline, No. 818 (RDB 818), photographed in April 1964 at Wood Lane terminus, Partington.

No. 234 (CDB 234), a Leyland PD2/1 with a Leyland body, is seen at Cannon Street, Manchester, working service 3 to Carrington Road, Flixton, in June 1965.

Service 12A followed, as one might expect, the route used by service 12. This variation of the Flixton services approached from Urmston itself, as did the 3 and 5 services, rather than from Davyhulme. Services 12 and 12A then worked along Church Road to Carrington Road, Flixton, terminus of the 12, with 12A continuing to Moss Lane, Carrington, but more often further on, to Partington itself. Manchester Depot operated the morning journey to Carrington Power-Station and also to Partington Gasworks, which was at the end of Broadway, Partington, the first turn left after passing under the low railway bridge on the approach to Partington Estates. A 12A, without any complications to the unwary, would terminate at the Greyhound Hotel.

In the city, service 3, alone, terminated at Cannon Street, Manchester, which was at the Cathedral end of Deansgate. This again produced the feeling of being out on a limb, with no other N–N bus in sight. The other Flixton services terminated at Piccadilly, with only service 12 leaving via a different route for Trafford Bar, using Stretford Road instead of the more common City Road route.

In the early days of my operation on Partington services, covering approximately three years, the Greyhound Hotel, Partington service was not as simple as it looked. Approaching from Manchester, the low bridge was passed, and then a short distance on the left was the public house, the King William, so that the road curved to the right past the church, and the stop was outside the Greyhound Hotel, either as a terminus or, for Wood Lane journeys, a stop. The

Greyhound looked an odd place, until I discovered that we were at the back of the pub. The long term plan was that the section of Manchester Road on which we stopped, would be replaced by a bypass which would then pass the front of the pub and disclose it to travellers in all its glory. Until this happened, in about 1966, we continued to provide a good service to the pub's back door. Wood Lane, Partington was a further three minutes run from the Greyhound, and after entering the estate, the road round the estate was traversed anticlockwise, although this was altered much later, after revisions to the services took place, to a clockwise circle. By then, the third option of Central Road had been added, but since this occurred not long before I left the depot, I cannot say how often I went to this terminus.

When the work began on the blocking of City Road, and the construction of an access to the Mancunian Way inner ring road, notices appeared warning drivers to use a diversion with effect from first journeys on a certain day. When these first journeys operated, it was still dark, being around 06.00. I was on a Partington run and was due to divert via Medlock Street and Jackson Street. Alas, I diverted, only to find the diversion not yet in use, so I bumped my Loline over a few areas of waste ground to rejoin City Road, and ignored the instruction. We later discovered that work was delayed, but no one had thought to tell the garage.

The older N–N timetables show service 27A as Mersey Square, Stockport to Buxton, via Long Hill.

The 13.20 departure from Buxton was operated by Buxton Depot, through to Manchester. The outward departure on service 27A was Manchester Depot's 09.30 off Lower Mosley Street Bus Station. I drove this journey on several occasions, and whilst the Buxton service generally was very slack in its timing, Long Hill was even worse. Since there was no demand for the service to stop at every stop along the route, an average speed of 18 m.p.h. still made it necessary to wait time at Disley and Whaley Bridge. To go faster, and wait longer, meant that no passengers would ever catch the service if they were using the Company's timetable. Departure from Whaley Bridge was at 4 or 34 minutes past each hour, to Buxton. Service 27A was at 10.34. On occasions, I have waited until 10.40 and then ambled up Long Hill at 20 m.p.h. only to find myself several minutes early at the top of Long Hill, which should be reached at 10.56, and have had to run the last half mile or so at a ridiculous crawl.

One amusing facet of bus operation is the number of rumours and tales that are passed around. Long Hill was no exception. It was said that if service 27A went past the farm at the top of Long Hill, then the occupants would telephone Buxton Office and report the crew. Since I never received any warnings from Buxton's inspectorate after arriving from a 27A journey, or a 27 for that matter, I assumed that this was a local rumour or my watch was reasonably accurate. Whatever the source of the tale, even the most hardened conductor would warn a driver if it seemed that the inevitable Tiger Cub was making too good a speed up the hill!

It was unfortunate that both routes to Buxton were along roads used by a large number of quarry wagons. I feel sure that they must have cursed the dawdling buses. Such running times had one good feature; there was plenty of time to stop half way up Long Hill and walk across a field to enable me to photograph the bus in its pleasant setting. How the passengers felt when the bus stopped and the driver walked away, I do not know. I did not ask them, but they seemed relieved when I returned.

The Macclesfield services had the odd variation, where certain morning journeys terminated at the Imperial Chemical Industries Limited offices at Nether Alderley. These journeys would operate 'Private' from Imperial Chemical Industries Limited to Alderley (District Bank) where service duplication would be operated, usually on service 52 or 500.

Service 52 itself had two terminal points at Alderley; the main one being the District Bank, later to become the National Westminster Bank, whilst the other terminal was 'The Circuit'. This was the name of a small crescent of houses at the end of a local road which was reached by crossing the railway bridge and turning first left. The Circuit was about a mile along that road. It was at this terminus, with its occasional Manchester operation, that the crews found that cups of tea were offered on one of the early morning journeys. This welcome offer ensured

that crews were helpful to the passengers in this area. The lady of the house was usually presented with a box of chocolates at Christmas as a token of appreciation, by the Manchester drivers and conductors.

Manchester Depot did not operate on the main service 31 to Jenny Lane, Bramhall. This was covered by Manchester Corporation and Stockport Depot, Manchester's share being confined to peak hour duplications. The variation of service 31A, which operated via Ack Lane, was also operated by both Manchester and Stockport Depots of N–N.

Service 51 operated from Chorlton Street Bus Station to Torkington which is part of Hazel Grove, Cheshire. The service wandered via Stockport Road, Kingsway, Parrswood Road and Kingsway extension, thus missing Cheadle, which all the other Manchester services in this direction served. At the Griffin, Heald Green, the route travelled along Turves Road, joining the 31 and 32 routes just before Cheadle Hulme. Service 51 approached Bramhall via Ack Lane, as did 32, whilst service 31 wandered off via Grove Lane. Service 51 left the other routes at Bramhall and went towards Stockport, turning up Bridge Lane, opposite Bramhall Park, approaching London Road, Hazel Grove via Bramhall Moor Lane, which passed the premises of Mirrlees Diesels, and Stepping Hill Hospital. After joining London Road at Brewers Green, the service turned into Commercial Road, and so through the estates to Torkington Road/Highfield Road, where a reverse was necessary. At this point, indicators were changed and the bus then operated on service 165 to Stockport. This inter-working allowed a neat scheduling package to be built up and the full round trip took three hours. Stockport Depot shared this service, and in order to balance the workings, Manchester Depot's 15.40 departure to Torkington, met Stockport's 16.30 ex-Torkington, at Bramhall Moor Lane when the crews changed buses. The Manchester crew would then travel back to Chorlton Street for 17.33, the 17.40 departure being the start of a late duty at Manchester Depot; virtually a day off prior to an evening's work.

This changeover system also took place on service 29, when the 22.10 departure from Manchester met the 22.15 ex-Macclesfield departure at the Blue Bell Hotel, Handford at about 22.55.

The changeovers on services 29 and 51 were daily occurrences. Saturday mornings also brought a changeover into operation on the 07.30 Buxton departure on service 27. The Manchester car changed with, I think, one of the Stockport workings coming from Buxton. Having worked this route once only, I seem to recall that the transfer of crews took place at Furness Vale.

Another rather vague changeover, which I think was necessary only on special holiday schedules, was on service 30, which operated to Macclesfield via Parrs Wood Road instead of Kingsway, as service 29 did. Service 27 was also noted at Manchester for having several oddities. The Ferodo diversion has been mentioned elsewhere. On the 07.30 from Manchester to

Buxton, the return journey from Buxton at 09.15 was met at High Lane by the local postman who then boarded the bus, chained a mail bag to the rail round the driver's cab and departed. At Mersey Square, Stockport, another postman appeared to collect the bag. This was one of the remaining examples of a once well-used method by which the Post Office moved its mail from outlying areas. It always seemed odd to me that this procedure took place in an area not very remote from Stockport.

The introduction of service 500 brought a new type of operation to Manchester Depot who shared its operation with Wilmslow Depot. This service covered the 52 route, but once at the Griffin Hotel, Heald Green, the service operated direct, and non-stop, via Kingsway extension and Kingsway to Chorlton Street.

Conductors dispensed tickets from a 'Setright' machine which, I always thought, seemed to be an unworthy receipt for the fare when compared to the earlier 'Willibrew' tickets of the Company. The Tyne-Tees—Merseyside Express services dispensed a variety of tickets from its various operators, but during my time at Manchester, the inevitable 'Setright' was used as a return ticket.

On local services where the route was 'by arrangement' with Manchester Corporation Transport, rather than a joint operation, all vehicles were from North Western garages. If a passenger boarded outside the Manchester boundary, but was travelling across the boundary towards Manchester, then, in addition to a normal 'Setright' ticket, a similar size, pre-printed and numbered 'NCV' ticket was issued, being punched in a clip on the side of the 'Setright' machine. The initials stood for 'No Cash Value' and was the source of costing by which the Corporation received its payment for passengers travelling on these services in the Manchester-controlled area.

Joint services, where operation was shared by the Company and one or other of the Corporation Transport Departments, did not need the 'NCV' ticket, since receipts were pooled and shared on a mileage basis.

Duties, Rosters and Scheduling

Manchester Garage was unique in its operations within the North Western empire. Whilst other garages had one or more express services based on the garage, Manchester stood alone in the number of all the year-round express and 'limited stop' services and, in summer, the weekend seasonal services came into operation. Almost half of the Manchester fleet of sixty six vehicles were coaches. Because of this, the peak hour, Monday to Friday, operation relied heavily on these thirty coaches, probably ten of which would be used on 'duplicate' operations to Cheadle Hulme and Bramhall, with the occasional appearance on the Flixton services. The fact that Cheadle Hulme and Bramhall were up-market commuter areas was, perhaps, offset by the fact that other areas served by North Western, Manchester,

demanded larger capacity single or double deck vehicles, which accounted for the rare appearance of coaches elsewhere. Despite this, the variants of service 12A to Partington (Gasworks) or Carrington (Power-Station) often had a coach allocated to them.

A typical operation for a coach would be the operation of a duplicate peak journey on service 31, returning on either 31 or its variants, or service 32, and operating from Chorlton Street Bus Station, on completion of the peak journey to Lower Mosley Street, for use on Nottingham (X2) or Chesterfield (X67) services. These journeys would be due into Manchester by 08.00, so they could easily work the express routes. This had the added bonus of warming the coach ready for the long distance passengers; a useful facility during the winter months.

Meal breaks in the duties tended to be in the region of twenty minutes or more, but many duties had no actual meal break scheduled. The three buses working service 32 from Lower Mosley Street, Manchester, to Higher Poynton or Middlewood, during the evening, each operated duties of three return trips. The thirty minute frequency arrived back at Lower Mosley Street at 22 or 52 minutes past each hour, departing thirteen minutes later at 5 or 35 minutes past. The two appearances in Lower Mosley Street were the only opportunities for food and drink, other than the flask and sandwich type. Unlike the Corporation lads, North Western crews rarely carried brew cans, even though the Corporation facilities were available at some points on the joint routes. The North Western habit was to know every café that existed within reasonable distance of the terminals. In some rural terminals, tea and toast for the odd early morning journey was offered to crews by local residents. It was customary to take more of an interest in passengers and potential passengers outside the 'Corpo' boundaries. Within the boundaries, the North Western staff tried to leave the Corporation to themselves although this was not always possible when a North Western bus was 'pushed' down the route by a Corporation bus. Then, North Western picked up, and had to like it. Since the work at the garage was remarkably varied, it was divided into a system of rosters. These were lettered 'A' to 'D' with the addition of 'E' roster in the summer operational months. The local stage carriage operations were mainly found in the 'D' sheet, as the rosters tended to be called, with similar work, plus some express work in the 'C' sheet. 'A' sheet contained mainly London service work with London 'duplicates' and other express work in 'B' sheet. Stockport Garage was also responsible for some London service and 'duplicate' work. The additional express and 'limited stop' work, resulting from the seasonal timetabled journeys during the summer, required the 'C' sheet diet to contain much more express work, with a slight increase in the amount of this work allocated to 'D' sheet. The displaced local work then went into the seasonal 'E' sheet, which gave drivers, who were normally on the spare sheet, awaiting a regular position on 'D' sheet, regular, scheduled work for the summer.

A Daimler Fleetline with an Alexander body, No. 102 (AJA 102B), at The Red Lion, when new, in September 1964.

North Western, Manchester was very class conscious. There were often un-filled lines of work on the 'E' sheet, which would be covered as overtime by crews on rest days. An 'A' sheet man, however, would not normally be called upon to work on the lowly 'Nags and Lions' (11X/23 services), unless he asked for this by way of a change. He would, no doubt, be allocated a Nottingham service journey off 'C' sheet, possibly left open due to holidays or sickness. The 'C' sheet man would also be given express work as overtime, leaving 'D' and 'E' sheets to mop up the stage operations, with the occasional crumb for 'E' sheet of an express journey. In earlier years, the failure of a top sheet driver to turn in for duty would result in a man from the same sheet being taken off stage work to operate the express journey, even though there may be a 'D' or 'E' sheet man available, on the spot, on spare. This man would then take over the stage carriage duty.

Whilst my scheduled work, during my first year with North Western, Manchester, rarely gave me any express runs, the inevitable demand for 'duplicates', or non-arrival of a crew, caught elsewhere in traffic hold-ups, enabled me to obtain some work of a more interesting nature.

Unlike Manchester Corporation, and several other municipalities, North Western did not allocate regular mates. In fact, it was discouraged, with drivers working down the roster weeks, whilst conductors worked up the list. The conductors' sheets did not include 'A' sheet work since London services were one man operated. It was about 1964 before Manchester's first 'normal' type of one man operation came into being, with the conversion of X12, the 'limited stop' Manchester–Halifax–Bradford service.

One or two contract journeys were maintained as spare duties worked only by drivers, such as the Loretto Convent School baths/playing fields contract, where a bus would be allocated for a morning, afternoon or full day. The full day contract operated between 09.00 and 16.00 approximately, a meal at lunchtime being supplied in the school kitchen, since there was no time to return to the bus station canteen. The contract was easy enough to operate but the travel to and from work then took place in the two peak hours which seemed difficult compared to normal duties.

On the occasion when I once operated this contract, my Crossley Regis car silencer was, to say the least, a trifle noisy. I would have preferred a quieter time on the roads so that I could have used less power and kept the noise down! This, I suppose, was preferable to leaving the garage at midnight after a late duty, only to discover that a tyre had ceased to be pneumatic. Wheel changing seems to be reserved for rainy nights, or dark streets, so that the wheel change is done by feel, and everything you feel is wet. At least the Regis had built-in jacks, which helped.

On Saturdays, North Western had several services to special schools or homes around Manchester, to which crews were allocated either for day off work or in exchange for the more mundane locals. These schools included Buglawton Hall and Soss Moss, near Alderley Edge, together with a service to Parkside Hospital at Macclesfield. I always remember this one because they had a Dennis Brothers Limited, Guildford, motorized lawn mower; the first I had seen. Dennis were well-respected for such machines, I later learned, and assumed, therefore, that it had no idiosynchrasies, like the gear change on the Dennis Loline Mark II!

At Manchester Garage, drivers signed-on at the garage office where an inspector or shift foreman would tell them the bus number, and tick their names off the duty sheet. That was the easy bit. A blank running sheet was obtained from a box and the great safari was on! If you were friendly with the 'man behind the counter', or were, in some way, favoured, a crumb of information such as 'your bus is in the top arch' or 'it's over the road' would direct your steps, and drastically reduce the time it took to find No. 224 or whatever was allocated. It was useful to be a bus enthusiast since one could at least concentrate, with No. 224, for example, on double decks. These PD2s were usually parked round the corner in Hulme Hall Road and you would probably have noticed it on the way into the garage. 'Over the road' covered the area against the fence on the canal side, as well as the various arches under the railway, outside the garage boundary.

I was once late for work, fortunately a rare occurrence, and was given bus No. 237. Somewhat surprised, since this vehicle, a PD2, usually lived at Altrincham Garage, I wandered off to search, without success. On returning to the office and feeling rather foolish, I asked where it was. After being directed round the corner, I came face to face with No. 237, a Trent Leopard. A further visit to the office revealed the delightful information that I had been allocated a Nottingham 'duplicate'. This was probably the only occasion where I benefited from a missed duty. It was certainly better than the expected 'Nags and Lions'.

At this point, I would direct the reader to Appendix 'B', which covers the Manchester duties.

Week 18 in the winter duties of 'D' sheet is, to me, an example of a most frustrating week's work. My comments on 'Nags and Lions' have been laboured elsewhere in this tale. Imagine my horror when being confronted with these elaborate routes, 11X and 23, not just as part of a duty's work, but for all of it. Week 18 excelled itself, with Saturday, Sunday, Monday and Thursday on these services. At least Thursday had three Partingtons in the second half of the duty. The other two working days, were the dear old Higher Poynton duties. To make matters worse, the week had only one rest day. No. 12 duty was the last journey whilst No. 14 duty was the middle of the three late Higher Poynton duties.

Higher Poynton was a pleasant enough route, but the generous running times for the rural service that it became after leaving the city, tended to make it boring to drive on, although this criticism could be levelled at several of the Company's routes, especially Buxton and Hayfield.

Before actually departing from the garage, it was the driver's duty to check the water level in the appointed vehicle. PDs were easy, since a visual check was possible and if full, could be driven off. Underfloor variants were more difficult to check so had to be topped up to be on the safe side. AEC Reliances were nuisances. They had to be topped up with engines running, to avoid air locks, and it paid to rev them and check again for safety. Apart from these complications, where it was necessary, or easier, to carry the water to the bus, rather than drive the bus to the watering points, a watering can had to be used. These were substantial watering cans with a hose extending the spout to ease the task of topping up the underfloor-engined vehicles. Normally, these cans would be left near the garage entrance but they often disappeared, so that the search for a can took longer than the rest of the operation.

Manchester Garage was too small to garage its full complement under cover. The coaches and better buses took pride of place inside, with whatever was left, outside. In winter, engines would be started at about 04.00 on the 'outside' fleet to overcome the effects of cold weather. However, at any time of the year, particularly on double decks which were often parked against the canal fence, handbrakes would have been pulled on hard, by the last driver of the previous night, so that the first driver of the day had to struggle to release it. If the engine could be started, all was well, since the air pressure would build up, and if the footbrake was applied hard, the handbrake would usually have enough movement for it to be released. If this handbrake condition coincided with a flat battery, then you had a chicken and egg situation. The handbrake could not be released until the air pressure was built up. The battery was flat so the engine could not be started to build up the air pressure. The handbrake being hard on, the bus could not be moved for a tow-start, and the time-consuming answer was to shift the next bus alongside to allow the battery trolley to be brought alongside to start the engine.

All road staff at Manchester worked on a system of alternating early and late weeks. Variation was possible since the duty worked would normally be different each day. Since the 'Corpo' (Manchester Corporation) catered for the majority of early 'works' journeys in the area, the earliest duty signed-on at 05.30. This service was 165 'Spare', the earliest working duty being No. 45 at 05.32 on Partington, whilst the latest arrival in garage at night was No. 42 duty at 00.07 from a duty working Partington, after starting on 'Nags and Lions' (11X/23). No. 44 duty, on a Sunday, worked Partington and returned to garage at 00.32.

In July 1962, No. 829 (RDB 829) stands at The Old Red Lion, Seacroft, Leeds, on a Melba Motors excursion to Scarborough. At this time, both Nos. 829 and 830 were in the blue and cream livery of Melba Motors Ltd.

Unlike many garages, Manchester was a hive of industry with coaches leaving in the late evening for the bus station, in order to take up service on the night London X5M service, as well as receiving the incoming day buses.

Work in the upper sheets was, of course, geared to the London and the express service departures, but 'C', 'D' and 'E' sheets tended to follow the standard rota pattern, with a few peculiarities of the Company's own.

Class distinction was apparent in the type of work allocated to the various sheets. In 'E' sheet, the new drivers and conductors had a number of split duties which were necessary to cover increased peak hour frequencies. These were scattered throughout the early weeks, so that it was possible for five days' work to include two split duties, which could finish at nearly 21.00, the remaining three early duties having finishing times which could range from 12.56 to 16.10. The following late week would then comprise full late finishing duties due into garage from 23.00 onwards. As staff progressed from 'E' sheet to vacancies on 'D' sheet, and so on to 'C' sheet, perks of the job were apparent for the longer serving occupants who reached 'C' sheet. These were in the form of any split duties worked being generally allocated to the late weeks, leaving early weeks with only normal early finishing duties. The inevitable dislike of crews having to work late finishes could, therefore, be reduced with this seniority perk. Since it was necessary to work for two to three years before reaching

the dizzy heights of 'C' sheet, it could be assumed that one was reasonably dedicated to the job by the time the more interesting conditions and content duties were reached. Particularly from a driver's point of view, the initial years could be likened to an apprenticeship, since the occasional long distance work, as overtime or day off work, would act as a gradual familiarization to this type of work with a, sometimes, experienced conductor as guide on an unknown route.

A similar attitude to apprenticeship was also taken on 'private hire' operation. It was only after three full years of driving experience with the Company that a driver's name was added to the list as being eligible to be used on 'private hire' work. Prior to this, only emergency cover in the unlikely event of a man missing duty for 'private hire' operation, or 'short private hires' (SPH), would give a new man experience of this work.

'SPHs' were short journeys, usually to or from a theatre or dance, that were allocated to anyone who would work them. Such journeys tended to be unpopular due to the unsocial hours of operation. A single journey at 01.00 from a Belle Vue dance hall, to some remote area of Manchester, did not always result in 'whippy', a monetary tip, or whip round, and the three hours' pay was not over-generous, bearing in mind that, officially, North Western staff had to pay their fares home on Manchester Corporation services, and double fares applied on night services.

'Sunday Morning Picnic' was another type of 'SPH',

An Alexander Y type-bodied Leyland Leopard, No. 146 (AJA 146B), similar to the type mentioned below, is seen, when new, at Clacton-on-Sea, in May 1964.

and this was the type where a group of men, usually from a works or club, would go to visit a pub or club about ten to twenty miles away for a 'breakfast'. The breakfast usually ended, coincidentally, with the beginning of lunch time opening hours at the bar. Often the return journey would not take place until 16.00 or so, making, under the circumstances, a remarkably long 'SPH'. The intake of ale, by the party, was not always compatible with retaining the interior of one's coach in a clean condition, especially since some ale was often taken on board to 'stop the lads getting thirsty' on the way to the venue.

I was not keen on these 'SPHs', particularly the 'breakfast' type, having experienced one where, from arrival at the club which was our destination, I was constantly offered drinks of alcohol, despite the party comprising mainly of lorry drivers from a national parcel delivery organization who should have known better!

Having a good general knowledge of Greater Manchester (in the older context of the phrase) made wanderings round the area after late night dances, etc., more acceptable to me. I had my trusty Regis to drive home in anyway!

One unexpected bonus came my way on an occasion where I was early spare, No. 165 duty, 05.30—13.30. This duty gave no guarantee that the finishing time of 13.30 would be adhered to and often, the relatively unpopular duties on 'Nags and Lions' would extend the duty to 15.35 or so. Modern bus drivers will, no doubt, be horrified that such extensions to finishing times existed.

On this occasion, a driver failed to appear for a 'private hire' from a junior school at Middleton Junction to York and Knaresborough. I was the lucky recipient and particularly so, when I found that an Alexander Y type-bodied Leopard was my steed; No. 149 (AJA 149B). The journey went without a hitch, except for the inevitable travel sickness, experienced by one child. Even then, things turned out well since the mess was on an engine access panel in the floor, which could be removed from the bus and cleaned outside the coach, with the least amount of inconvenience; one appreciates such niceties after a time! A pleasant stay in York was followed by a run to Knaresborough, where tea was booked, and the run for home was through Harrogate.

This was my first run through Harrogate, although I know it better now that I have been on several Trans-Pennine rallies, and I remember thinking that I had to journey to Harrogate on the B6162, then take the A61, south. It was only when I reached a signpost in Harrogate, not realizing it was the centre of Harrogate at the time, that I saw that the B6162 was the road across the roundabout that I was approaching. Round the roundabout we went on to the B6162, and I suddenly realized that the A61 to Leeds and home, was the road I had just crossed. Fortunately, modesty allows me to admit to a good sense of direction and a rather pleasant country run along the B6162 and B6161 terminated at Pool-in-Wharfedale, from whence a few recognizable names, such as Otley and Shipley, led me to Bradford and on to home. No one in the adults of the party, seemed to have noticed anything amiss with the route, and they seemed to have enjoyed the day. I certainly did.

Duty changes were made to the schedules by the traffic staff at Charles Street head office, Stockport. Generally, two major revisions a year tended to take place to introduce summer workings for Whit Weeks, with the other change, at the end of September, when winter operations came into effect. Naturally, small amendments could be made, at any time during the year, to sort out odd problems of works or schools that had changed their hours of operation, or to re-time a journey by a few minutes to ensure connecting facilities. Changes necessary to ensure that a cinema crowd were picked up were never popular with the road staff.

The main scheduling records consisted of two graphs per garage which were 'duty' and 'car' graphs. These were held by the scheduler who looked after the particular garage, and they were kept in large cardboard folders to ensure that they stayed in good condition and did not become bent or scuffed. Both graphs were set out, with the hours of the day across the top of the sheet, with duty numbers shown down the left-hand margin against which would be shown, by lines, the work allocated to each duty. In the case of the buses, the car numbers were shown in the left-hand margin, and the work against each number was the work that that bus did for the day. Further information included in the car numbers was as follows:

Car 1 etc: This would indicate a 35 seat saloon or single deck bus.

Car 1 D/D etc: This showed the required vehicle was a double deck bus, which would generally be a 53 seater, although some of the PD2s were 55 seaters. In the case of the PD2/20s, the 58 seater, an additional note, '58' would be added to denote the large capacity scheduled. A similar arrangement for the 71 seat Lolines was made later.

Car 1 L/C etc: This would indicate that a single deck saloon, of larger capacity than the 35 seater, was required. Normally it would mean a 44 seater saloon. Where coaches were used in large numbers, such as at Manchester and Stockport garages, then a 41 seater could replace a 44 seater, although the few 37 seater coaches had to be monitored carefully by garage staff to ensure that there were no embarrassing moments.

I always felt that the use of graphs gave a good picture of the allocation of buses and staff, so that additional work could be inserted into the gaps that could physically be seen on the paper. Mind you, this was not easy. Whenever an extra journey was needed, it seemed to be at the time of maximum traffic requirements, so that there were no gaps in the graph at the time when an extra journey was required.

For mileage purposes, a list of the day's work for a bus would be typed, and this would show individual journey mileages as well as the daily and weekly totals. This 'car schedule', as it was known, had individual mileages shown, so that any changeovers that were necessary during the day could be allocated the correct proportion of mileage with minimum difficulty. I think most problems here arose from the fact that a driver would write his running sheet out at the start of his duty, as a reminder of where he was going, and if he needed to changeover, he rarely altered his sheet at the appropriate point, but just wrote out a new sheet for his changeover bus.

Staff working instructions were provided in the form of duty boards, similar to the following example of a Manchester Garage operation on service 32; Lower Mosley Street to Higher Poynton, or Middlewood.

MANCHESTER GARAGE
Car 6   *12 Duty*

Driver Gar. 4.15 p.m.   Con. on 4.25 p.m.

4.35 p.m. – 5.41 p.m. – Mcr. LMS – Middlewood
5.46 p.m – 6.52 p.m. – Middlewood – Mcr. LMS
7.05 p.m. – 8.07 p.m. – Mcr. LMS – Higher Poynton
8.20 p.m. – 9.22 p.m. – Higher Poynton – Mcr. LMS
9.35 p.m. – 10.41 p.m. – Mcr. LMS – Middlewood
10.46 p.m. – 11.52 p.m. – Middlewood – Mcr. LMS

Driver Gar. 12.01 a.m.   Con. off 11.57 p.m.

Driver Hours = 7.46   *Con. Hours = 7.30*

It should be noted that, if the driver had signed-on at Lower Mosley Street, he would have been signed-on at 4.17 p.m., five minutes prior to the arrival of the bus in the bus station at 4.22 p.m. He, and not the relieved driver, would be responsible for the bus.

No. 633 (KDB 633) poses on Long Hill, between Whaley Bridge and Buxton, in April 1965, whilst on the variation of service 27, Manchester to Buxton.

The Company worked on the system where only basic instructions were given to the driver, since he should be aware of the route from his initial training, whilst the conductor was in charge of timing, being issued with a Company timetable when commencing his employment and, in which, full details of intermediate timing points were to be found.

Additional information would sometimes be given to the driver on his duty board to remind him of his route (e.g. Manchester to Buxton, via Chapel-en-le-Frith, and Manchester to Buxton, via Long Hill).

Generally, the system worked well. A good percentage of the road staff at Manchester Garage, whilst I was employed there, were long service men plus staff who had been employed for, perhaps, five years or more. This meant that the young tearaway types were in the minority and, depending on the circumstances, the bad ones rarely stayed longer than a season, or were despatched as the result of disciplinary action, whichever was the earlier. One of the idiosyncrasies of the industry, I felt, was to be found in the operation of the last journeys. Timetabled last journeys tend to be fairy tale operations with most bus companies. Some drivers tend to leave the town terminus on a last journey, on time, mainly since the point is supervized. These drivers, despite any comments from their timekeeping conductors, will rush to the outer terminus and back to garage, irrespective of the official time of departure from the outer terminus. This is wrong, I feel, my own

personal method being to depart from the outer terminus up to two minutes late and then go like hell! Whilst this is still not perfection in the eyes of the Company, or its timetable, it does, at least, give the potential passenger a fighting chance. On a route such as my beloved Partington, there was a major timing point at Manor Avenue, Ashton-on-Mersey which was fifteen minutes from Wood Lane terminus, or twelve minutes from the Greyhound. Since the road between Partington and Manor Avenue was excellent for making up time, I always ensured that I was on time, and not early, at Manor Avenue. I feel sure that most 'last bus' passengers are aware of the need to be early at the bus stops, and read the timetable in order to arrive at their stop well in advance of the published time. At least, my method ensured as good a chance as any. Leaving the outer terminus early always seemed to be cheating to me, and any driver could be early in depot with that method.

During the day, I felt that good timekeeping was imperative, since many of the Company's services went into rural areas around Manchester where patronage was essential for the services to remain viable. It was not always a popular move with some conductors, who felt that 'pushing' the 'Corpo' down the road was part of the job. Despite this, and my strict timekeeping on departure of journeys running into garage, my track record of early arrival into garage, and, therefore, arrival at Lower Mosley Street for the conductor to pay in, maintained a certain popularity with the conducting staff. They usually relied on the 'Corpo's' all-night services for transport home.

It was on these garage journeys that my use of the 'clutch stop' on crash gearboxes came into its own. I have mentioned elsewhere my lazy attitude to gearchanging where clutchless gearchanges were the norm, except when speed in the peak period traffic rendered clutch use necessary. On garage journeys, speed and fast gearchanges rendered the use of the 'clutch stop' imperative, and I think that my last journey running times reflected the full usage, made by me, of the gearbox. Dennis Lolines of the Mark III variety in particular, and the Tiger Cubs, were my favourites. Mark II Dennis Lolines were not to be sneezed at, of course.

Bearing in mind the cuts in service over the years, on the routes that seemed so stable whilst I was at Manchester, one hopes that any early running at Manchester was not the culprit.

Returning to the office, I was always impressed whilst working in the Charles Street offices, with the pencils issued to the traffic department employees. These were black lead HB type, finished in a red colour with gold lettering stating 'North Western Road Car Co. Ltd'. I still have a few and have written parts of this manuscript with one. An interesting point that I did not discover until my office career ended, was that the indelible pencils which were used in Traffic Records, and in other departments, were purple with silver lettering, whilst I find that my collection also includes a yellow example with silver lettering. I think, but cannot confirm, that these latter pencils were used in the wages office.

On the stationery front, the Company's letter-headings, both large and small, maintained the old-fashioned N−N title, similar in lettering to the pre-war fleetname, but with 'Road Car Co. Ltd' below the underlining. As far as I can see, the only updating was the inclusion of the post code, in the later years of the Company's life, but that was after I left Manchester Garage. Whilst working on Bank Holiday schedules at Greater Manchester's Central East Office, years later, I came across correspondence with North Western over jointly-operated routes. The letter-heading still looked as impressive as ever, so I photographed it for posterity!

Having digressed from schedules to last journeys and pencils, let us return to schedules!

The rotary schedule was compiled to indicate to drivers and conductors their work for the week. The total hours of work was shown against each week and this was a total as near as possible to 48 hours, until the beginning of the 1966 summer season, when the 40 hour week was introduced. It was always a scheduler's problem, to maintain the weekly hours as near to the correct figure as possible. Where hours totalled less than the official week, then the Company would need to pay out unnecessary money to make up the week's pay, whilst hours worked over the basic week would incur overtime payments.

The industry has, for many years, paid penalty payments for work done after 1.00 p.m. on Saturdays, and for Sunday work. Naturally, higher overtime payments are made, when these days are worked as rest day overtime work, the basic rate then being compounded into high overtime rates. The trend for transport to be needed in, basically, two 'peaks', calls for staff to be used during these peaks but not necessarily between them. The universal answer used by N−N, and other undertakings, was to employ 'split' or part-day duties, where a crew would work for up to four hours in each 'peak', the start and finish times spreading over twelve or more hours. For this, a nationally agreed penalty payment rate was paid over and above the normal eight hours pay for the day, although Manchester Corporation employees had negotiated a much higher penalty rate than North Western. A rather interesting situation arose, that concerned me more later in my career than whilst I was driving, but it is worth a mention. The penalty payment was, I always felt, a payment that the Company made since they asked staff to go to work twice in the eight hour working day, which was, in these cases spread over twelve or more hours. Whenever the Company could reduce the number of split duties, which were not popular, this reduced the spreadover penalty payment. Unfortunately, from a driver's point of view, it reduced his pay for the week. Only eight hours per day, instead of eight plus penalty! He, therefore, objected and tried to ensure that he continued to get the split duties, despite the fact that he didn't like them. As they say in Lancashire, 'There's nowt so queer as folk.'

A crew's wage could be further enhanced by the payment of a minimum 'call-out' payment of three hours pay, if it was necessary to undertake work for even one hour, as overtime. The normal work available as overtime, due to holidays and sickness, has generally given N−N staff a reasonable (to them) supply of overtime. The necessity to withdraw stage carriage service journeys, on busy summer season weekends, in order to cover long distance express and 'limited stop' work, would probably lead the Company to consider the overtime to be less than reasonable. In the section dealing with Lower Mosley Street, mention has been made of the hiring arrangements that were made to try to cover all the garage's work.

Duties operated at Manchester, during my employment there, are included in Appendix 'B'. A selection of the 'C' and 'D' sheet duties, both winter and summer timetable-based, shows the variety of work available. Manchester's earliest start was 5.30 a.m., whilst several duties will be seen to sign-off after midnight. The special duties, working summer seasonal journeys to mid-Wales or the East Coast, could give a driver a particularly long day, especially when the usual summer holiday traffic was encountered in some of the country's worst traffic 'black spots'. These latter workings formed duties which tended to be allocated to longer service drivers, generally from

'C' sheet, in place of their scheduled work which, in turn, would be given out to other drivers as 'day off' work, or, to the favoured, given as a day's work, so throwing open stage carriage work which invariably ended up with a 'spare' man.

The duties shown in Appendix 'B' are scheduled duties only. Rest day working would provide the opportunity for working any duty not covered, due to holidays, sickness or staff shortage, from either a driver's current sheet or a more senior one. At various times, one or two 'open' duties existed. These were pieces of work made into a three hour portion of work to which no regular driver was allocated. They would not be included in a week's work due to their short length. Such duties also tended to be in a 'peak' period.

Open duties 'A' and 'B' existed during my time at Manchester. I note that overtime for me, on 13th May 1964, was Duty 'A', 07.18 (garage) to 09.29; 2 hours 11 minutes. Services worked were 30 and 52. I again operated this duty on 25th November 1964, and 4th February 1965, by which time the work had become 06.38 (garage) to 09.41; 3 hours 3 minutes, with no record, I'm afraid, of the work content. Duty 'B', worked again as overtime, on 29th December 1965, consisted of 06.45 (garage) to 08.59; 2 hours 14 minutes, working 31 and 51 services.

A rather interesting point is that in order for head office schedules to be transmitted to their respective garages, many copies of the duty boards were required. I think seven copies were needed and these were made using carbon paper, a long way from the present method of using a photocopier to make as many copies as required. Needless to say, the garage always needed a spare copy to combat the crew who lost their board, or to replace it when it became too worn to read.

Modern technology enables schedules to be produced by computer but, like the National Bus Company livery, N–N were never subject to such events!

Awaiting departure from Moss Lane, Bramhall in May 1966, is No. 741 (LDB 741), a Weymann-bodied AEC Reliance, on a morning peak 31 service.

Chapter Eleven ~ Finale

My career with North Western, Manchester Garage, ended on 3rd February 1967. Having decided that I must do something other than drive buses and enjoy myself, I had obtained a job with the Civil Service. Like many transport men, this departure from the industry was short-lived and, after ten months, I returned to what I realized was my main interest, at Salford City Transport in their Main Offices. But that is another story . . .!

After a bout of influenza, I returned to work at Manchester on Wednesday, 1st February to work for my last three days as a full time PSV driver. No. 16 duty, three 'Higher Poyntons', was Wednesday's lot, followed by No. 10 duty on Thursday. Three journeys with service 222, with the 20.00 to Buxton was to follow. Fate smiled on me as I had a Leopard on the Buxton. The last day of all was No. 50 duty: three on service 23 and two journeys on service 5. Not the most devastating work, as my thoughts of service 23 were never complimentary. A Fleetline, No. 175 (DDB 175C), was mine for the first part of the duty. This passed without anything of interest happening. In view of my liking for Dennis Lolines, I felt that I should end the day with one of these. We took another Fleetline 'off' at Lower Mosley Street, inward-bound to Piccadilly where I quickly phoned the garage to try to organize a Loline. They had nothing on hand, but they suggested that I see what was on the spare stand at Lower Mosley Street and agreed I could take what I wanted. Service 5 departed Piccadilly amidst an air of expectation. At Lower Mosley Street all we could find was No. 669, a PD2/20 with Weymann bodywork. At least it had gears rather than the 'softie' transmission of a Fleetline. I took it. Alas, my poor condcutor was not particularly impressed but suffered in silence for the next three hours. Just three hours to him, but my last! A friend boarded for the last journeys and I showed off by changing down the gears to first, fortunately quite smoothly (not like a Leyland National).

I returned to garage at quite a modest speed for a last journey of a duty and set the conductor down at Lower Mosley Street. Then to garage for the last time. Photographs were taken at Carrington Road, Flixton, the outer terminus of service 5, together with a view of me going through the bus wash. No. 669 was parked inside the garage for once, a luxury of the almost completed extension to Manchester Garage, with its modernization and enlargement. I felt rather sad as I left the garage for the last time.

The beginning of the end. No. 175 (DDB 175C), an Alexander-bodied Daimler Fleetline, is seen on the first part of the author's last duty on 3rd February 1967, service 23. It is photographed at Manchester Piccadilly.

Appendix A (i) ~ Internal Company Fleet List of 11th April 1962

NORTH WESTERN ROAD CAR COMPANY LIMITED
Summary of Single Deck Fleet

Fleet No.	Registration No.	Make and Type	Year	Engine	Make and Type of Body	Body Year	Seat and Entrance	Door	Moquette	Weight	C/N	Boot	Total
87–100	BJA 403–5/407–411/413–417/426	Bristol L	1946	Gardner 5LW	MCW	1949	35 R	S	L	6.10.0	–	No	14
261–279	BJA 406/12/18–25/27–35	Bristol L	1946	Gardner 5LW	Willowbrook	1952/3	38 R	S	F	6. 7.0	–	No	19
193–212	CDB 193–212	Bristol L	1949/50	Gardner 5LW	MCW	1949/50	35 R	S	L	6. 7.0	52	Yes	20
293–299	DDB 293/301/295–6/303/298/306	Bristol L	1950	Gardner 5LW	MCW	1950	32 R	S	F	6. 7.2	224	Yes	7
300–310	DDB 300/294/302/297/304/305/299/307–310	Bristol L	1950	Gardner 5LW	MCW	1950	35 R	S	L	6. 7.2	224	Yes	11
311–320	EDB 311–320	Bristol L	1950	Gardner 5LW	MCW	1950	35 R	S	L	6. 7.2	173	Yes	10
321–325	ERR 601–605	Bristol L	1939	Gardner 5LW	Burlingham	1950/1*	35 R	S	L	6.11.1	243	No	5
326–376	JA 7739/44/58/67 AJA 109/11/12/14/16–20/25/27/30/32/36/38/40	Bristol L	1938	Gardner 5LW	Burlingham	1950/1*	35 R	S	L	6.11.1	243	No	13
394–5	EDB 321–322	Atkinson PM746H	1951	Gardner 6HLW	MCW	1951	42 R	S	L	7.12.0	301	Yes	2
396–7	EDB 323–324	Leyland/MCW Olympic	1951	Leyland 0 600	MCW	1951	44 F	G	B	7. 4.0	–	Yes	2
500–509	FDB 500–509	Atkinson PM746H	1952	Gardner 6HLW	MCW	1952	42 R	S	L	7.19.2	363	Yes	10
510–511	FDB 510–511	Atkinson PM745H	1953	Gardner 5HLW	MCW	1953	42 R	S	L	7.17.0	363	Yes	2
512–513	FDB 512–513	Atkinson PL745H	1952	Gardner 5LW	Willowbrook	1952	44 R	S	L	5. 8.3	399	No	2
514–549	FDB 514–549	Leyland Royal Tiger	1953	Leyland 0 600	MCW	1953	44 F	G	L	7. 3.3	401	Yes	36
556–559	FDB 556–559	AEC Reliance	1954	AEC AH410	MCW	1954	44 F	G	L	5.10.3	498	Yes	4
560–563	FDB 560–563	Leyland Tiger Cub	1954	Leyland 0 350	MCW	1954	44 F	G	L	5.16.2	500	Yes	4
577–596	FDB 577–596	Leyland Tiger Cub	1955	Leyland 0 350	MCW	1955	44 F	G	L	5.16.0	575	Yes	20
616–625	HJA 616–625	AEC Reliance	1955	AEC AH410	Burlingham	1955	44 F	G	L	5.13.0	576	Yes	10
631–660	KDB 631–660	Leyland Tiger Cub	1956	Leyland 0 350	MCW	1956	44 F	G	L	6. 0.2	627	Yes	30
671–700	KDB 671–700	Leyland Tiger Cub	1957	Leyland 0 350	MCW	1957	44 F	G	L	6. 1.0	711	Yes	30
714–719	LDB 714–719	Albion Aberdonian	1957	Leyland 0 350	MCW	1957	42 F	G	L	4.19.3	769	No	6
720–739	LDB 720–739	AEC Reliance	1958	AEC AH410	MCW	1958	43 F	G	L	5.18.2	762	Yes	20
746–760	LDB 746–760	AEC Reliance	1959	AEC AH470	Willowbrook	1959	43 F	G	F	5.14.3	819	Yes	15
761–765	LDB 761–765	Leyland Tiger Cub	1959	Leyland 0 350	Willowbrook	1959	43 F	G	D	6. 2.3	818	Yes	5
782–796	LDB 782–796	Leyland Tiger Cub	1960	Leyland 0 350	Willowbrook DP	1960	43 F	G	L	6. 2.1	850	Yes	15
797–811	LDB 797–800, RDB 801–811	AEC Reliance	1960	AEC AHU470	Willowbrook DP	1960	43 F	G	L	5.16.2	881	Yes	15
852–871	RDB 852–871	AEC Reliance	1961	AEC AHU470	Willowbrook DP 1961		43 F	J	F	5.16.2	60/5	Yes	20

Summary of Double Deck Fleet

Fleet No.	Registration No.	Make and Type	Year	Engine	Body Year	Make and Type of Body	Seat and Entrance	Door	Moquette	Weight	C/N	Boot	Total
10–30	BJA 89–90, 131–140, 107–109 181–186	Guy Arab	1944	Gardner 5LW	1951*	Willowbrook	53(26L)R	–	L	7.11.2	245	–	21
223–236	CDB 223–236	Leyland PD2/1	1947	Leyland 0 600	1947	Leyland	53(26L)R	–	B	7. 5.3	21	–	14
237–244	CDB 237–244	Leyland PD2/1	1949	Leyland 0 600	1949	Leyland	53(26L)R	–	W	7.12.0	72	–	8
245–250	CDB 245–250	Leyland PD2/1	1949	Leyland 0 600	1949	Leyland	57(26L)R	J	L	8. 1.0	72	–	6
251–260	DDB 251–260	Leyland PD2/1	1949	Leyland 0 600	1949	MCW	53(26L)R	–	L	7.13.0	133	–	10
400–423	JA 7716–27, 7784–95	Bristol K	1938	Gardner 5LW	1951/2*	Willowbrook	53(26L)R	–	L	7. 0.1	244	–	13
424–463	AJA 144–183	Bristol K	1939	Gardner 5LW	1951/2*	Willowbrook	53(26L)R	–	L	7. 0.1	244	–	33
464	EDB 325	Leyland PD2/10	1952	Leyland 0 600	1952	Leyland	55(28L)R	–	B	7.18.0	398	–	1
550–555	FDB 550–555	Leyland PD2/12	1953	Leyland 0 600	1953	MCW	53(26L)R	–	F	7. 5.3	402	–	6
661–670	KDB 661–670	Leyland PD2/21	1956	Leyland 0 600	1956	MCW	58(28L)R	J	L	6.19.2	626	–	10
812–814	RDB 812–814	Dennis Loline	1960	Gardner 6LX	1960	East Lancs	71(32L)F	SL	L	8.12.2	924	–	3
815–826	RDB 815–826	Dennis Loline	1960	Leyland 0 600	1960	East Lancs	71(32L)F	SL	L	8.12.2	924	–	12
872–906	RDB 872–900, VDB 901–906	Dennis Loline	1962	Gardner 6LX	1962	Alexander	71(32L)F	SL	L	7.19.2	60/43	–	35

Summary of Coach Fleet

Fleet No.	Registration No.	Make and Type	Year	Engine	Make and Type of Body	Seat and Entrance	Door	Moquette	Weight	C/N	Boot	Total
570	FDB 570	AEC Reliance	1954	AEC AH470	MCW	37 F	S	L	6. 6.0	550	Yes	1
571–576	FDB 571–576	Leyland Tiger Cub	1955	Leyland 0 350	Burlingham	41 F	S	L	6. 6.0	569	Yes	1
626–630	KDB 626–630	AEC Reliance	1956	AEC AH470	MCW	37 F	S	L	6. 4.0	628	Yes	6
701–712	LDB 701–712	Leyland Tiger Cub	1957	Leyland 0 350	Burlingham	41 F	S	L	6.13.0	712	Yes	12
713	LDB 713	AEC Reliance	1957	AEC AH470	Burlingham	41 F	S	F	6. 8.0	727	Yes	1
740–745	LDB 740–745	AEC Reliance	1957	AEC AH470	MCW	41 F	G	F	6. 8.0	713	Yes	6
766–775	LDB 766–775	Leyland Tiger Cub	1959	Leyland 0 350	Willowbrook	41 F	S	F	6. 5.2	818	Yes	10
776–781	LDB 776–781	AEC Reliance	1959	AEC AH470	Harrington	41 F	S	L	6. 4.0	875	Yes	6
827–831	RDB 827–831	AEC Reliance	1960	AEC AHU470	Willowbrook	41 F	J	F	6. 2.1	947	Yes	5
832–851	RDB 832–851	AEC Reliance	1961	AEC AHU470	Alexander	41 F	J	L	5.17.2	60/37	Yes	20
907–916	VDB 907–916	Leyland Leopard	1962	AEC AHU470	Alexander	49 F	J	H	7. 5.0	61/57	Yes	10

KEY

DOORS
J – Jack-knife
SL – Sliding
S – Single panel

MOQUETTE
L – Listers
W – Woods
B – Unknown
F – Firths
H – Holdsworths
Melba Motors Limited Nos. 701, 702, 703, 829, 830

BODY
DP – Dual-purpose
SC – Semi-coach
* – Chassis rebuilt to take new body

Appendix A (ii) ~ Internal Company Vehicle Allocation List of 24th May 1961, with notes of general variation

Notes on Company Fleet Allocation List of 24th May 1961

The allocation was basically similar to that of the years 1963–7, the period of my driving career at Manchester.

During the course of the years, new buses and coaches would be allocated to Manchester to replace vehicles withdrawn or relocated and, generally, such alterations would substitute double deck for double deck, and coach for coach. The main changes to the 1961 allocation were as follows:

Double Decks

Dennis Lolines of the Mark III type supplemented the Mark IIs, whilst the old Leyland PD1s were withdrawn. The Mark III Lolines involved were Nos. 888–893, although No. 888 later went to Wilmslow; an unpopular move for Manchester men since No. 888 was a good bus. Leyland PD2s were increased in numbers by the arrival of Nos. 224–229/231, whilst Nos. 249 and 250 went, it is thought, to Macclesfield. The rather smart Weymann-bodied PD2s, Nos. 552 and 554, went to Stockport whilst the older Weymann PD2s, Nos. 258 and 259, arrived at Manchester later. Additional PD2s, of the sole examples of the 'tin front' type, arrived at Manchester, No. 670 coming from Northwich and showing, very much, the high maintenance standards of that garage, being complete with its front wheel Leyland nut guards, which were items that rarely stayed on N–N vehicles for very long. Later, AEC Renowns of the early series of No. 970 etc., appeared and, in 1964, the inevitable Daimler Fleetlines, Nos. 100–102 came on the scene. The 1965-built Fleetlines were Nos. 175–179, with Nos. 194–196 arriving in 1966.

Single Decks

Nos. 396 and 397, the solitary Leyland Olympics in the fleet, were augmented by Atkinson Alphas during the period in question with examples of the AEC Reliance class, Nos. 617–625, with Burlingham bodies, being shuffled in and out of Manchester as garages tried to off-load them. Unfortunately, Manchester seemed to lose out and kept them longer than other places.

The introduction of one man operation brought the Reliance/Weymann down-rated dual-purpose vehicles to Manchester. These were of the 720–739 batch, which were equipped for OMO and which were used on the recently-converted X12 Manchester to Bradford service.

Dual-purpose/Semi-coach

These types had a very narrow definition, the semi-coaches being fitted, as far as one could tell, with slightly better seats with some semblance of a head rest. Later 'DPs', as they were universally called, I never heard semi-coach used officially, despite the headings used by the engineering department in its lists) came into the fleet and several came to Manchester. The Willowbrook-bodied vehicles on Tiger Cub and Reliance chassis included ten semi-coaches on Tiger Cub chassis in the 766–775 batch, which were officially listed as coaches. These were painted in the coach livery of cream with a red band, the more usual 'DP' livery being red below a cream

waist band with black round the windows and over the roof, so earning the name 'Black Tops'.

The Tiger Cub coaches were used a great deal on the London motorway service since the older Burlingham Seagull-bodied Tiger Cubs were not officially presentable enough for such premier service!

Coaches

These tended to drift around the Company's empire as the work load necessitated. Manchester, with its hard core of express services, and particularly the London service, did keep a reasonably constant fleet of coaches. Basically, the Reliance Highlanders and the 740-type Fanfares stayed at Manchester, whilst the Harrington Contenders and Willowbrook Viking types went the rounds.

By the time I arrived at Manchester, the solid, reliable but sadly-maltreated Leyland Royal Tiger coaches were a thing of the past, but in my eyes, their replacement with Leyland Leopards did a lot to compensate for this. The Royal Tiger, with its Leyland coachwork, was the type most often found on the express services of Ribble during my enthusiast years which had left me with many happy memories of the type. As it happened, it was on the Ribble and Standerwick examples that my experience of driving the type was gained, since they appeared on Derby and Nottingham, as well as Blackpool services, during the course of N–N duties.

The new Manchester coach fleet came to include 36 ft. long Highlander Leopards and what almost became a 'standard' N–N coach; the Y type by Alexander.

General

Apart from the general allocation, weekend duplication was catered for by a temporary input of vehicles on a Friday evening, to be returned to the parent garage, usually Stockport, on Sunday night. This temporary allocation included single and double deck Bristols up to their withdrawal in 1964 and 1965 respectively. No. 406, a K5G, was to be found almost permanently at Manchester in its final year. Atkinson Alphas were also sent to Manchester, together with coaches allocated for specific work.

From about 1960, the rather small number of good coaches, from a passenger point of view, made it necessary to introduce a system whereby each coach would be allocated to specific work, particularly over the weekend period. A further complication was the number of extended tours which were operated on behalf of the Co-operative Travel Service for which N–N supplied the coaches. These were for parties of old age pensioners travelling to holiday resorts around Britain. It was necessary to ensure that the Co-op had decent coaches although the tour season tended to be during May and early June and in September and early October so that, in theory, the summer season for the Company did not clash. However, at the same time, the Company's not inconsiderable private hire trade needed to be maintained and this could only be done by giving good service, which it did, and good vehicles, which it provided to the best of its ability. The continued growth of the private hire side of the Company must reflect a contented customer.

NORTH WESTERN ROAD CAR COMPANY LIMITED

Fleet Allocation – 1st June 1961

Depot	Double Deck	Single Deck	Large Capacity	OMV	Dual-purpose	Semi-coach	Coach	Depot Total
Altrincham	15	21	6	4	3	2	3	54
Biddulph	5	1	—	8	3	—	2	19
Buxton	—	13	9	12	5	—	4	43
Glossop	8	4	2	2	2	—	2	20
Macclesfield	8	20	10	12	5	—	5	60
Manchester	22	—	2	—	4	8	30	66
Matlock	—	6	8	8	2	—	2	26
Northwich	28	12	6	8	7	2	9	72
Oldham	8	2	—	10	4	2	5	31
Urmston	6	2	13	—	5	—	2	28
Wilmslow	7	—	—	9	3	—	2	21
Stockport	43	24	36	14	6	6	21	150
NWRC TOTAL	150	105	92	87	49	20	87	590
Delicensed	—	—	—	—	—	—	—	—
Melba Motors	—	—	—	—	—	—	5	5
TOTAL FLEET	150	105	92	87	49	20	92	595

One of the first two Atkinson Alphas in the fleet, No. 394 (EDB 321), with Weymann bodywork, is seen, in January 1962, at Stockport Garage.

Fleet summary table — vehicles by type and depot

	Coach													Semi-coach	Dual-purpose				OMV						Single Deck									Double Deck							
TOTALS	Highlander 41	Royal Tiger 41	Cub 57 41	Cub 55 41	Cub 54 41	Cub W/B 41	AEC W/B 41	AEC S/G 41	AEC Har 41	AEC W/B 41	AEC F/F 41	AEC Har 37	AEC F/F 37	AEC 61 43	Cub 60 43	AEC 60 43	AEC 59 43	AEC 58 43	Cub 44	AEC 44	Royal Tiger 44	Cub 59 43	AEC 58 43	Albion 42	AEC 44	Cub 44	Royal Tiger 44	Olympic 44	AEC 58 43	Atkinson 42	Bristol 38	Bristol 35	Bristol 32	Guy 53	Bristol 53	Bristol 53	Leyland 53	Leyland 49	Leyland 58	Dennis 71	Location
54		1												2		3					4				5				1			20	1		7		3	2	5		Altrincham
19	1	1															3		5				3									1		5							Biddulph
43	1							2			1						3	1	12				13			9	1														Buxton
20	1														2				1				4			1					2		1				2		6		Glossop
60		3	1	1					2							1	2	2	9			3					10		5			15		3			1	4	11	6	Macclesfield
66	7	5	4	1			2	1			3	1		8			1	2			2						2								11	13	6	2	6	3	Manchester
26	1	1		2														2	6				2				8		2			4									Matlock
72	2	2			1	3				3				2	2		3	2			5		2				4		6			6		7	13	6	6	2			Northwich
31	2				3									2	4				4				6									2					6	6		2	Oldham
28		1	1	1											5										7				6			2	2		1	5					Urmston
21	1	1													3								7							2				3	4	1					Wilmslow
150	8				2	1	1		3		2	3	2	6											11		17	5	10	4	16	19	14	8	79	7	2	11	13	15	4	Stockport
590	20	16	9	6	10	4	3	3	6	3	6	1	3	20	15	15	15	4	4		49	14	4	5	8	6	2	8	16	19	79	7	35	22	2	8	16	5	4	49	10	Licensed Fleet
																																									Delicensed
5		3								2																															Melba Motors
595	20	16	12	6	10	4	3	3	6	5	6	1	3	20	15	15	15	4	4		49	14	4	5	8	6	2	8	16	19	79	7	35	22	2	8	16	5	4	49	10	Total Fleet

ALTRINCHAM

Van No. NDB 506

Double Deck		Single Deck			DP	SC	Coach	
Leyland PD2	Bristol K	Bristol L	AEC	OMV (AEC)	AEC	AEC	Cub	RT
237	433	89	616	556A	797	861	566	614
238	434	91	619	557A	798	862	704	
239	435	92	620	558A	799			
661	436	95	621	559A				
662	437	96	622					
663	437	97	732					
664	438	98						
665	458	99						
		193						
		194						
		206						
		295						
		309						
		310						
		311						
		312						
		325						
		341						
		366						
		367						
		370						
8	7	21	6	4	3	2	2	1
15		31			3	2	2	1
54								

BUXTON

Van No. MDB 560

Single Deck			DP	Cub	Coach	AEC
Bristol L	Cub	OMV (Cub)	AEC	W/B	AEC S/Gull	Hil'd
100	631	560A	731	766	713	849
200	632	561A	757	767		
201	633	562A	809			
300	634	563A	810			
313	635	584A	811			
314	636	585A				
315	637	586A				
320	638	690A				
332	644	692A				
334		697A				
373		699A				
374		700A				
376						
13	9	12	5	2	1	1
34			5		4	
43						

GLOSSOP

Van No. NDB 502

Double Deck		Single Deck			DP	Coach	
Leyland PD2	Bristol K	Bristol L	OMV (Cub)	Cub	Cub	Royal Tiger	Cub
229	406	316	578A	640	786	611	575
230	413	317	765A	641	791		
	414	318					
	415	321T					
	416						
	417						
2	6	4	2	2	2	1	1
8		8			2	2	
20							

BIDDULPH

Double Deck	Single Deck			DP	Coach	
Bristol K	Bristol L	OMV (AEC)	OMV (Cub)	AEC	Cub	RT
418	319	720A	593A	749	573	610
428		726A	594A	759		
429		735A	595A	760		
455			596A			
457			680A			
5	1	3	5	3	1	1
5	9			3	2	
19						

MACCLESFIELD — Van No. NDB 505

Double Deck		Single Deck				DP		Coach	
Leyland PD2	Guy	Bristol L	Royal Tiger	OMV Royal Tiger	OMV Cub	AEC	Cub	Royal Tiger	Cub
245	10	87	514	526A	588A	733	782	603	571
246	11	88	515	527A	589A	750		604	706
247	12	198	530	528A	590A	800		612	
248		204	534		673A	801			
464		205	535		674A				
		207	536		675A				
		345	537		676A				
		356	538		677A				
		358	539		681A				
		359	540						
		360							
		362							
		363							
		364							
		365							
		262							
		263							
		265							
		270							
		274							
5	3	20	10	3	9	4	1	3	2
8		42				5		5	
60									

MATLOCK — Van No. OJA 9

Single Deck				DP	Coach	
Bristol L	Royal Tiger	OMV(AEC)	OMV Royal Tiger	AEC	Cub	Royal Tiger
301	516	727A	520A	754	705	601
302	517	728A	521A	758		
303	518		522A			
372	519		523A			
296	531		524A			
297	532		525A			
	533					
	541					
6	8	2	6	2	1	1
22				2	2	
26						

WILMSLOW

Double Deck		Single Deck	DP	Coach	
Dennis	Bristol K	OMV Cub	Cub	Cub	Royal Tiger
824	460	580A	784	708	605
825	461	581A	785		
826	462	582A	796		
	463	583A			
		587A			
		682A			
		688A			
		761A			
		762A			
3	4	9	3	1	1
7		9	3	2	
21					

URMSTON — Van No. NDB 503

Double Deck		Single Deck			DP	Coach	
Leyland PD2	Bristol K	Bristol L	Atkinson	Cub	Cub	Royal Tiger	Cub S/G
232	427	322	395	639	783	615	707
233		368T	505	642	792		
550			506	646	793		
551			507	647	794		
553			512	648	795		
			513	649			
				650			
5	1	2	6	7	5	1	1
6		15			5	2	
28							

NORTHWICH
Van No. OJA 8

Leyland PD1	Leyland PD2	Bristol K	Guy	Bristol L	Royal Tiger	AEC	OMV AEC	OMV Royal Tiger	AEC	AEC	Royal Tiger	Cub S/G	AEC F/F	Cub W/B	AEC Hil'd
Double Deck				Single Deck					DP	SC	Coach				
213	669	430	13	191	542	730	723A	529A	722	853	602	569	626	768	850
214	670	442	14	208	543	738	724A	546A	725	854	613			769	851
215		444	15	209	544		737A	547A	748					770	
216		445	16	210	545			548A	755						
217		446	17	211				549A	756						
218		448	18	212					807						
		449	19	261					808						
		450		271											
		451		276											
		452		277											
		453		278											
		454		279											
		456													
6	2	13	7	12	4	2	3	5	7	2	2	1	1	3	2
28				26					7	2	9				

Total 72

MANCHESTER
Van No. OJA 7

Den	Leyland PD1	Leyland PD2	Oly	AEC	AEC	AEC F/F	AEC Har	AEC F/F	Hil'd	AEC Har	AEC W/B	Cub W/B	Cub S/G	Royal Tiger
Double Deck			Single Deck	DP	SC	37 Seat		Coach				41 Seat		
813	219	234	396	746	852	628	781	740	842	779	831	771	567	600
818	220	235	397	747	863	630		741	843	780		772	572	606
819	221	242		802	864	570		742	844				709	607
820	222	243		803	865				845				710	608
821		244			866				846				711	609
822		249			867				847				712	
		250			868				848					
		552			869									
		554												
		666												
		667												
		668												
6	4	12	2	4	8	3	1	3	7	2	1	2	6	5
22			2	4	8	3	1		30					

Total 66

STOCKPORT

Van No. OJA 10

Double Deck				Single Deck							DP	SC	37 Seat		Coach		41 Seat		AEC
Dennis	Leyland PD2	Bristol K	Guy	Bristol L	Atkinson	AEC	Cub	Oly	OMV AEC	OMV Cub	AEC	AEC	AEC F/F	AEC Har	AEC F/F	AEC Har	AEC W/B	Cub S/G	Hil'd
814	223	400	20	90	394	617	643		736A	577A	751	855	627	776	743	778	827	564	832
815	224	401	21	94	500	618	645			579A	752	856	629	777	744		828	574	833
816	225	402	22	195	501	623	651			591A	753	857			745			576	834
817	226	403	23	196	502	624	652			592A	804	858							835
	227	404	24	197	503	625	653			671A	805	859							836
	228	410	25	202	504	721	654			672A	806	860							837
	231	420	26	203	508	729	655			689A									838
	236	422	27	264	509	734	656			691A									839
	255	423	28	266	510	739	657			693A									
	256	425	29	267	511		658			698A									
	257	431	30	268			659			763A									
	258	432		272			660			764A									
	259	459		273			684			683A									
	260			275			685												
	555			293			686												
				294			687												
				304			696												
				305															
				306															
				307															
				308															
				323															
				324															
4	**15**	**13**	**11**	**24**	**10**	**9**	**17**		**1**	**13**	**6**	**6**	**2**	**2**	**3**	**1**	**2**	**3**	**8**
43				**74**							**6**	**6**			**21**				

150

OLDHAM

Van No. NDB 504

Double Deck		Single Deck			DP	SC	Coach		
Dennis	Leyland PD2	Bristol L	OMV Albion	OMV Cub	Cub	AEC	W/B Cub	AEC	Hil'd
812	240	298	714A	678A	787	870	773	840	
823	241	299	715A	679A	788	871	774	841	
	251		716A	694A	789		775		
	252		717A	695A	790				
	253		718A						
	254		819A						
2	**6**	**2**	**6**	**4**	**4**	**2**	**3**	**2**	
8		**12**			**4**	**2**	**5**		

31

Altrincham Coachways:
Bedford Duple: 1, 2, 3, 4, 5, 6, 7, 8
TOTAL = 8

Melba:
Bristol L: 287, 288, 289, 290
Cub S/G 1954: 565, 568
Cub S/G 1957: 701, 702, 703
AEC W/B 1960: 829, 830
TOTAL = 11

Appendix A (iii) ~ List of North Western and Other Operators' Vehicles driven by the Author

Other Operators : Vehicles Driven

East Midland Motor Services

LA27 (FVO 427D)

Hebble Motor Services

164 (CJX 65)

Lancashire United Transport

521 (STF 206)	3 (243 GTJ)	87 (277 STF)	146 (8090 TE)
626 (432 DTF)	32 (125 MTE)	88 (278 STF)	
628 (434 DTF)	33 (126 MTE)	92 (616 WTE)	

Northern General Transport

1683 (ECN 683)	1717 (FCN 717)	1755 (GCN 55)	1921 (KCN 921)	2519 (CCN 719D)
1686 (ECN 686)	1746 (GCN 46)	1852 (JCN 452)	1955 (MCN 55)	2608 (PCN 8)
1715 (FCN 715)	1753 (GCN 53)	1914 (KCN 914)		

Ribble Motor Services

548 (ARN 548B)	727 (TCK 727)	768 (TRN 768)	990 (LCK 704)	1268 (RRN 417)
543 (UCK 543)	754 (TRN 754)	813 (ARN 813C)	999 (LCK 713)	1272 (RRN 421)
714 (TCK 714)	762 (TRN 762)	921 (FCK 421)	1001 (LCK 725)	1282 (RRN 431)
724 (TCK 724)	764 (TRN 764)	954 (GCK 289)	1077 (FFR 360)	

Sheffield Joint Omnibus

228 (NWA 928)

Starks (Scottish Omnibuses)

ZB 672S (SWS 672)

Trent Motor Traction

124 (GRC 124)	176 (VCH 176)	204 (204 CCH)	227 (ACH 227B)	238 (ECH 238C)
134 (CRC 134)	188 (YRC 188)	205 (205 CCH)	229 (ACH 229B)	239 (ECH 239C)
164 (VCH 164)	201 (201 CCH)	207 (207 CCH)	231 (ACH 231B)	240 (ECH 240C)
169 (VCH 169)	202 (202 CCH)	210 (210 CCH)	237 (ECH 237C)	241 (ECH 241C)

United Automobile

BUT 17 (17 BHN)

West Yorkshire Road Car Company

CUG 1 (LWR 406)	CUG 18 (OWX 135)	CUG 22 (VWU 233)	EUG 78 (YWT 292)
CUG 2 (LWR 407)	CUG 19 (OWX 136)	CUG 26 (7937 WU)	EUG 89 (7910 WY)

Wilts & Dorset Motor Services

912 (BMW 137C)

Yorkshire Woollen District

759 (AHD 822)	765 (BHD 705)	781 (CHD 366)	886 (GHD 758)	889 (GHD 761)
761 (AHD 824)	779 (CHD 364)	785 (CHD 370)	888 (GHD 760)	

North Western : Vehicles Driven — Registration numbers are in alphabetical order, and where fleet numbers are different from the registration this is shown in brackets.

JA 7719 (403)	AJA 140 (Ambulance)	BJA 186 (30)	RDB 802	VDB 901	YJA 1	AJA 100B
JA 7720 (404)	AJA 145 (425)	BJA 146	RDB 804	VDB 903	YJA 2	AJA 101B
JA 7722 (406)	AJA 152 (432)	BJA 422 (267)	RDB 805	VDB 904	YJA 3	AJA 102B
JA 7726 (410)	AJA 156 (436)		RDB 806	VDB 905	YJA 16	AJA 111B
JA 7792 (420)	AJA 165 (445)		RDB 812	VDB 907		AJA 114B
JA 7795 (423)	AJA 183 (463)		RDB 813	VDB 908		AJA 130B
JA 7724 (408) Training Bus			RDB 814	VDB 909		AJA 140B
			RDB 817	VDB 910		AJA 141B
CDB 202	DDB 254	EDB 321 (394 — Atkinson)	RDB 818	VDB 911		AJA 142B
CDB 224	DDB 255	EDB 323 (396 — Olympic)	RDB 819	VDB 912		AJA 143B
CDB 225	DDB 258	EDB 324 (397 — Olympic)	RDB 820	VDB 913		AJA 144B
CDB 226	DDB 259	EDB 325 (464 — PD2/10)	RDB 821	VDB 914		AJA 145B
CDB 227	DDB 260		RDB 822	VDB 915		AJA 146B
CDB 228	DDB 293		RDB 824	VDB 916		AJA 147B
CDB 229	DDB 300	FDB 257C (Landrover)	RDB 825	VDB 917		AJA 148B
CDB 231			RDB 826	VDB 918		AJA 149B
CDB 233			RDB 827	VDB 920		
CDB 234			RDB 829	VDB 921		FJA 194D
CDB 238			RDB 830	VDB 922		FJA 195D
CDB 241			RDB 831	VDB 929		FJA 196D
CDB 242			RDB 832	VDB 932		FJA 216D
CDB 243			RDB 833	VDB 933		FJA 218D
			RDB 834	VDB 937		FJA 220D
			RDB 836	VDB 938		FJA 222D
FDB 500	HJA 617	KDB 627	LDB 701	RDB 837	VDB 945	FJA 223D
FDB 504	HJA 618	KDB 628	LDB 702	RDB 838	VDB 946	FJA 224D
FDB 508	HJA 620	KDB 630	LDB 703	RDB 839	VDB 947	FJA 226D
FDB 509	HJA 621	KDB 631	LDB 718	RDB 841	VDB 948	FJA 229D
FDB 510	HJA 624	KDB 632	LDB 721A	RDB 843	VDB 949	
FDB 511	HJA 625	KDB 633	LDB 722*	RDB 844	VDB 952	
FDB 515		KDB 634	LDB 728A	RDB 845	VDB 953	
FDB 530		KDB 639	LDB 729	RDB 846	VDB 954	
FDB 537		KDB 641	LDB 730	RDB 847	VDB 955	
FDB 538		KDB 643	LDB 731	RDB 848	VDB 956	
FDB 541		KDB 644	LDB 732	RDB 850	VDB 957	
FDB 543		KDB 646	LDB 734A	RDB 851	VDB 958	
FDB 555		KDB 647	LDB 735	RDB 852	VDB 959	
FDB 570		KDB 648	LDB 736A	RDB 853	VDB 960	
FDB 572		KDB 649	LDB 737	RDB 855	VDB 962	
FDB 580		KDB 651	LDB 738	RDB 857	VDB 963	
FDB 586A		KDB 652	LDB 740	RDB 858	VDB 970	
FDB 591		KDB 653	LDB 741	RDB 859	VDB 973	
		KDB 654	LDB 742	RDB 860	VDB 974	
		KDB 655	LDB 744	RDB 863	VDB 978	
DDB 155C		KDB 656	LDB 746	RDB 864		
DDB 156C		KDB 657	LDB 750	RDB 865		
DDB 157C		KDB 658	LDB 751	RDB 866		
DDB 160C		KDB 659	LDB 752	RDB 867		
DDB 161C		KDB 660	LDB 754A	RDB 868		
DDB 163C		KDB 661	LDB 758	RDB 869		
DDB 168C		KDB 662	LDB 765	RDB 875		
DDB 172C		KDB 663	LDB 766	RDB 880		
DDB 173C		KDB 665	LDB 768	RDB 881		
DDB 175C		KDB 666	LDB 770	RDB 881		
DDB 176C		KDB 667	LDB 771	RDB 882		
DDB 177C		KDB 668	LDB 772	RDB 884		
DDB 178C		KDB 669	LDB 773	RDB 885		
DDB 179C		KDB 678	LDB 774	RDB 886		
		KDB 679	LDB 775	RDB 888		
		KDB 684	LDB 776	RDB 889		
		KDB 693	LDB 777	RDB 890		
		KDB 694	LDB 778	RDB 891		
		KDB 700	LDB 779	RDB 892		
			LDB 780	RDB 893		
			LDB 786	RDB 894		
			LDB 787	RDB 896		
			LDB 790A	RDB 897		
			LDB 791A	RDB 898		
			LDB 792A	RDB 899		
			LDB 793	RDB 900		
			LDB 795			

*No. 722 was still in 'Black Top' livery on 18th May 1966

Appendix B ~ Extract of Duties on Manchester Garage 'C' and 'D' Sheets, showing Winter and Summer variations

'D' Sheet: — Summer 19 weeks: From week 5, 16th May 1964, to week 23, 19th September 1964. (end of summer season)

Winter 20 weeks: From week 5, 9th January 1965, to week 24, 22nd May 1965. (end of winter season)

'C' Sheet: — Summer 17 weeks: From week 21, 28th May 1966, to week 7, 23rd September 1966. (end of summer season)

Winter 17 weeks: From week 4, 12th February 1966, to week 20, 21st May 1966. (end of summer season)

Manchester duty extracts from 'D' and 'C' sheets

The following lists are extracts from my diaries for 'D' and 'C' sheets following the winter and summer roster and duty patterns.

In order to try to give a straight comparison, the number of weeks for the summer period is directly comparable with the same roster weeks for the winter period for both sheets.

The working week commenced on a Saturday, so that in the early days, one Friday rest day would be followed by a Saturday and Sunday rest day, making a three day break. After the introduction of the 40 hour week at the start of the 1966 summer season, both weeks would have two rest days, so that the addition of a Thursday would make a four day break for those wishing to have time off.

The column headings are self-explanatory; the 'hours' column shows the 'paid' hours for the duty, a '+1.30', for example, denoting a penalty payment of one hour, thirty minutes paid for a split duty. Minimum payment for a day's work was six hours forty minutes.

The routes worked show either the actual number of journeys, working by the duty, (i.e. 2 x 28 or 2 x 222; 23/11/23), or the general routes worked (i.e. 11/23). In this latter case, several journeys on services 11 and 23 would be worked, but my records do not denote how many of each.

Where the route is shown as 2 x 222, the two journeys operate both directions on service 222. No. 222/3 shows that the outward journey is 222, returning as 223. Similarly, 31/32 denotes out 31, back as 32.

In some cases, notes of interest are included such as 'Blue Bell' changeover on the 22.10 service 29, to Macclesfield.

Duties shown 'spare' indicate that the crew are not allocated work but stand by to cover for any staff who may miss duty due to sickness or oversleeping. Very rarely did a spare man sit on his back-side for a full eight hours! If not called upon to actually do some work, he would doubtless be used to take a changeover bus to drivers suffering breakdowns or defects. The garage invariably found a driver some work by sending him to Stockport Charles Street Stores for spare parts in the garage Landrover.

Once a driver had found his line of duties from the roster, he usually headed for the display cases which contained the copies of the duties, so that he could see exactly what he was in for during the coming week, or even further, if he wished!

In common with all other N—N garages, Manchester had the duties in a glass-fronted case, glued to a linen roll which could be turned with a handle, just like a bus indicator. It certainly brought out the gricer in one!

Unfortunately, I have no record of the conductors' signing-on and signing-off times so I will not try to be specific here. For the record, the signing-on and signing-off times for the driving staff were as follows:

Signing-on

Bus from garage:	20 minutes
At the bus station:	5 minutes, prior to the arrival of the bus in the bus station
At a point away from Lower Mosley Street:	5 minutes, plus travelling time
Second part of split duty:	No signing-on time paid

Signing-off

At garage:	5 minutes
At any other point:	Only walking time to Lower Mosley Street from a relieving point

No. 260 (DDB 260), a Leyland PD2 with a Weymann body, is seen at the terminus of service 28, Royal Hotel, Hayfield, in August 1965.

NORTH WESTERN'S MANCHESTER GARAGE : 'D' SHEET DUTIES : SUMMER

Day	Duty	Sign-on	Place	Sign-off	Hours/Minutes	Routes Worked
Week 5 : 16th May 1964						
Sat.	20	14.25	Chorlton Street	23.34	9.09	2 x 30:52
Sun.		Rest Day				
Mon.	37	07.05	Garage	09.22 (Chorlton St.)	7.20	52: 31/32: 222
		15.20	Chorlton Street	19.22	+1.30	
Tue.	167	07.00	Garage	15.00	8.00	Spare
Wed.	73	06.17	Garage	10.18	7.20	X99: 51 changeover
		15.28	Chorlton Street	17.33	+.45	
Thu.	9	06.20	Garage	12.56	6.40	30/52: 27A
Fri.		Rest Day				
Week 6 : 23rd May 1964						
Sat.	65	07.05	Garage	15.20	8.15	3 x 64: 20
Sun.	168	14.00	Lower Mosley Street	22.00	8.00	Spare
Mon.	50	16.29	Lower Mosley Street	23.26	6.57	2 x 23: 2 x 5
Tue.	12	16.19	Lower Mosley Street	23.56	7.37	3 x 32
Wed.	68	17.16	Lower Mosley Street	23.45	6.40	2 x 51/165
Thu.	34	15.29	Lower Mosley Street	23.50	8.21	3 x 11: 11X/23/11X
Fri.		Rest Day				
Week 7 : 30th May 1964						
Sat.	14	15.47	Lower Mosley Street	23.31	7.44	3 x 32
Sun.	121	08.25	Garage	18.26	10.01	2 x X60
Mon.		Rest Day				
Tue.	31	06.31	Garage	15.24	8.53	2 x 5: 23/11X/23/11X
Wed.	9	06.20	Garage	12.56	6.40	30/52: 27A
Thu.		Rest Day				
Fri.	65	07.05	Garage	15.20	8.15	3 x 64: 20
Week 8 : 6th June 1964						
Sat.	139	07.20	Garage	14.46	7.26	31A/51: X97 (Leeds)
Sun.	6	16.25	Lower Mosley Street	23.18	6.53	27: 28
Mon.	14	15.47	Lower Mosley Street	23.31	7.44	3 x 32
Tue.	50	16.29	Lower Mosley Street	23.26	6.57	2 x 23: 2 x 5
Wed.	46	14.35	Lower Mosley Street	23.22	8.47	5 x 222
Thu.		Rest Day				
Fri.	30	15.35	Lower Mosley Street	00.06	8.31	2 x 222: 23/11X/23
Week 9 : 13th June 1964						
Sat.	12	16.17	Lower Mosley Street	00.01	7.44	3 x 32
Sun.		Rest Day				
Mon.	47	06.15	Garage	14.09	7.54	2 x 3: 3 x 5
Tue.	45	05.32	Garage	13.04	7.32	5 x 222
Wed.		Rest Day				
Thur.	61	06.58	Garage	08.58 (Lower Mosley St)	7.20	31A
		17.09	Lower Mosley Street	20.18	+1.45	2 x 5
Fri.	13	06.25	Garage	14.18	7.53	2 x 32: 64
Week 10 : 20th June 1964						
Sat.		Rest Day				
Sun.	34	17.04	Lower Mosley Street	23.28	6.40	5: 11X/23/11X
Mon.	66	14.30	Garage	23.15	8.45	2 x 52: 2 x 64
Tue.	68	17.16	Lower Mosley Street	23.45	6.40	2 x 51/165
Wed.	44	15.50	Garage	22.57	7.07	12A: 23: 222: 223
Thu.	66	14.30	Garage	23.15	8.45	2 x 52: 2 x 64
Fri.	18	14.50	Garage	23.42	8.52	2 x 222: 52: 30

Day	Duty	Sign-on	Place	Sign-off	Hours/Minutes	Routes Worked
Week 11 : 27th June 1964						
Sat.	22	12.50	Lower Mosley Street	21.49	8.59	2 x 222 : 52 : 30
Sun.		Rest Day				
Mon.		Rest Day				
Tue.	23	07.35	Garage	15.52	8.17	23X : 222 : 32 : 32 changeover
Wed.	23	07.35	Garage	15.52	8.17	23X : 222 : 32 : 32 changeover
Thu.	19	07.15	Garage	16.05	8.03	31A : 2 x 29
Fri.	43	06.45	Garage	15.10	8.25	5 x 222
Week 12 : 4th July 1964						
Sat.	39	08.30	Garage	15.50	7.20	51/32 : 12A : 2 x 222
Sun.	10	15.20	Chorlton Street	23.35	8.15	20 : 2 x 52
Mon.	42	15.48	Garage	00.07	8.19	11/23X : 3 x 222
Tue.		Rest Day				
Wed.	38	07.12	Garage	09.01	7.20	23
		14.01	Lower Mosley Street	17.48	+.30	2 x 64
Thu.	28	15.20	Chorlton Street	23.30	8.10	2 x 20 : 11X/23/11X
Fri.	166	14.45	Chorlton Street	22.00	7.15	Spare
Week 13 : 11th July 1964						
Sat.	54	11.50	Garage	19.07	7.17	4 x 222
Sun.		Rest Day				
Mon.	38	07.12	Garage	09.01	7.20	23
		14.01	Lower Mosley Street	17.48	+.30	2 x 64
Tue.	53	07.20	Garage	09.37	7.20	604/52
		15.40	Garage	19.59	+1.30	12A : 32X
Wed.	67	07.20	Garage	15.33	8.13	501/2 : 2 x 51
Thu.		Rest Day				
Fri.	35	05.43	Garage	14.10	8.27	2 x 11 : 3 x 3
Week 14 : 18th July 1964						
Sat.	39	08.30	Garage	15.50	7.20	51/32 : 12A : 2 x 222
Sun.	10	15.20	Chorlton Street	23.35	8.15	20 : 2 x 52
Mon.	42	15.48	Garage	00.07	8.19	11/23X : 3 x 222
Tue.		Rest Day				
Wed.	38	07.12	Garage	09.01	7.20	23
		14.01	Lower Mosley Street	17.48	+.30	2 x 64
Thu.	28	15.20	Chorlton Street	23.30	8.10	2 x 20 : 11X/23/11X
Fri.	166	14.45	Chorlton Street	22.00	7.15	Spare
Week 15 : 25th July 1964						
Sat.		Rest Day				
Sun.		Rest Day				
Mon.	7	06.12	Garage	14.09	7.57	222/223 : 2 x 28
Tue.	41	06.25	Garage	14.40	8.15	12A/222 : 2 x 222 : 223
Wed.	11	06.40	Garage	13.52	7.12	32/31 : 2 x 32
Thu.	7	06.12	Garage	14.09	7.57	222/223 : 2 x 28
Fri.	61	06.58	Garage	08.58	7.20	31A
		17.09	Lower Mosley Street	20.18	+1.45	2 x 5
Week 16 : 1st August 1964						
Sat.	148	13.13	Lower Mosley Street	21.27	8.14	X97
Sun.	20	16.00	Lower Mosley Street	23.44	7.44	2 x 29 : 29 changeover
Mon.		Rest Day				
Tue.	29	07.00	Garage	09.25	7.20	31A/31
		14.55	Garage	19.22	+1.15	2 x 52
Wed.	2	14.30	Garage	23.15	8.45	2 x 52 : 2 x 64
Thu.	20	16.00	Lower Mosley Street	23.44	7.44	2 x 29 : 29 changeover
Fri.	12	16.19	Lower Mosley Street	23.56	7.37	3 x 32

Day	Duty	Sign-on	Place	Sign-off	Hours/Minutes	Routes Worked
Week 17 : 8th August 1964						
Sat.	168	14.00	Lower Mosley Street	22.00	8.00	Spare
Sun.	39	07.30	Garage	15.55	8.25	5 x 222
Mon.	137	09.58	Garage	16.54	6.56	X97 (Leeds): 23
Tue.	5	07.10	Garage	11.05	7.20	27
		15.50	Garage	17.59	+.30	Wilcox (Works)
Wed.	165	05.30	Garage	13.30	8.00	Spare
Thu.		Rest Day				
Fri.		Rest Day				
Week 18 : 15th August 1964						
Sat.	165	05.30	Garage	13.30	8.00	Spare
Sun.	10	15.20	Chorlton Street	23.35	8.15	2 x 52: 27 (27 Calls Ferodo on last journe
Mon.	28	15.20	Chorlton Street	23.30	8.10	2 x 20: 11X/23/11X
Tue.	14	15.47	Lower Mosley Street	23.31	7.44	3 x 32
Wed.	52	16.35	Lower Mosley Street	23.18	6.43	2 x 222: 28
Thu.		Rest Day				
Fri.	20	16.00	Lower Mosley Street	23.44	7.44	2 x 29: 29 changeover
Week 19 : 22nd August 1964						
Sat.	82	14.13	Lower Mosley Street	22.27	8.14	2 x X12
Sun.	45	08.30	Garage	15.25	6.55	4 x 222
Mon.	165	05.30	Garage	13.30	8.00	Spare
Tue.	27	05.50	Garage	14.10	8.20	2 x 222: 2 x 11X/23
Wed.	53	07.20	Garage	09.37	7.20	604/51
		15.40	Garage	19.13	+1.00	12A: 32
Thu.		Rest Day				
Fri.		Rest Day				
Week 20 : 29th August 1964						
Sat.		Rest Day				
Sun.	32	17.11	Lower Mosley Street	23.55	6.44	11X/23: 23/11X/23
Mon.	46	14.35	Lower Mosley Street	23.22	8.47	5 x 222
Tue.	36	16.40	Lower Mosley Street	00.01	7.21	32: 11X/23: 2 x 11X
Wed.	50	16.29	Lower Mosley Street	23.26	6.57	2 x 23: 2 x 5
Thu.	18	14.50	Garage	23.42	8.52	2 x 222: 2 x 20
Fri.	14	15.47	Lower Mosley Street	23.31	7.44	3 x 32
Week 21: 5th September 1964						
Sat.	46	14.45	Lower Mosley Street	23.22	8.37	5 x 222
Sun.		Rest Day				
Mon.		Rest Day				
Tue.	47	06.15	Garage	14.09	7.54	2 x 3: 3 x 5
Wed.	27	05.50	Garage	14.10	8.20	2 x 222: 23/11X/23
Thu.	67	07.20	Garage	15.33	8.13	501/502: 2 x 51/165
Fri.	29	07.00	Garage	09.25	7.20	31A
		14.55	Garage	19.22	+1.15	2 x 52
Week 22 : 12th September 1964						
Sat.		Rest Day				
Sun.	18	17.18	Lower Mosley Street	23.42	6.40	3 x 20
Mon.	8	14.15	Lower Mosley Street	20.18	6.40	2 x 28
Tue.	46	14.35	Lower Mosley Street	23.22	8.47	5 x 222
Wed.	22	15.15	Lower Mosley Street	23.34	8.19	2 x 23: 2 x 52
Thu.	14	15.47	Lower Mosley Street	23.31	7.44	3 x 32
Fri.	48	15.10	Lower Mosley Street	23.12	8.02	X60: 2 x 3

Day	Duty	Sign-on	Place	Sign-off	Hours/Minutes	Routes Worked

Week 23 : 19th September 1964

Day	Duty	Sign-on	Place	Sign-off	Hours/Minutes	Routes Worked
Sat.	2	15.46	Lower Mosley Street	23.15	7.29	4 x 64
Sun.	167	07.00	Garage	15.00	8.00	Spare
Mon.	45	05.32	Garage	13.04	7.32	4 x 222
Tue.		Rest Day				
Wed.		Rest Day				
Thu.	15	06.50	Garage	15.22	8.32	29: 2 x 32
Fri.	37	07.10	Garage	09.39	7.20	52
		16.05	Garage	20.04	+1.30	32/31: 222

End of summer season

NORTH WESTERN'S MANCHESTER GARAGE : 'D' SHEET DUTIES : WINTER

Week 5 : 9th January 1965

Day	Duty	Sign-on	Place	Sign-off	Hours/Minutes	Routes Worked
Sat.	18	17.08	Lower Mosley Street	23.42	6.40	3 x 20
Sun.		Rest Day				
Mon.	43	06.45	Garage	15.10	8.25	223/2: 4 x 222
Tue.	3	06.05	Garage	10.30	7.20	31: 32
		15.28	Chorlton Street	17.33	+.45	51 changeover
Wed.	3	06.05	Garage	10.30	7.20	31: 32
		15.28	Chorlton Street	17.33	+.45	51 changeover
Thu.		Rest Day				
Fri.	35	Garage		14.10	8.27	2 x 11: 3 x 3

Week 6 : 16th January 1965

Day	Duty	Sign-on	Place	Sign-off	Hours/Minutes	Routes Worked
Sat.	13	06.25	Garage	14.22	7.57	3 x 32
Sun.	2	16.45	Lower Mosley Street	23.15	6.40	Spare: 3 x 64
Mon.	22	15.45	Garage	23.34	7.49	32: 501/2: 2 x 52
Tue.	14	15.47	Lower Mosley Street	23.31	7.44	3 x 32
Wed.	36	16.40	Lower Mosley Street	00.01	7.21	32: 23: 11X
Thu.	46	14.35	Lower Mosley Street	23.22	8.47	5 x 222
Fri.		Rest Day				

Week 7 : 23rd January 1965

Day	Duty	Sign-on	Place	Sign-off	Hours/Minutes	Routes Worked
Sat.	34	18.05	Lower Mosley Street	23.44	6.40	222: 30: 29
Sun.		Rest Day				
Mon.		Rest Day				
Tue.	37	07.10	Garage	09.39	7.20	52
		16.05	Garage	20.04	+1.30	32/31: 222
Wed.	23	07.35	Garage	16.03	8.28	23X/222: 2 x 64
Thu.	23	07.35	Garage	16.03	8.28	23X/222: 2 x 64
Fri.	41	06.25	Garage	14.40	8.15	12A/222: 4 x 222

Week 8 : 30th January 1965

Day	Duty	Sign-on	Place	Sign-off	Hours/Minutes	Routes Worked
Sat.	39	08.30	Garage	15.55	7.25	51/32: 12A: 222
Sun.	38	15.30	Chorlton Street	23.04	7.34	20: 2 x 52
Mon.	2	14.30	Garage	23.15	8.45	2 x 52: 2 x 64
Tue.	50	16.14	Garage	23.26	7.12	2 x 23: 2 x 5
Wed.	20	16.00	Lower Mosley Street	23.44	7.44	2 x 29: 29 changeover
Thu.		Rest Day				
Fri.	10	15.50	Garage	23.35	7.45	2 x 222/3: 27

Week 9: 6th February 1965

Day	Duty	Sign-on	Place	Sign-off	Hours/Minutes	Routes Worked
Sat.	20	14.25	Chorlton Street	23.34	9.09	2 x 30: 52
Sun.		Rest Day				
Mon.		Rest Day				
Tue.	23	07.35	Garage	16.03	8.28	23X: 222: 2 x 64
Wed.	9	06.20	Garage	13.05	6.45	30: 27A
Thu.	61	06.45	Garage	09.07	7.20	31A
		17.09	Chorlton Street	20.18	+2.00	2 x 5
Fri.	69	06.55	Garage	09.01	7.20	12A/23X
		16.54	Chorlton Street	20.19	+1.45	2 x 23

Day	Duty	Sign-on	Place	Sign-off	Hours/Minutes	Routes Worked

Week 10 : 13th February 1965

Day	Duty	Sign-on	Place	Sign-off	Hours/Minutes	Routes Worked
Sat.	54	11.50	Garage	19.07	7.17	4 x 222
Sun.	4	14.50	Chorlton Street	23.34	8.43	4 x 52
Mon.	36	16.40	Lower Mosley Street	00.01	7.21	32: 11X: 23
Tue.	52	16.35	Lower Mosley Street	23.18	6.43	2 x 222: 28
Wed.		Rest Day				
Thu.	51	06.50	Garage	10.55	7.20	31A: 51
		15.55	Garage	18.02	+.45	32
Fri.	2	14.30	Garage	23.15	8.45	2 x 52: 2 x 64

Week 11: 20th February 1965

Day	Duty	Sign-on	Place	Sign-off	Hours/Minutes	Routes Worked
Sat.	46	14.45	Lower Mosley Street	23.22	8.37	5 x 222
Sun.	11	07.15	Garage	13.58	6.43	2 x 20: 23
Mon.	29	07.00	Garage	09.25	7.20	31A/31
		15.25	Chorlton Street	19.20	+1.15	2 x 20
Tue.		Rest Day				
Wed.	7	06.12	Garage	14.09	7.57	222/3: 2 x 28
Thu.	67	07.20	Garage	1533	8.13	501/2: 2 x 51/165
Fri.		Rest Day				

Week 12 : 27th February 1965

Day	Duty	Sign-on	Place	Sign-off	Hours/Minutes	Routes Worked
Sat.	7	08.00	Garage	15.52	7.52	2 x 28: 32
Sun.	44	16.20	Lower Mosley Street	00.32	8.12	3 x 222: 223: 222
Mon.	46	14.35	Lower Mosley Street	23.22	8.47	5 x 222
Tue.	20	16.00	Lower Mosley Street	23.44	7.44	2 x 29: 29 changeover
Wed.	10	15.50	Garage	23.35	7.45	2 x 222: 27
Thu.	12	16.19	Lower Mosley Street	23.56	7.37	3 x 32
Fri.		Rest Day				

Week 13 : 6th March 1965

Day	Duty	Sign-on	Place	Sign-off	Hours/Minutes	Routes Worked
Sat.	50	17.04	Lower Mosley Street	23.26	6.40	4 x 5
Sun.	43	08.45	Garage	16.25	7.40	32: 222: 223: 222
Mon.	40	06.27	Garage	08.22	7.20	222
		14.09	Lower Mosley Street	17.09	+.30	2 x 5
Tue.	67	07.20	Garage	15.33	8.13	501/2: 2 x 52
Wed.		Rest Day				
Thu.		Rest Day				
Fri.	67	07.20	Garage	15.33	8.13	501/2: 2 x 52

Week 14: 13th March 1965

Day	Duty	Sign-on	Place	Sign-off	Hours/Minutes	Routes Worked
Sat.	67	07.05	Garage	15.33	8.28	31A/32: 2 x 51/165
Sun.		Rest Day				
Mon.	14	15.47	Lower Mosley Street	23.31	7.44	3 x 32
Tue.	28	14.50	Garage	23.30	8.40	2 x 52: 11X: 23: 11X
Wed.	52	16.35	Lower Mosley Street	23.18	6.43	2 x 222: 28
Thu.	22	15.45	Garage	23.34	7.49	32: 502/1: 2 x 52
Fri.	50	16.14	Garage	23.26	7.12	2 x 23: 2 x 5

Week 15 : 20th March 1965

Day	Duty	Sign-on	Place	Sign-off	Hours/Minutes	Routes Worked
Sat.	48	15.28	Chorlton Street	23.26	7.58	51 changeover: 11X: 23
Sun.		Rest Day				
Mon.	27	05.50	Garage	14.10	8.20	223/2: 222: 11X: 23
Tue.	11	06.40	Garage	13.52	7.12	32/31: 2 x 32
Wed.		Rest Day				
Thu.	41	06.25	Garage	14.40	8.15	12A/222: 2 x 222: 223
Fri.	13	06.25	Garage	13.00	6.40	2 x 32: Spare

Day	Duty	Sign-on	Place	Sign-off	Hours/Minutes	Routes Worked
Week 16: 27th March 1965						
Sat.	33	07.05	Garage	14.54	7.49	52: 11X: 23
Sun.	24	15.46	Lower Mosley Street	23.12	7.26	64: 3 x 3
Mon.	166	14.45	Chorlton Street	22.00	7.15	Spare
Tue.	18	14.50	Garage	23.42	8.52	2 x 222: 2 x 20
Wed.		Rest Day				
Thu.	34	15.29	Lower Mosley Street	23.50	8.21	11X/23
Fri.	68	17.16	Lower Mosley Street	23.45	6.40	2 x 51/165
Week 17 : 3rd April 1965						
Sat.		Rest Day				
Sun.	23	09.30	Lower Mosley Street	15.22	6.40	2 x 23: 32
Mon.	61	06.45	Garage	09.07	7.20	31A
		17.09	Lower Mosley Street	20.18	+2.00	2 x 5
Tue.	45	05.32	Garage	13.04	7.32	222/3
Wed.	15	06.50	Garage	15.22	8.32	29: 2 x 32
Thu.		Rest Day				
Fri.	27	05.50	Garage	14.10	8.20	222: 11X/23
Week 18 : 10th April 1965						
Sat.	27	05.50	Garage	13.21	7.31	11X/23
Sun.	34	17.00	Lower Mosley Street	23.28	6.40	11X/23
Mon.	34	15.29	Lower Mosley Street	23.50	8.21	11X/23
Tue.		Rest Day				
Wed.	12	16.19	Lower Mosley Street	23.56	7.37	3 x 32
Thu.	42	15.48	Garage	00.07	8.19	11X: 23: 3 x 222
Fri.	14	15.47	Lower Mosley Street	23.31	7.44	3 x 32
Week 19 : 17th April 1965						
Sat.	12	16.17	Lower Mosley Street	23.56	7.39	3 x 32
Sun.	3	10.50	Garage	16.55	6.40	32: 2 x 3
Mon.	9	06.20	Garage	13.05	6.45	30: 27A
Tue.		Rest Day				
Wed.		Rest Day				
Thu.	27	05.50	Garage	14.10	8.20	2 x 222: 11X/23
Fri.	5	07.10	Garage	15.52	8.42	27: 32: 32 changeover
Week 20 : 24th April 1965						
Sat.	35	06.15	Garage	14.27	8.12	3 x 23: 30
Sun.	14	15.47	Lower Mosley Street	23.31	7.44	3 x 32
Mon.	28	14.50	Garage	23.30	8.40	2 x 52: 11X/23
Tue.	22	15.45	Garage	23.34	7.49	32: 502/1: 2 x 52
Wed.	68	17.16	Lower Mosley Street	23.45	6.40	2 x 51/165
Thu.	10	15.50	Garage	23.35	7.45	2 x 222: 27
Fri.		Rest Day				
Week 21 : 1st May 1965						
Sat.	30	14.49	Lower Mosley Street	23.13	8.24	11X/23
Sun.	15	09.10	Garage	15.52	6.42	27A: 32
Mon.	7	06.12	Garage	14.09	7.57	222/3: 2 x 28
Tue.	40	06.27	Garage	08.22	7.20	222
		14.09	Lower Mosley Street	17.09	+.30	2 x 5
Wed.		Rest Day				
Thu.		Rest Day				
Fri.	40	06.27	Garage	08.22	7.20	222
		14.09	Lower Mosley Street	17.09	+.30	2 x 5

Day	Duty	Sign-on	Place	Sign-off	Hours/Minutes	Routes Worked

Week 22 : 8th May 1965

Day	Duty	Sign-on	Place	Sign-off	Hours/Minutes	Routes Worked
Sat.	49	06.31	Garage	15.40	9.09	3 x 5: 2 x 3
Sun.	10	15.20	Chorlton Street	23.35	8.15	2 x 52: 27
Mon.	68	17.16	Lower Mosley Street	23.45	6.40	2 x 51
Tue.	34	15.29	Lower Mosley Street	23.50	8.21	11X/23
Wed.	50	16.14	Garage	23.26	7.12	2 x 23: 2 x 5
Thu.	68	17.16	Lower Mosley Street	23.45	6.40	2 x 51/165
Fri.		Rest Day				

Week 23 : 15th May 1965

Day	Duty	Sign-on	Place	Sign-off	Hours/Minutes	Routes Worked
Sat.	10	15.45	Lower Mosley Street	23.35	7.50	11X/23: 27
Sun.	67	09.20	Garage	15.33	6.40	2 x 51/165
Mon.		Rest Day				
Tue.		Rest Day				
Wed.	67	07.20	Garage	15.33	8.13	501/2: 2 x 51/165
Thu.	37	07.10	Garage	09.39	7.20	52
		16.40	Lower Mosley Street	18.44	+1.00	32/31: 222
Fri.	7	06.12	Garage	14.09	7.57	222/3: 2 x 28

Week 24 : 22nd May 1965

Day	Duty	Sign-on	Place	Sign-off	Hours/Minutes	Routes Worked
Sat.		Rest Day				
Sun.	18	17.18	Lower Mosley Street	23.42	6.40	2 x 20
Mon.	10	15.50	Garage	23.35	7.45	2 x 222/3: 27
Tue.	46	14.35	Lower Mosley Street	23.22	8.47	5 x 222
Wed.	28	14.50	Garage	23.30	8.40	2 x 52: 11X: 23: 11X
Thu.	36	16.40	Lower Mosley Street	00.01	7.21	32: 11X/23
Fri.	28	14.50	Garage	23.30	8.40	2 x 52: 11X: 23: 11X

End of winter season

NORTH WESTERN'S MANCHESTER GARAGE : 'C' SHEET DUTIES : WINTER

Week 3 : 12th February 1966

Day	Duty	Sign-on	Place	Sign-off	Hours/Minutes	Routes Worked
Sat.	8	12.28	Lower Mosley Street	20.18	7.50	X20: 28
Sun.		Rest Day				
Mon.	33	06.38	Garage	15.34	8.56	11X/23
Tue.	131	05.50	Garage	13.35	7.45	2 x 11: X19
Wed.		Rest Day				
Thu.	1	07.05	Garage	15.20	8.15	3 x 64: 20
Fri.	145	08.17	Garage	14.00	6.40	X97 (Liverpool)

Week 4 : 19th February 1966

Day	Duty	Sign-on	Place	Sign-off	Hours/Minutes	Routes Worked
Sat.	35	06.15	Garage	14.27	8.12	3 x 23: 30
Sun.	144	09.17	Garage	18.27	9.10	2 x X97 (Liverpool)
Mon.	32	12.55	Lower Mosley Street	20.15	7.20	27: 2 x 12
Tue.	128	14.40	Lower Mosley Street	23.12	8.32	X60: 2 x 12
Wed.	132	14.04	Lower Mosley Street	21.44	7.40	2 x 5: X19
Thu.		Rest Day				
Fri.	42	15.50	Garage	23.27	7.37	12A: 3 x 222

Week 5: 26th February 1966

Day	Duty	Sign-on	Place	Sign-off	Hours/Minutes	Routes Worked
Sat.	168	14.00	Lower Mosley Street	22.00	8.00	Spare
Sun.	1	06.50	Garage	14.18	7.20	223/23: 29: 63
Mon.	167	07.00	Garage	15.00	8.00	Spare
Tue.	5	07.10	Garage	15.52	8.42	27: 2 x 32
Wed.	40	06.50	Garage	10.55	7.20	No record
		15.24	Lower Mosley Street	16.54	+.15	
Thu.		Rest Day				
Fri.		Rest Day				

Day	Duty	Sign-on	Place	Sign-off	Hours/Minutes	Routes Worked
Week 6: 5th March 1966						
Sat.		Rest Day				222: X70/60
Sun.	124	16.05	Garage	22.50	6.45	Spare
Mon.	168	14.00	Lower Mosley Street	22.00	8.00	23: X70
Tue.	122	15.15	Lower Mosley Street	23.22	8.06	27: 2 x 12
Wed.	32	12.55	Lower Mosley Street	20.15	7.20	29: 27
Thu.	4	13.05	Lower Mosley Street	19.56	6.51	23: X70
Fri.	122	15.15	Lower Mosley Street	23.22	8.06	
Week 7 : 12th March 1966						
Sat.	134	13.47	Lower Mosley Street	20.42	6.55	32: X20
Sun.		Rest Day				
Mon.	31	06.31	Garage	15.24	8.53	2 x 5: 23/11X
Tue.	38	06.45	Garage	09.01	7.20	12A/23: 63: 64
		15.46	Lower Mosley Street	19.54	+1.45	
Wed.	29	07.00	Garage	09.25	7.20	31A/31: 2 x 20
		15.25	Lower Mosley Street	19.20	+1.15	
Thu.		Rest Day				
Fri.	15	06.50	Garage	15.22	8.32	29: 2 x 32

Note: At this point, I was moved further along the roster to week 11, without working weeks 8, 9 or 10

Day	Duty	Sign-on	Place	Sign-off	Hours/Minutes	Routes Worked
Week 11 : 19th March 1966						
Sat.		Rest Day				
Sun.		Rest Day				
Mon.	11	06.40	Garage	13.52	7.12	31/31: 2 x 32
Tue.	119	06.40	Garage	14.41	7.59	52/500: X60
Wed.	33	06.38	Garage	15.34	8.56	11X/23
Thu.	7	08.08	Lower Mosley Street	16.25	8.17	2 x 28: 222
Fri.	73	06.17	Garage	10.27	7.20	X97: 32
		14.05	Lower Mosley Street	16.24	+.15	
Week 12 : 26th March 1966						
Sat.	31	06.38	Garage	14.43	8.05	11X/23
Sun.	36	12.04	Garage	19.45	7.41	11X/23: 2 x 222
Mon.	122	15.15	Lower Mosley Street	23.22	8.06	23: X70
Tue.	16	15.17	Lower Mosley Street	23.01	7.44	3 x 32
Wed.		Rest Day				
Thu.	166	14.45	Chorlton Street	22.00	7.15	Spare
Fri.	16	15.17	Lower Mosley Street	23.01	7.44	3 x 32
Week 13 : 2nd April 1966						
Sat.	40	14.04	Lower Mosley Street	21.27	7.23	28: X12 (Dup)
Sun.	167	07.00	Garage	15.00	8.00	Spare
Mon.	41	06.25	Garage	14.45	8.20	12A/222: 3 x 222
Tue.	27	05.45	Garage	14.10	8.25	223/2: 222: 11X/23
Wed.	35	05.43	Garage	13.54	8.11	2 x 11: 3 x 12
Thu.		Rest Day				
Fri.		Rest Day				
Week 14 : 9th April 1966						
Sat.	15	08.20	Garage	15.22	7.02	30 changeover (Ret. 29) 3 x 222
Sun.	8	14.04	Lower Mosley Street	20.18	6.40	2 x 28
Mon.	8	14.04	Lower Mosley Street	20.18	6.40	2 x 28
Tue.	11	06.40	Garage	13.52	7.12	32/31: 2 x 32
Wed.	134	13.30	Lower Mosley Street	22.32	9.02	X19: X67
Thu.		Rest Day				
Fri.	4	13.05	Lower Mosley Street	19.56	6.51	29: 27

Day	Duty	Sign-on	Place	Sign-off	Hours/Minutes	Routes Worked
Week 15 : 16th April 1966						
Sat.	122	14.10	Lower Mosley Street	23.50	9.40	2 x X60
Sun.		Rest Day				
Mon.		Rest Day				
Tue.	165	05.30	Garage	13.30	8.00	Spare
Wed.	13	06.25	Garage	15.20	8.55	2 x 32: 20
Thu.	73	06.17	Garage	10.27	7.20	X97: 32
		14.05	Lower Mosley Street	16.24	+.15	
Fri.	23	07.17	Garage	16.03	8.46	23X: 223: 63 : 64
Week 16 : 23rd April 1966						
Sat.		Rest Day				
Sun	134	13.53	Lower Mosley Street	21.27	7.34	11X/23: X12
Mon.	128	14.40	Lower Mosley Street	23.12	8.32	X60: 2 x 12
Tue.	24	14.05	Lower Mosley Street	20.27	6.40	11X: X97
Wed.	168	14.00	Lower Mosley Street	22.00	8.00	Spare
Thu.	128	14.40	Lower Mosley Street	23.12	8.32	X60: 2 x 12
Fri.	166	14.45	Chorlton Street	22.00	7.15	Spare
Week 17 : 30th April 1966						
Sat.		Rest Day				
Sun.		Rest Day				
Mon.	13	06.25	Garage	15.20	8.55	2 x 32: 20
Tue.	15	06.50	Garage	15.22	8.32	29: 2 x 32
Wed.	71	07.18	Garage	09.03	7.20	2 x 23: 2 x 12
		13.49	Lower Mosley Street	16.54	+.15	
Thu.	11	06.40	Garage	13.52	7.12	32/31: 2 x 32
Fri.	35	05.43	Garage	13.54	8.11	2 x 11: 3 x 12
Week 18 : 7th May 1966						
Sat.	133	06.25	Garage	14.59	8.34	12A/222: X20: 23
Sun.	122	14.10	Lower Mosley Street	23.26	9.16	X60: 2 x 5
Mon.		Rest Day				
Tue.	123	07.00	Garage	09.39	7.29	52: X60
		15.00	Garage	19.50	+1.30	
Wed.	166	14.45	Chorlton Street	22.00	7.15	Spare
Thu.	166	14.45	Chorlton Street	22.00	7.15	Spare
Fri.	50	16.29	Lower Mosley Street	23.26	6.57	2 x 23: 2 x 5
Week 19 : 14th May 1966						
Sat.	166	14.45	Chorlton Street	22.00	7.15	Spare
Sun.		Rest Day				
Mon.		Rest Day				
Tue.	41	06.25	Garage	14.45	8.20	12A/222: 3 x 222
Wed.	11	06.40	Garage	13.52	7.12	32/31: 2 x 32
Thu.	47	06.18	Garage	13.05	6.47	2 x 12: 29
Fri.	1	07.35	Garage	16.26	8.51	2 x 64: 27
Week 20 : 21st May 1966						
Sat.	27	05.50	Garage	13.21	7.31	11X/23
Sun.	166	14.45	Chorlton Street	22.00	7.15	Spare
Mon.	44	15.50	Lower Mosley Street	22.57	7.07	12A: 32: 222: 222/3
Tue.		Rest Day				
Wed.	124	06.45	Garage	08.59	7.35	31/51: X70
		13.00	Garage	18.22	+1.00	
Thu.	122	15.15	Lower Mosley Street	23.22	8.06	23: X70
Fri.	168	14.00	Lower Mosley Street	22.00	8.00	Spare

End of winter season

NORTH WESTERN'S MANCHESTER GARAGE : 'C' SHEET DUTIES : SUMMER

Day	Duty	Sign-on	Place	Sign-off	Hours/Minutes	Routes Worked
Week 21 : 28th May 1966 *(Start of summer season)*						
Sat.	124	14.10	Lower Mosley Street	23.50	9.40	2 x X60
Sun.		Rest Day				
Mon.		Rest Day				
Tue.	23	07.18	Garage	15.33	8.15	23 : 222 : 2 x 64
Wed.	9	05.30	Garage	12.56	7.26	222/3 : 222 : 27A
Thu.	39	07.10	Garage	15.05	7.55	12A/23 : 3 x 222
Fri.	55					No record
Week 22 : 4th June 1966						
Sat.	137	08.25	Garage	18.26	10.01	X67 : X60
Sun.	122	16.20	Lower Mosley Street	22.35	6.40	X60
Mon.	52	16.00	Garage	23.18	7.18	32/31 : 222 : 28
Tue.	128	15.10	Lower Mosley Street	23.50	8.40	X60 : 23/11X
Wed.		Rest Day				
Thu.		Rest Day				
Fri.	126	14.10	Lower Mosley Street	23.50	9.40	2 x X60
Week 23 : 11th June 1966						
Sat.	128	13.30	Lower Mosley Street	23.07	9.37	X19 : X60/70
Sun.	15	09.10	Garage	17.35	8.25	27 : X19
Mon.	47	06.18	Garage	13.05	6.47	2 x 12 : 29
Tue.	5	07.10	Garage	15.52	8.42	27 : 2 x 32
Wed.	165	05.30	Garage	13.30	8.00	Spare
Thu.		Rest Day				
Fri.		Rest Day				
Week 24 : 18th June 1966						
Sat.	147	06.15	Garage	15.30	9.15	X97 (Round trip)
Sun.	148	12.34	Lower Mosley Street	21.44	9.10	5 : 28 : X97
Mon.		Rest Day				
Tue.		Rest Day				
Wed.	52	16.00	Garage	23.18	7.18	32/31 : 222 : 28
Thu.	42	15.50	Garage	23.12	7.12	12A : 11 : 222
Fri.	146	11.25	Lower Mosley Street	20.44	9.19	X97 : X99
Week 25 : 25th June 1966						
Sat.	150	12.35	Lower Mosley Street	21.54	9.19	X97 : 2 x 222
Sun.		Rest Day				
Mon.		Rest Day				
Tue.	27	07.15	Garage	15.04	7.49	31A : 23/11X
Wed.	17	07.17	Garage	15.24	8.07	23 : 2 x 20 : 12
Thu.	149	07.15	Garage	17.09	9.54	X97/9 : 2 x 5
Fri.	47	06.18	Garage	13.05	6.47	2 x 12 : 29
Week 26 : 2nd July 1966						
Sat.	83	10.25	Garage	16.10	6.40	X1
Sun.	144	12.15	Garage	22.39	10.24	X97 (Round trip)
Mon.	126	14.10	Lower Mosley Street	23.50	9.40	2 x X60
Tue.	120	16.25	Garage	00.20	7.55	32 : X60
Wed.	130	15.10	Garage	23.07	7.48	32 : X60
Thu.		Rest Day				
Fri.		Rest Day				
Week 27 : 9th July 1966						
Sat.	158	15.20	Garage	00.44	9.24	X72 : X60 (Dup)
Sun.	151	09.40	Garage	17.28	7.43	X2
Mon.	123	07.00	Garage	15.11	8.11	52 : X60
Tue.	43	06.15	Garage	15.00	8.45	222
Wed.	39	07.10	Garage	15.05	7.55	12A/23 : 3 x 222
Thu.		Rest Day				
Fri.		Rest Day				

Day	Duty	Sign-on	Place	Sign-off	Hours/Minutes	Routes Worked

Week 28 : 16th July 1966

Day	Duty	Sign-on	Place	Sign-off	Hours/Minutes	Routes Worked
Sat.		Rest Day				
Sun.		Rest Day				
Mon.	128	15.10	Lower Mosley Street	23.50	8.40	X60: 11X/23
Tue.	52	16.00	Garage	23.18	7.18	32/32: 222: 28
Wed.	166	14.45	Chorlton Street	22.00	7.15	Spare
Thu.	126	14.10	Lower Mosley Street	23.50	9.40	2 x X60
Fri.	30	15.48	Garage	00.06	8.18	11X/23

Week 29 : 23rd July 1966

Day	Duty	Sign-on	Place	Sign-off	Hours/Minutes	Routes Worked
Sat.	120	14.40	Lower Mosley Street	00.20	9.40	2 x X60
Sun.	141	09.15	Garage	17.16	8.01	X99: 11X/23
Mon.	29	06.18	Garage	09.50	7.44	2 x 12
		15.25	Chorlton Street	19.32	+1.45	2 x 20
Tue.		Rest Day				
Wed.	35	05.43	Garage	13.54	8.11	2 x 11: 3 x 12
Thu.		Rest Day				
Fri.	27	07.15	Garage	15.04	7.49	31A: 11X/23

Week 30 : 30th July 1966

Day	Duty	Sign-on	Place	Sign-off	Hours/Minutes	Routes Worked
Sat.	125	09.10	Garage	15.50	6.40	X60: 11X
Sun.	158	12.45	Garage	20.56	8.11	32: X72
Mon.		Rest Day				
Tue.		Rest Day				
Wed.	128	15.10	Lower Mosley Street	23.50	8.40	X60: 11X/23
Thu.	44	15.35	Garage	22.57	7.22	12A/32: 222
Fri.	126	14.10	Lower Mosley Street	23.50	9.40	2 x X60

Note: End of roster. Next week restarts at week 1.

Week 1 : 6th August 1966

Day	Duty	Sign-on	Place	Sign-off	Hours/Minutes	Routes Worked
Sat.	136	10.49	Lower Mosley Street	19.50	9.01	2 x 12: X60
Sun.	125	08.55	Garage	15.11	6.40	X60
Mon.	145	07.20	Garage	17.30	10.10	2 x Leeds
Tue.	39	06.45	Garage	15.05	8.20	222
Wed.		Rest Day				
Thu.		Rest Day				
Fri.	165	05.30	Garage	13.30	8.00	Spare

Week 2 : 13th August 1966

Day	Duty	Sign-on	Place	Sign-off	Hours/Minutes	Routes Worked
Sat.	143	08.15	Garage	18.30	10.15	2 x Leeds
Sun.	126	13.10	Garage	21.50	8.40	64: X60
Mon.	4	13.05	Lower Mosley Street	20.05	7.00	29: 27
Tue.		Rest Day				
Wed.		Rest Day				
Thu.	38	06.45	Garage	09.01	7.20	12A/23: 64: 63
Fri.	16	15.17	Lower Mosley Street	23.01	7.44	3 x 32

Week 3 : 20th August 1966 and Week 4 : 27th August 1966 — No record, due to holidays

Week 5 : 3rd September 1966

Day	Duty	Sign-on	Place	Sign-off	Hours/Minutes	Routes Worked
Sat.	140	15.25	Lower Mosley Street	23.44	8.19	2 x Liverpool
Sun.		Rest Day				
Mon.		Rest Day				
Tue.	17	07.17	Garage	15.24	8.07	23/23X: 2 x 20: 12
Wed.	47	05.50	Garage	13.05	7.15	2 x 11: 29
Thu.	27	07.15	Garage	15.04	7.49	31A: 11X/23
Fri.	147	06.15	Garage	15.30	9.15	X97/99: X97

Day	Duty	Sign-on	Place	Sign-off	Hours/Minutes	Routes Worked

Week 6: 10th September 1966

Day	Duty	Sign-on	Place	Sign-off	Hours/Minutes	Routes Worked
Sat.	11	06.45	Garage	14.01	7.16	31A: 2 x 32
Sun.	119	11.20	Garage	19.41	8.21	52X: X60
Mon.	168	14.00	Lower Mosley Street	22.00	8.00	Spare
Tue.	144	13.47	Lower Mosley Street	22.39	8.52	32: X99
Wed.	20	16.00	Lower Mosley Street	23.42	7.42	29: 2 x 20
Thu.		Rest Day				
Fri.		Rest Day				

Week 7 : 17th September 1966

Day	Duty	Sign-on	Place	Sign-off	Hours/Minutes	Routes Worked
Sat.	50	17.04	Lower Mosley Street	23.26	6.40	4 x 5
Sun.	147	06.45	Garage	15.30	8.45	X97
Mon.	119	06.40	Garage	14.11	7.31	52/500: X60
Tue.	149	07.15	Garage	17.09	9.54	X97/9: X60
Wed.	7	06.05	Garage	14.09	8.04	31: 2 x 28
Thu.		Rest Day				
Fri.		Rest Day				

End of summer season

No. 907 (VDB 907), a 36 ft. Leyland Leopard with Alexander Highlander coachwork, passes The Crescent, Salford, in June 1966, with an X60 service to Blackpool.

Appendix C ~ List of Services operated by Manchester Garage
with notes on Stage Carriage Services

Express services operated by Manchester Garage

X1	Manchester to Derby
X2	Manchester to Nottingham
X3	Manchester to Barmouth
X4	Manchester to Aberystwyth
X11	Manchester to Southend
X12	Manchester to Bradford
X13	Manchester to Cleethorpes
X15	Manchester to Whitby
X19	Manchester to Barnsley, via Holmfirth
X20	Manchester to Barnsley, via Penistone
X24/34	Manchester to Llandudno
X25	Manchester to Scarborough
X44	Manchester to Bangor
X48	Manchester to Sheffield, via Woodhead
X60	Manchester to Blackpool, via Bolton, Chorley and Preston
X67	Manchester to Chesterfield
X70	Manchester to Blackpool, via Westhoughton, Chorley and Preston
X74	Manchester to Pwllheli
X92	Liverpool to Nottingham
X97	Liverpool to Newcastle upon Tyne
X98	Liverpool to Newcastle upon Tyne, (non-stop Liverpool to Manchester)
X99	Liverpool to Middlesbrough
X5	Manchester to London

A suffix indicated the route as follows:

B:	via Stockport, Buxton and M1
D:	via Stockport, Macclesfield, Newcastle under Lyme, M6 and M1
E:	via Stockport, Macclesfield, Biddulph, Newcastle under Lyme, Wolverhampton, Birmingham, Coventry and Oxford
L:	via Altrincham, Newcastle under Lyme, Birmingham, Coventry, M1, Dunstable and St. Albans
M:	(night) via Altrincham, Knutsford, Newcastle under Lyme, Birmingham, Coventry, M1, Dunstable and St. Albans
N:	(night) via Altrincham, Knutsford, Newcastle under Lyme, M6 and M1
P:	via Altrincham, M6, Wolverhampton and Birmingham (terminus)
Z:	via Altrincham, M6 and M1 (express)

For the summer season, commencing 28th May 1966, the Company issued, to all its drivers, a handbook of 'Operating Instructions' giving the detailed routes of a selection of seasonal express and 'limited stop' services. The official routes, with detailed information for each town were shown, together with lists of picking-up points. The production of the instructions was made necessary by an increase in the seasonal operations.

The types of service covered by the handbook were those to places such as Aberystwyth, Barmouth, Skegness, etc., although more frequent services, including Manchester to Llandudno, were also included. The production of the instructions was made necessary by an increase in the seasonal operations.

North Western stage carriage routes from Manchester operated by Manchester Depot

3:	Cannon Street	Flixton, via Flixton Road
5:	Piccadilly	Flixton, via Flixton Road
11:	Piccadilly	Moss Lane, Carrington, with short workings to Flixton (11); Nags Head, Davyhulme (11X)
12:	Piccadilly	Flixton, via Church Road
12A:	Piccadilly	Partington, via Church Road, Flixton and Carrington
20:	Chorlton Street	Poynton, Lostock Road
20A:	Chorlton Street	Woodford
23:	Piccadilly	Red Lion, Flixton, via Nags Head, Davyhulme
23X:	Piccadilly	Red Lion, Flixton, via Nags Head and Union Inn, Davyhulme
27:	Lower Mosley St.	Buxton, via Chapel-en-le-Frith
27A:	Lower Mosley St.	Buxton, via Long Hill
28:	Lower Mosley St.	Hayfield
29:	Lower Mosley St.	Macclesfield
30:	Chorlton Street	Macclesfield
31:	Chorlton Street	Bramhall, via Grove Lane
31A:	Chorlton Street	Bramhall, via Ack Lane
32:	Lower Mosley St.	Higher Poynton/Middlewood
51:	Chorlton Street	Torkington, via Ack Lane
52:	Chorlton Street	Alderley
64:	Piccadilly	Moss Nook/Ringway/Styal
165:	Torkington	Stockport (Interworked with serice 51)
222:	Piccadilly	Partington (Greyhound/Wood Lane/Central Road)
223:	Piccadilly	As 222, but operated through the works of Shell Chemicals Limited (Petrochemicals)
500:	Chorlton Street	Alderley (Non-stop between Griffin Hotel, Heald Green and Aytoun Street, Manchester)

The front end of No. 555 showing the destination panel.

NORTH WESTERN ROAD CAR COMPANY

Additional background notes on services operated from
Manchester Depot; 1963—1967

3 : Manchester to Flixton

This service had its origins in 1928 when the Manchester Corporation 'limited stop' service, between Cornbrook and Rochdale, was extended to Urmston Station, jointly with NWRCC, forming part of an extensive network of cross-Manchester express services. In the same year the service was further extended to run between Bacup and Flixton Station, via Flixton Road. Following the deliberations, of 1931/2, of the Traffic Commissioners, the route was split up to form service 17, Manchester to Rochdale. The Flixton section ran briefly through to Heywood, in 1932, before being curtailed at Cannon Street. The Carrington Road terminus at Flixton opened in April 1933. The service has survived as Greater Manchester Transport service 254.

5 : Manchester to Flixton

This service also originated as part of the 1928 express network. In fact, it started in October 1927 as Urmston Station to Hollinwood. However, this route was short-lived and, in 1928, it was curtailed at Lower Mosley Street. Extensions followed to Flixton Station, via Flixton Road, in 1929, and to the Carrington Road terminus in 1933. The Manchester terminus moved to Piccadilly in 1934, but the route via City Road continued until 1970 when the diversion, via Chester Road and Great Bridgewater Street, took place. After the integration of North Western into the SELNEC Passenger Transport Executive in 1973, this service became PTE service 255. In 1979, it was extended to Partington.

11 : Manchester to Flixton

A service between Lower Mosley Street and the western part of Flixton started in 1929 by arrangement with Manchester Corporation, although North Western had operated over the route before this. Initially, service 11 terminated at the Red Lion, then in 1933 it was extended to Carrington Road, via Irlam Road. By 1938, as the Davyhulme area expanded, some buses were running via Hayeswater and Bowfell Roads instead of Cornhill and Moorside. In February 1940, the Moorside Road service became 23, leaving service 11 as the peak period service to Carrington Road, via the new route. In 1947, some journeys on service 11 were extended to Carrington. Service 11X was used for short workings to Nags Head, Davyhulme, and also for the occasional journeys to Selby Drive, Davyhulme, via Woodhouse Road, which started in May 1967. The latter service survives as Greater Manchester Transport service 259, although the route was altered in 1979. Meanwhile, service 11 had become 256, and when the service was re-routed via Moorside Road, Cornhill Road and Irlam Road, in 1979, the original route of nearly 50 years before had been re-created.

12 : Manchester to Flixton

Service 12 was another very early-established North Western route, dating from the 1920s, and operating on a similar route to service 5, except that Church Road was used between Urmston and Flixton. The route via All Saints and Stretford Road was adopted in January 1940, but again the wheel was destined to go full circle, as in October 1981, the service was diverted via City Road. By this time service 12 had become Greater Manchester Transport service 253.

12A : Manchester to Partington

This was originally an independent service by Messrs Cash, whose business was taken over by North Western in 1932.

The Partington terminus was at the Greyhound Hotel, until 1954, when the route was extended to the housing estate at Wood Lane. The service was withdrawn in 1970.

20/20A : Manchester to Woodford

These services had their origins in Sharp's service, Manchester to Woodford and the Manchester Corporation/North Western express service between Stockport, Dailstone Lane and Bury (1927). The Bury section did not survive long, but the Poynton and Woodford services continued until 1964, when they were combined, and formed SELNEC service 190 in 1973.

23 : Manchester to Flixton

This service dates from 1940 (see notes for service 11) when it became the regular service to the Red Lion, Flixton. Some peak period journeys started operating via the full length of Davyhulme Road in May 1961. The routes survive as Greater Manchester Transport services 257 and 258 respectively.

27 : Manchester to Buxton

A service between Stockport and Buxton was started in 1921, and extended to Lower Mosley Street in March 1928 under the Company's agreement with Manchester Corporation. It is not clear when journeys commenced operating via Long Hill, but the service survived, basically unchanged, until the decline of the 1970s affected the Company's network considerably. Long Hill journeys were withdrawn in 1971 and the service no longer ran through to Manchester on weekdays, being curtailed at Stockport. On the split of the Company in 1972, the Buxton service went to Trent as service 3 and later 199. Sunday journeys ceased to run to Manchester in 1975. In some North Western timetables, service 27A was used for short workings between Stockport and Buxton, but this practice ceased in 1960.

28 : Manchester to Hayfield

This was another pioneering service, dating from 1921, between Stockport and New Mills. Extensions followed to Hayfield in 1922 and to Manchester in March 1928. In 1971, the service was curtailed at Stockport on weekdays, and on Sundays in 1975, but the Stockport to Hayfield section survives as Greater Manchester Transport service 358.

29/30 : Manchester to Macclesfield

North Western's service between Macclesfield and Cheadle was one of its first motor bus ventures during World War I. The extension to Manchester as service 29 was another result of the Manchester Corporation agreement in 1928. Service 30 is of more recent origin, dating from 1931 when Goodfellow's service between Piccadilly and Alderley was taken over. Single deck buses predominated on these services until 1961, and service 30 terminated at Chorlton Street, Manchester between 1958 and 1968. In 1972, these services were transferred to Crosville's newly-acquired Macclesfield Depot, and although the 30 route was abandoned for a time, in the late 1970s, both survive as part of the GMT/Crosville joint operation between Manchester and Macclesfield.

31/31A : Manchester to Bramhall

These services date from 1928 and operated via Stockport Road and Parrs Wood Road until 1940, when the present route, via Wilmslow Road, was adopted. In 1968, double deck buses were used for the first time, and further re-routing took place as part of Manchester Corporation's extensive re-modelling of Wilmslow Road routes. As SELNEC services 148/149, the extension to Woodford followed in 1973. Later the routes were again renumbered 157/158.

32 : Manchester to Middlewood

A service between Cheadle and Higher Poynton had operated since the early 1920s. Following the extension to Manchester a succession of service numbers was used. The Middlewood extension followed in 1947, and the service passed to SELNEC as 232. However, the timetable has suffered severe curtailments in more recent years and is now a mere shadow of its former self.

51 : Manchester to Torkington

This had its origins in Goodfellow's service to Macclesfield, via Didsbury and Cheadle, which was taken over by Manchester Corporation and North Western in 1931, and curtailed at Bramhall so as not to duplicate services 29 and 30. Parrs Wood Road was served from 1940, and the route was extended to Bridge Lane in 1946, and Torkington in 1953. In April 1963 buses were re-routed to avoid Cheadle. After the demise of the North Western bus operations in 1972, this service passed to SELNEC Passenger Transport Executive as 151, being operated from Stockport, and was later re-numbered 366. In 1980, buses ceased to run north of Cheadle Hulme.

52 : Manchester to Alderley

Originally an independent service by Coopwood, in 1927 this passed to Goodfellow, and then to North Western in 1931. Between 1931 and 1940 buses continued through to Macclesfield, augmenting service 29. Parrs Wood Road was served from 1946, and Alderley Circuit from 1948. Service 52 later became SELNEC service 152, and was subsequently withdrawn in the extensive service revisions of 1980.

64 : Manchester to Ringway

Bus services between Piccadilly and Moss Nook date from 1933 when Manchester Corporation and North Western commenced joint operation. Styal was originally the province of independents Bailey and Organ & Wachter, who later sold out to the joint operators, and Ringway was served from 1931. North Western ceased operation on this service in 1968 when the Wilmslow Road reorganization reduced the number of 'limited stop' services. In return, MCT gave up some operation on service 31. Services to Ringway are now numbered 44, but Styal has not been served by through buses from Manchester since 1973.

165 : Stockport to Torkington

In 1963, this service operated through to Woodley, via Chadkirk, Romiley and Greave. Some journeys continued to operate to Greave until March 1971. The Torkington service became SELNEC service 365.

222/223 : Manchester to Partington

In 1960, when the Manchester Corporation service 91 to Ashton-on-Mersey was extended to Partington, operation was taken over by North Western. In September 1961, new 'limited stop' service 222 took over, and service 91 reverted to Manchester operation on a peak period basis. MCT did not operate to Partington until 1965 when the Corporation acquired low-height buses. Journeys to the Central Road estate began in September 1966, and in December 1967, the Wood Lane circular route was reversed, only to be reinstated anti-clockwise in 1976. In 1971, the service was re-routed via Chester Road, instead of City Road, although there was no stop at Knott Mill until 1979. By this time, service 222 had become Greater Manchester Transport 252, with a different route, via Sale centre. In 1980, the low bridge at Partington was rebuilt to accommodate standard buses. The service 223 variation, via Petrochemicals Works at Carrington, was withdrawn in April 1973.

500 : Alderley (District Bank) to Manchester (Parker Street)

This service started on 7th December 1959 to cater for commuters from the Alderley/Wilmslow areas. It picked up as far as The Griffin, Heald Green from where it travelled non-stop to Parker Street, via Kingsway, Slade Lane and Stockport Road. On 25th September 1961, the route was amended to Birchfields Road instead of Slade Lane and Stockport Road. After being transferred to Chorlton Street Bus Station for the City terminus at an unknown date, the service was withdrawn on 28th May 1971.

501 : Albert Square to Cheadle Hulme, via Birchfields Road, Kingsway and Schools Hill
502 : Albert Square to Cheadle Hulme, via Birchfields Road, Kingsway and Turves Road

Both services were introduced on 16th April 1963. Both were early OMO conversions; 502 on 7th August 1967 and 501 on 23rd October 1967. Double deck operation followed on 2nd January 1968, possibly by Manchester Corporation alone. On 30th September 1967, MCT ceased their operation on service 501, and service 502 was withdrawn completely. Service 501 was re-routed via Turves Road and still survives, unchanged, as Greater Manchester Transport service 150.

504 : Manchester to Bramhall (Grove Lane)

This service ran from 1956 to 1970, originally starting in Parker Street, but later being moved to Chorlton Street Bus Station. It was joint with MCT but the Corporation never operated on the route. The actual destination was shown on the blinds as 'CCPRO' — which stood for Central Civilian Pay and Records Office (of the Royal Air Force). The destination was later re-styled 'Air Ministry'.

The last of the Weymann-bodied Leyland Tiger Cubs of this batch, No. 700 (KDB 700), stands in Lower Mosley Street, in April 1965, ready to depart to Higher Poynton on service 32.

Appendix D ~ Staff Circular on Coach Heating and Ventilating Controls

North Western Road Car Co. Ltd.

COACH HEATING AND VENTILATING CONTROLS

The following illustrations show the position of the Heating and Ventilating controls on specific coaches, for which Fleet Nos. are shown : —

General Notes

1. Do not switch on Heater until engine has 'warmed up'.

2. Heater and Demister Blowers only work when engine is running, but Rack Blowers will work whenever they are switched on.

3. All Demisters can be used to supply 'COOL' air for ventilation. Note switches have two positions 'FAST' and 'SLOW'.

4. Most Heaters will supply 'COOL' air for ventilation, see notes on illustrations.

5. If vehicle is stopped with passengers on board or moving slowly in traffic during warm weather, the Rack Blowers should be kept running.

6. During 'warm' or 'close' weather the 'Lift Up' Roof Vents should be opened to face rearward even if it is raining. If the coach has become excessively Hot then the front vent can be opened to face forward for a while. See Notice to Drivers. DATE : — July 6th. 1965.

7. The Side Window Demisters depend on ram effect and therefore only work when the vehicle is moving.

915-916
Leopard Highlander

Heaters will supply HOT air only
Demister will supply HOT or COOL air
Rack Vents will supply COOL air only

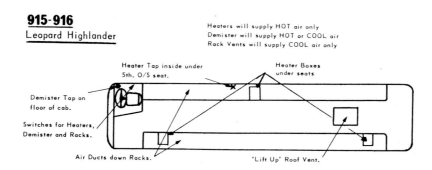

Heater Tap inside under 5th. O/S seat.

Heater Boxes under seats

Demister Tap on floor of cab.

Switches for Heaters, Demister and Racks.

Air Ducts down Racks.

'Lift Up' Roof Vent.

150-154
Leopard Harrington

Heaters will supply HOT or COOL air
Demister will supply HOT or COOL air
Rack Vents will supply COOL air only
Window Demisters will supply COOL air only
Dash Vents will supply COOL air only

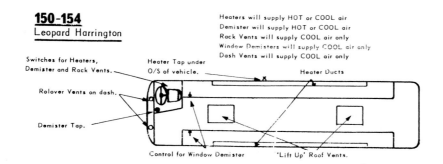

Switches for Heaters, Demister and Rack Vents.

Heater Tap under O/S of vehicle.

Heater Ducts

Rolover Vents on dash.

Demister Tap.

Control for Window Demister

'Lift Up' Roof Vents.

127

952-961, 140-149 *
Leopard Travelmaster

Heaters will supply HOT or COOL air
Demister will supply HOT or COOL air
Rack Vents will supply COOL air only

* On 149 only the Heater top is under the O/S of the vehicle.

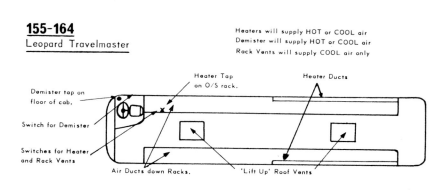

Heater Tap inside under 4th. O/S seat.

Heater Ducts

Demister Tap on floor of Cab.

Switches for Heaters Demister and Rack Vents.

Air Ducts down Racks.

'Lift Up' Roof Vents

155-164
Leopard Travelmaster

Heaters will supply HOT or COOL air
Demister will supply HOT or COOL air
Rack Vents will supply COOL air only

Heater Tap on O/S rack.

Heater Ducts

Demister tap on floor of cab.

Switch for Demister

Switches for Heater and Rack Vents

Air Ducts down Racks.

'Lift Up' Roof Vents

962-963
Leopard Plaxton

Heaters will supply HOT air only
Demister will supply HOT or COOL air
Rack Vents will supply COOL air only
Window Demisters will supply COOL air only

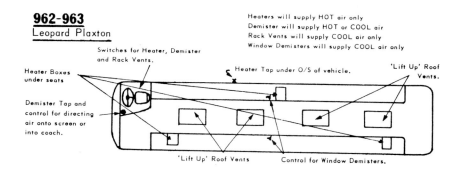

Switches for Heater, Demister and Rack Vents.

Heater Tap under O/S of vehicle.

'Lift Up' Roof Vents

Heater Boxes under seats

Demister Tap and control for directing air onto screen or into coach.

'Lift Up' Roof Vents

Control for Window Demisters.

907-914
Leopard Highlander

Heaters will supply HOT air only
Demister will supply HOT or COOL air

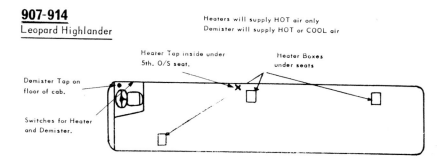

Heater Tap inside under 5th. O/S seat.

Heater Boxes under seats

Demister Tap on floor of cab.

Switches for Heater and Demister.

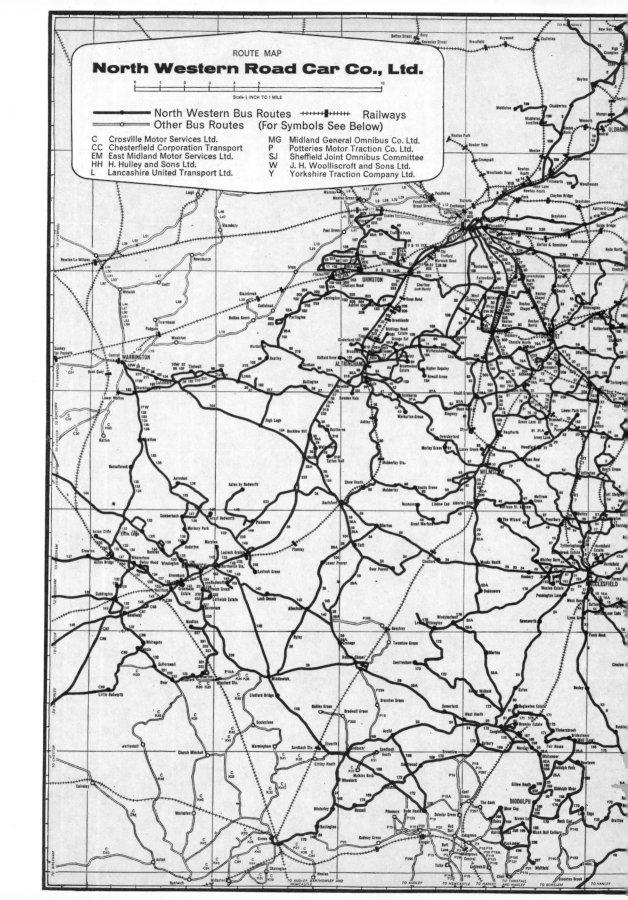

ROUTE MAP
North Western Road Car Co., Ltd.

Scale ¼ INCH TO 1 MILE

●——— North Western Bus Routes   ＋＋＋＋■＋＋＋ Railways
○——— Other Bus Routes   (For Symbols See Below)

C   Crosville Motor Services Ltd.
CC Chesterfield Corporation Transport
EM East Midland Motor Services Ltd.
HH H. Hulley and Sons Ltd.
L   Lancashire United Transport Ltd.

MG Midland General Omnibus Co. Ltd.
P   Potteries Motor Traction Co. Ltd.
SJ Sheffield Joint Omnibus Committee
W   J. H. Woolliscroft and Sons Ltd.
Y   Yorkshire Traction Company Ltd.